NEVER FORGOTTEN

CHRISTOPHER D. RANSOM

Copyright © 2022 Christopher D. Ransom

ALL RIGHTS RESERVED. This book contains material protected under International and Federal Copyright Laws and Treaties. Any unauthorized reprint or use of this material is prohibited. No part of this book may be reproduced or transmitted in any form or by any means, electronic or mechanical, including photocopying, recording, or by any information storage and retrieval system without express written permission from the author/publisher.

Scripture is taken from the New King James Version®. Copyright © 1982 by Thomas Nelson. All rights reserved.

Book Cover Design: Prize Publishing House

Printed by: Prize Publishing House, LLC in the United States of America.

First printing edition 2022.

Prize Publishing House
P.O. Box 9856, Chesapeake, VA 23321
www.PrizePublishingHouse.com

ISBN (Hardcover): 979-8-9858926-7-3
ISBN (E-Book): 979-8-9858926-8-0

Library of Congress Control Number: 2022909431

Disclaimer

This book is based on notes and recollections of Christopher D. Ransom. Last names and some locations have been changed or omitted to protect the privacy of individuals. In passages containing dialogue, quotation marks are used when the author was reasonably sure that the speaker's words were close to verbatim and/or that the speaker's intended meaning was accurately reflected.

To anyone who has repeatedly questioned their value.
Oh, and to all children who ever felt *different*.

CONTENTS

Foreword ix
Introduction xi

Chapter 1   **Genesis** 1
Chapter 2   **Burden** 13
Chapter 3   **Labeled** 21
Chapter 4   **Heaven & Hell** 53
Chapter 5   **Chaos** 69
Chapter 6   **Curiosity Killed Chris/Trying To Fit** 76
Chapter 7   **Identity Crisis** 85
Chapter 8   **Summer Of Suffering** 99
Chapter 9   **Marcy Day** 106
Chapter 10   **Mission Bay** 116
Chapter 11   **Ball Player?** 126
Chapter 12   **Senior Year** 136
Chapter 13   **G-House** 158

Chapter 14	**Jail**	165
Chapter 15	**Depression**	184
Chapter 16	**The First**	192
Chapter 17	**Savannah**	202
Chapter 18	**Wearing a Mask**	212
Chapter 19	**Noisy Heart**	221
Chapter 20	**Jordan**	225
Chapter 21	**Jeff**	245
Chapter 22	**Longing For a Happy Ending**	256
Chapter 23	**Free**	269

Acknowledgments. 279

FOREWORD

"Indeed our survival and liberation depend upon our recognition of the truth when it is spoken and lived by the people. If we cannot recognize the truth, then it cannot liberate us from untruth. To know the truth is to appropriate it, for it is not mainly reflection and theory. Truth is divine action entering our lives and creating the human action of liberation."

– James Cone

Cone, James. Black Theology and Black Power, 1969.

IT BRINGS ME IMMENSE PLEASURE, JOY, AND APPRECIATION TO write the foreword for Chris' first book, *Never Forgotten*. It's an experience I would not trade for anything. For the past several years, I've had the honor of working alongside Chris. I was there when he was ordained as a minister. We've flown to various parts of the country to lobby politicians and have walked various parts of our city to speak to community members. Collaborating with him to make our hometown, San Diego, CA, a better place for all is what we do. Even while writing this, we're working towards ending pretext stops in our city. While many see this as an immovable mountain, we both recognize that time changes all, so we should change things for our people today.

We spend much of our lives telling people who we are. I learned incredibly young in life that it's not what people say but what they do. Since day one, Chris has been A-1. I recall our first meeting during a community gathering in the iconic Fellowship Hall at City of Hope International Church. I was told by folks that he was a "good" young man. In many spaces, good works, but the organizing tradition requires more than that. It requires one to continuously self-evaluate WITH community. This is what Chris delivers, the curiosity to ask the tough questions and the courage to pursue the answers or lack thereof.

Never Forgotten is a memoir of a man, a minister, a brother, and a son who is willing to expose the soil of his story while he's still unearthing it. Many folks wait until they've figured things out to share while Chris takes the path least followed – that scary road, that back alley of the spirit and soul and walks with us! No, there aren't any streetlights here, but there is a magnificent light, a light that shines from Chris' spirit guiding us through his memoir.

Jeffrey Alonzo Karahamuheto

INTRODUCTION

You could say that San Diego is where California began since Spanish settlers established the region's very first mission here in 1769. Today, many people refer to San Diego as *America's Finest City*. To some extent, that is true. It's difficult to deny a label as such when the county has anywhere between twenty-three and thirty-one beaches and what many would say is the best weather in the world. It's ranked twenty-eight in the biggest cities internationally, eighth in the United States, and second in California. It's sunny and green (in most places), diverse, and maintains cool, calm, dry weather anywhere between sixty and eighty degrees all year long. It barely rains and never snows. There are hundreds of activities going on during the weekend and sporting events, and the closer you are to the Mexico border, the better tasting the Mexican food gets.

However, just like every big city in America, there's a ghetto that's hardly ever mentioned on the news for the right reasons. There's a race of people America has continued to neglect, Black people. According to many Black people, we refer to San Diego as *Daygo*. Why? Well, it's our way of staying connected and knowing who's who since we make up roughly six percent of the *fine* city and predominantly live in the ghetto parts. See, San Diego is made up of nine major districts, and most Black people live in the fourth, better known as the southeast.

The southeast is made up of several different neighborhoods: Paradise Hills, South Bay Terrence, North Bay Terrence, Lomita Village, Skyline, Alta Vista, O'Farrell, Jamacha, South Encanto, North Encanto, Valencia Park, Lincoln Park, Emerald Hills, Broadway Heights, Mt. View, Oak Park, Webster, Ridgeview, Chollas View, and Mt. Hope. These communities build certain personalities and personas in Black people, which means on any given day, you could be somewhere enjoying yourself at a cookout or in the middle of gunfire; it just depends.

In August of 2010, I was fourteen and living in Paradise Hills. They say thirteen and fourteen are the ages when things begin to change for teenage boys. Things like puberty, social status, and other assets are accomplished in the southeast. In the southeast, the average fourteen-year-old kid who grew up around the same neighborhoods had a lot more edge, swagger, and experience. Most Black boys grew up fast in the southeast, very fast. Most Black boys owned cell phones, had street experience, a girlfriend, or all three. If you weren't hopping trolleys, gang banging (or knew someone that was), or having sex with as many girls as possible, you were considered less important.

You guessed correctly. Many would've labeled me a less important teen for two reasons: I wasn't partaking in any of that, and I barely began to show signs of puberty. Fourteen was the age at which I was no longer a little kid. So many changes took place after my fourteenth birthday. I stood at a staggering six feet one inch, which was very tall for a fourteen-year-old kid. It wasn't hard to spot me from afar because of my height and how goofy I walked. I was a pretty goofy-looking kid with very long legs. I was quiet too, but for some reason, people (somewhat) knew who I was both at school and in my neighborhood.

My mustache was nonexistent, but I spent hours in mirrors, hoping a little peach fuzz would appear. That was a part of my nature. I was a curious kid who thought, hoped, and wished for what others had that interested me. I wasn't passionate about much, but I was indeed caring. Compassion was my niche, but it wasn't thought of as cool, so I hid it. I had a thing for watching people, for good and bad reasons. I was also very moody and had mixed emotions about nearly everything. Boy, I was such a complex kid.

Everyone mostly knew me as the tall, chubby kid who always had a pair of crutches locked under his armpits. Per day, at least ten kids would ask me the same question, "What happened?" I had surgery because I was born with a bone disease. I didn't even understand it myself, so it wasn't easy to convey. My legs looked nothing like the average kids', and for a tall Black kid, I had no game on the court. In fact, most of the Blacks didn't pick me in pick-up games. Instead, I was the last man standing as the obligatory player to complete the team. That was a painful feeling, but I learned my place during those moments.

I was the complete opposite of what society figured the "average Black teenager" was. I couldn't play any ball, and I lacked social skills – hell, I was even afraid of girls. Although I was the anomaly, I didn't think much of it because I was quite used to who I was due to my earlier years in elementary school. Fourteen was a part of continuous years of being introverted. Since I learned to enjoy isolation, I formed a love for arts and crafts. Creating was my safe place and my way of expressing myself. By the time I was fourteen, I could draw nearly anything I had imagined in my mind: my family, musicians, cartoon characters, athletes, etc. It wasn't long before my dream job was a tattoo artist. Whenever I completed a masterpiece, I honored it by placing it in a secret place. I prided myself on my artwork.

The scary truth is I enjoyed drawing, painting, and all other solo projects under the sun more than I enjoyed talking to people. I didn't know how to, so I was uncomfortable talking to others. To me, that was a good thing until I found myself in situations where I had to socialize. Usually, during classroom projects or whenever my mother called me out of my room for dinner was when I had to come out of my world, and it sucked. Sometimes I'd prolong my stay in my room and wait for my food on the dining table to get cold, so I wouldn't have to come out of my safe haven. Solitude just felt that good to me.

One day, unexpectedly, my little world was shaken. It shocked me, frightened me, and made me want to crawl under a rock and never come out. As a teenager, I hated surprises, so it made me extremely uncomfortable when sudden changes took place. Whether or not your world is similar to mine, I think everyone goes through a pivotal moment in their life that alters them spiritually, physically, emotionally, and or mentally. It's almost like life has something hidden around the corner for us all, and when we meet it, we are never the same after that.

Mine? Well, it happened to me when I was fourteen. It was easily one of the strangest days of my life. My mom asked me to go with her to Bible Study on a Wednesday evening – just the two of us. She was remarried and had four of my brothers to choose from, but instead, she decided to ask me to tag along, so I did. On this particular night, when she knocked on my door and asked me if I wanted to go with her to Bible Study, I replied, "Yeah, sure." I enjoy going to church, so I planned on going regardless, but it rubbed me with interest to see that it was just her and I on that evening.

That sent a signal through my mind that said *something isn't right*. I knew something was off, but I didn't have enough courage to say anything, so I just went along with the evening. We went to Bible Study together, and afterward, we stopped in the drive-thru of a local Wendy's fast-food restaurant. "Are you hungry? Let's go to Wendy's," she asked me. *Yes,* I nodded. I wasn't, but I wasn't going to pass up on 99-cent chocolate Frosty. The Wendy's was a few blocks down from our church, so it was a short drive. I rolled my window down to enjoy the cool night breeze.

She ordered food. I didn't ask for food, just the Frosty, but I took both and called it a night. I wanted to know what was causing so much generosity, but I didn't have enough courage to ask. I didn't have to because she opened up the floor. My mom pulled into the vacant parking lot, and from there, we could see an empty freeway: nothing but a breeze blowing through our ears. "Son, I want to tell you something," she said. "Tell me what," I replied. There was a super long pause. I turned and looked at her as I waited for her to tell me what she needed to. My eyes were glued to her while she stared through the front windshield.

My mom was a confident and bold woman, so I knew this wasn't anything simple because if it were, she would've been comfortable enough to look at me. Suddenly, in a monotone voice and in a short sentence, she uttered, "Son, I was raped. Mike is not your dad." My face frowned, and I almost dropped my Frosty. *Huh?* I repeated back to her what she said to me a few times, just to make sure it wasn't what I actually heard. Indeed, it was. She was raped, and that's how she became pregnant with me.

Mike was who I believed to be my biological father. He was the biological father of three of my four brothers. My mom and Mike were divorced, but he had promised my mom a few times that he would show up to tell me during this moment. He didn't show up. I was shocked at what had just happened. A part of me could not comprehend what my mom was telling me and another part refused to believe it. It just did not make enough sense to me. None of it added up. I was lost.

So many thoughts began circling my mind... *Why did he rape you? Where is he? Wait, so my brothers are only half?* I paused in mid-thought. My mom began to cry even harder. I hated seeing anyone cry, so the entire world stopped when I saw tears roll down her face and the stumbling of her words. Even at a young age, I realized that she was hurting too, so if there were any anger within me, I wouldn't have shown any of it. For years, she held in the truth, and it was time for her to let it go. Seeing her cry made me cry, but I did not know how to feel because I was too curious.

My brain was loaded with thousands of spontaneous questions... *Who else knows? Why hasn't anyone else said anything? Wait, does this mean Donte knew about this? Jhamir?*

"Mike was supposed to be here by now, but I just could not hold it in anymore. I am sorry, Chris," she said. "Why didn't he show up, mom?" I replied. She could not stop crying, so I never got an answer. Instead, I just rolled down my window and stared with hopes that she would pull off. She did, and I was glad that she did.

I was trying my best to process the conversation so much to the degree that I did not feel the dry tears on both sides of my face or my runny nose. In addition to that, I developed a headache, and it was hard to breathe. For the rest of the night, my mind raced. I just wanted to go home. Just before she pulled into the car garage, I accepted that I was shook and would be in shock for however long that was going to be. This was the turning point in my life; in some horrible way, the defining point. A part of me died then. I became a fourteen-year-old boy who, emotionally, physically, and spiritually, started to feel like a small orphan who was taking up space in a big city.

1

GENESIS

My granny and poppa fell in love at Booker T. Washington High as sophomores in Shreveport, Louisiana, back in 1963. Granny was a mild-mannered, reserved girl, while poppa was an outgoing hustler. Shreveport is where the two were born, raised, married, and birthed my aunt Lashonda, uncle Greg, and my mom, Rotunda. My mom was born on April 4, 1971, in Los Angeles, California, in the midst of traveling, but when she was one year old, granny and poppa moved to Galveston, Texas, just southeast of Houston. My mom vividly remembers her weekends spent in Texas as a girl that consisted of going to the beach with granny and poppa on Saturdays and church on Sundays. Especially Sunday mornings, she spent downtown in the cornerstone church after service enjoying cake and soda. Those weekends lasted for years until granny was diagnosed with cancer caused by the air in Houston, so by the time my mom was twelve, she was living in San Diego, California.

San Diego developed the tomboy in my mom. She was the

middle child who was always into some type of trouble (we have this in common). She was also hot-tempered and had thin patience. If you ask the right people, they would tell you that she was either a bully or the girl who would bully the person who bullied other people. She was a dawg, and as she grew into a teenager and adulthood, she was known in multiple communities. She didn't dress or behave like the average woman. She didn't wear makeup or lashes, and she barely wore heels except for Sunday service. She had a hard nose persona that was well represented by her tattoos and piercings, but to many men around the city, she was pretty and the one to get. I think her personality also had much to do with this as well. However, none of this mattered on the night of September 9, 1995, when she was taken advantage of. That's the night I was conceived, but as for her, it was a night she would never forget as long as she was alive.

The summer was ending, and the weather in San Diego was slowly changing. Everything was changing, including my mom's lifestyle and mental health. My mom was living on her own, but after that night, she was afraid to stand at a gas station by herself. It's like she wanted to be alone but couldn't stand being alone because of the memories it brought. My granny knew about what happened, my poppa knew about what happened, my aunt LaShawnda and uncle Greg knew about what happened, and the couple of friends she did have, she trusted enough to tell them about what happened.

In February of 1996, my mom was conversing with a friend named Sherry who she went to middle school with. Sherry and her remained friends for years. When Sherry found out about her pregnancy, she tried her best to convince her that the best decision was to get an abortion. The two had many phone conversations, but my mom never fully committed to the first steps of getting an abortion. "Girl, yes, you should get an abortion. I had my first baby at fourteen and was pregnant at twelve," Sherry said. "I understand, but I am just not sure," my mom replied. "I think it is the best decision for you," Sherry implied again.

March 1996

Instead of following through and setting an appointment to have an abortion, my mom went shopping because it was therapeutic for her. Shopping was her escape from reality. It was her getaway from the storms in her life. So instead of taking her friend's advice, she wandered around at any and every clothing store she liked. One of her favorite department stores was Ross. On the rainy weekdays of February, she went looking for anything and ended up only disciplining my brothers in the back of the store. Donte (the oldest) was seven years old, and Jhamir (the second oldest) was two years old. The two of them were touching stuff, and her patience was wearing thin. "Put that back! Come here! Jhamir! Donte... No!" she yelled out loud over and over.

She was just about to crack open a Pepsi she bought, and from a distance, she heard, "Aye, pregnant lady in the back! You with them kids!" It was someone's voice, but she wasn't sure whose because it didn't sound familiar. She stood still and hid herself between a rack of purses. In denial, she thought to herself, *she is not talking about me. How can she even see me? I am not showing.* There was a silence from the voice, but she heard footsteps coming toward her, and they were getting closer. "Me?" my mom abruptly replied while pointing her finger towards her chest as if she were in trouble. "Yeah, you," she said back.

Before she knew it, an elderly woman who stood about five feet tall, Black, and could have been anywhere between eighty-five and one hundred years old, made it to the same aisle she was on. She looked her square in the eye and said, "This was a peculiar pregnancy, do not hide it. God gave you that child. That's a male child. He is going to be the one who is going to take care of you when you are old." She said nothing more, turned around, and walked out of the store. Tears flowed from my mom's face because she knew that had to be the voice of God speaking through the stranger. Neither had she known who my mom was, nor was there much evidence of pregnancy. She was only five months pregnant.

Sunday, The Day of Pentecost, May 26, 1996, 12:00 a.m.

My mom was expecting to meet me on Sunday, July 26, but I made my entrance into the world eight weeks earlier than expected. She had been in pain all night and could not bear another set of contractions. About fifty minutes later, the amniotic sac covering my body began to make its way outside her womb without any warning. The nurses immediately commanded her to stop pushing because of the speed at which I was moving. She was perplexed because she never tried to push. "Huh, I am not pushing!" she yelled back at the nurses. Dr. Hill, who was the overseer, made an intuitive decision to reach in as far as he could and pop the sac.

Once the sac popped open, my mom mustered up just enough strength to push me straight out. My head faced an upward upstream position as if I were swimming up a river stream. This was bad because babies usually come out of the womb face down. I was out, and so was the umbilical cord wrapped around my neck, choking me greatly. The team of nurses quickly unwrapped and cut the cord. I was born at 12:56 a.m. on Sunday, the Day of Pentecost, May 26, 1996.

My mom was able to peek an eye over at the table Dr. Hill sat me on just to make sure I was okay. I was; however, the nurses weren't. The nurses were unsure about my condition because I didn't appear as well. Looking down at me with a perplexed look, Dr. Hill said, "Hmm, six pounds, ten ounces...he is a heavy one. Pretty big for premature birth, but light for a full term. Pretty rare." I was not as reactive as most babies born with the same weight and time frame as I, and because of that, I was diagnosed with Extremely Low Birthweight Down Syndrome (ELBW).

I was born with the rarest blood type in the world — AB negative. AB negative is associated with being spiritual, intuitive, friendly, empathic, trusting, emotional, and passionate. Little did I know that as I grew into a boy, teenager, and man, the traits associated with my blood type would show up consistently in many different circumstances in my life. Dr. Hill smiled, looked over at my mom, and said, "He is going to make it. Do not worry." Though she was unsure, my mom nodded back. The color of my eyes appeared as a dry yellow, and after testing, he diagnosed me with neonatal jaundice (Hyperbilirubinemia). Dr. Hill immediately ordered nurses to prepare the incubator for a few months because I would be staying for a while until my eyes improved.

The umbilical cord wrapped around my neck caused my brain to receive an improper amount of oxygen, so I suffered from brain damage. Dr. Hill also picked up on the sound of my wheezy cough and rapid breathing and was overly concerned by it. Brain damage was just the start. The choking caused me to suffer from

Bronchopulmonary Dysplasia (BPD) (undeveloped lungs). I began to receive treatment for all of these issues, one by one. I was being watched minute by minute and hour by hour. I was not healthy, but everyone remained optimistic that I would make it. There was a lot of silence throughout the morning, so my mom began to lose her state of tranquility. She was worried about her baby.

My granny, who had been present since my mom arrived that night, left before the sun came up, so it was just my mom and I. By this time, I was well asleep, and it was so quiet that you could hear a pin drop in the room. My mom lay next to me all morning long and refused to distance herself. For most of the day, she talked to me (as if I were talking back) and prayed over me as if I could pray with her. These practices kept her sane.

That following Tuesday, my granny showed back up and asked my mom if she had a name for me yet. "So Tee, what are you going to name him?" my Granny asked. "Christopher Dominique. His first name will be Christopher, and his middle name will be Dominique. The Lord gave it to me," my mom replied.

This was the second time God spoke on my behalf, but this time it came directly from a spirit and through a human. Not just any spirit, my mom felt she heard from the Holy Spirit because my name held a divine meaning. Christopher was of Greek origin (Χριστόφορος), and it means "bearing Christ." When Christ (Χριστός) is combined with phero (φέρω), it means "to bear, or to carry." The early Christians in the Bible used it as a metaphorical name, expressing that they carried Christ in their hearts. Dominique (Dominicus) means "of the Lord" and is traditionally given to a child born on Sunday. My first and middle names served as evidence of her encounter with the elderly lady back in February.

Wednesday was the day my mom had to leave me at the hospital until I was healthy enough to leave. Dr. Hill was not quite sure how long it would take for my lungs to fully develop, so he could not promise her a day for my exit. It was a gamble for me. On her way out of the room, she gazed at me, tubes attached to my body, lying under the incubator, as caffeine flowed into my nostrils. Although Dr. Hill tried to reassure her, she was not greatly confident in a soon return.

In June, I made enough progress to become registered in the state of California. Towards the end of the month, my mom was able to make an appearance during the registration process. She was excited. My birth certificate was signed off, and under the father section, she filled out her maiden last name, "Turner." Christopher Dominique Turner. Shortly afterward, I was released from the hospital.

There was just one problem. I didn't have a home to go to. My mom had only lived in her apartment for a little while before she was homeless. Before giving birth to me, she moved out of my granny's home prematurely, assuming that she had received access to Section 8 housing, but she was misinformed. Instead of going back to granny's home, my mom decided to live in her car with my oldest brothers, Donte and Jhamir, and I. She was twenty-five, Donte was six, Jhamir was seventeen months, and there I was, just weeks old, living in a car for three weeks.

Living on four wheels ended once Mike returned to my mom's life. The two wanted to make a blended family work. This is who we were: my mom had Donte when she was eighteen by her boyfriend at the time and met Mike a few years later. Mike was not Donte's biological father either, but he was Jhamir's. In 1994, Mike and my mom shared Jhamir before they eventually split. When the two split, she became pregnant with me. As parents, they were willing to make things right for the better of us all, so we moved into my granny's house until we found a place to call home.

Mike was a working man, and my mom stayed home with my brothers and I, but we all went to church on Sundays no matter the circumstance. This Is The Way was the name of the church my family and I faithfully attended. Mike and my mom were well-known members who served in any and every way they possibly could. A few weeks after being home from the hospital, I was scheduled to be christened. It was a Sunday, and everyone was dressed up for the occasion. It was said that clergy members of This Is The Way were going to hand-select my Godparents. What a time it was.

This Is The Way was a classic corner store-looking Pentecostal church. Just like in my neighborhood, the church members were predominantly Black. The building was small, and the members were minimal, but the service was long. It was very traditional. The necessities for praise and worship were emphasized. Pastor Taylor was the head pastor of the church. She was a stern old Black woman who didn't play any games. She ran off of a set of strict rules that said: women couldn't wear jeans, no cell phones during service, everything started on time and ended when she decided. She ran the show, which was probably why there were more women than men.

One of the clergy members, who was also a woman, christened me on my first Sunday in church. She was ordained to teach and preach as a minister, but everyone called her Pastor Sanders. She grabbed me from my mother's arms, stared me in my eyes, and immediately said, "He doesn't need no Godparents. I hear the Lord saying pastor. He's going to be a pastor." The church was silent as she continued to speak over the destiny of my life. It moved my mom to tears, and from that day forward, everyone in the church began calling me Pastor Chris at an incredibly young age.

For years, my family and I faithfully served as members at This Is The Way. When service on Sundays started at 10 a.m. sharp, we were there. When Wednesday night Bible Study started at 6 p.m., we were there. On Friday youth nights, Donte showed up at 6 p.m. sharp, and my mom sang in the choir, so she was on time every Saturday at noon. We didn't miss a beat. Nine times out of ten, my family was at church and on time.

1997

My family and I moved to another city within San Diego named La Mesa. La Mesa wasn't in district four. In fact, it was nowhere near it. However, it was much bigger, and everything was tangible: grocery stores, restaurants, malls, you name it, we had it. The five of us lived with my granny. 7251 El Cajon Blvd; this was another pretty small apartment. They all were; a bunch of units in one huge three-story building. We resided on the third floor. By this time, I was a one-year-old.

A lot of new changes and adjustments were taking place. My legs were bowing further out by the minute, and my mom was pregnant again. I did not move much like most babies. I sat still on average, and it began to concern my parents. But when I did make a move, I made a move! I was a chubby toddler who started showing signs of early walking, which worried people, so she wasted no time setting a doctor's appointment.

I was admitted to Rady Children's Hospital. This was the main campus located in the northern area of San Diego, known as Kearny Mesa. There, my mom was introduced to Dr. Dennis R. Wenger. Dr. Wenger, at the time, was a fifty-three-year-old White man with a very raspy voice. He stood at about five-foot-six-inches tall, had a comb-over, and never stopped smiling. Disregarding his smile, my mom sized him up as she did most people she entrusted with her kids. There was only one thing that set Dr. Wenger apart from his team of doctors, and that was his very raspy voice. You would have thought he smoked three packs of cigarettes every day by how his voice sounded.

He specialized in orthopedic surgery and was given *me* as his task. Little did we know that he and I would spend the next fifteen years of my life together. "Yes, mom, this is Blount's. He has got Tibia Vera," he said. "What is that?" my mom replied. "He has a rare bone disease, but with orthopedic procedures, he will be fine. We must take progress as it comes," he said. "What does that mean, and what is orthpe.. or whatever you just said?" she asked.

He looked at my mom nonchalantly and said, "Blount's disease is an autosomal recessive disorder. In others, you and his father carried the abnormal genes that gave the disease an opportunity to develop while he was stationed in your womb." She was still confused. The two conversed for a few hours, and at the end of the appointment, the respect and trust for Dr. Wenger were earned by my mom.

Floppy Infant Syndrome (Hypotonia) and Cerebral Palsy were other issues of mine. She explained to him that I rarely got myself into trouble like most babies do and rarely moved. She felt that me sleeping too much was a sign of something not so well. Laughing and crying constantly, but I was not sitting up or turning over, neither often nor correctly. Dr. Wenger then explained that being born too early may have caused my muscles not to have enough time to develop, which caused the Hypotonia. "What about his legs?" my mom asked. "Usually, this is caused by positioning in your womb for much of the pregnancy, causing his lower body to grow in such a direction. He didn't move much," he answered. The news kept getting worse and worse.

I lacked basic proper muscle tone that would've enabled me to flex and flail my limbs which explained why it was not wiggling around. My entire upper body movements were weak. I had poor head control due to weak neck muscles. I was missing milestones like turning over on my stomach and lifting my head forward, backward, or to the side. My mom then explained how "limp" I felt when reaching to pick me up. When she would grab me under my armpits, my arms would raise without me resisting as if I were going to slip right through her hands. Dr. Wenger kindly stated things should get much better as weeks went by for my muscle tone. But as far as my bones, there was a lot of work that needed to be done. After being thoroughly examined and diagnosed, paperwork was processed. My mom was sadder than she had ever been.

Dr. Wenger wasted no time. In December, my first orthopedic operation was in full throttle. The mission was to align my inner tibia so that it would grow congruently with my outer fibula. I was hooked up, diapered up, and breathing silently while my mom slept in the waiting room adjacent to me. The operation took about two hours. Coming around third base, the nurses prepared a custom-made body cast to place me in. It was not in stock or a usual tangible cast, so I was lucky that it came in time. A metal bar was connected between the legs of my cast to hold my lower body together and an attachable and detachable bag for me to urinate and pass stool safely. My first operation was in the books, and I began physical therapy to strengthen my bones as they grew.

Right before the 12th of December (the day my younger brother, Jhavari, was born), I began therapy for all the concerning issues. The beginning of therapy was like teaching a fish how to ride a horse - it looked impossible. Thankfully, I had a group of persistent doctors. My mom woke up early in the morning to drop Mike at work and take me to physical therapy. The first two hours contained playful toys and obstacles that required me to stretch my body but have a blast at the same time.

1998

In February, my second operation was underway. To prevent my tibia and fibula from growing incorrectly, Dr. Wenger broke the middle of both tibia bones during surgery. For the bones to grow properly, they needed to be broken right in the middle—mission complete. Now my lower body managed to straighten just enough to transition from a full body cast to an individual cast. Making it back home that same night, I was as free as a bird. I was a tad bit more mobile, so I took some of my first steps. In my head, I was liable to have fun, so I got my hands on anything I could potentially reach. The only other times I was not having fun was when I was asleep.

The progress in my muscle tone was apparent. It seems as if overnight, I became strong, stronger than ever. My regular visits to Rady Children's Hospital continued for both Hypotonia and Blount's. The staff knew me by face. It did not take quite long for me to become a regular. The waiting room was always cold. I would see hundreds of other kids in the parking structure, waiting room, or the McDonald's that was built on the inside. Black, Mexican, Caucasian, Asian, fat, skinny, short, tall, older, younger. It did not take me long to realize that they, too, had an issue. Sometimes I would see another kid with a cast on, and other times it would be the complete opposite. No matter what, I rarely saw a peer without their parent or guardian.

2

BURDEN

My progress visually and physically began showing so well that my mom discussed starting me off at daycare soon after turning two. San Miguel Preschool & Daycare was the name, and I was joining Jhamir. Jhamir was one year ahead of me, and it gave my mom confidence that I would be under good supervision and support if I needed it. I was only two, but she was determined to get me going early.

My checkup took place one week into September, my first week of school. After my exam, I was diagnosed with Infant Apraxia because I failed basic steps like understanding many vowels and consonant sounds, saying my first words on time, or saying any at all. On top of that, my mom let the doctor know that she had issues feeding me. In addition, I failed my eye exam and was diagnosed with Strabismus. When I was asked to locate words on the chart, my right eye did not look in the exact same direction at the same time as my left. The clinic prescribed me a pair of glasses that would align my right eye with my left over time, but it was said that I might have a lazy eye for the rest of my life. Daycare soon went from promising to uncertain.

Since I spent so much time around my mom, I suffered from separation anxiety in daycare, and because of that, I didn't care enough to do what I was told. When the teacher taught, I seldom paid attention, and when I did, it was only for a few seconds. I roamed around the classroom for most of the day while the other kids sat still. Whatever I could get my hands on, I did just that: toys, snacks, blocks, books, crayons, trucks, cars, and balls. Basketballs and books always grabbed my attention more than anything else. I was the first toddler to grab the basketball during playtime. I threw the ball around the room until my teacher could not put up with it anymore.

One day my teacher had a sit down with my mom and explained to her that she felt I was more of a distraction to the other kids. She felt like I was not ready yet. I showed little interest in doing activities in class, and this too concerned her. No matter how often she would call my name to attention, I didn't respond. My mom agreed with her idea because, to her, it was evident as well that it was a tad bit too soon. Paperwork was processed by the end of the year, and I was officially removed from daycare.

1999

In February, my mom received a notice in the mail stating my ability to return to school. Assembly Bill 2726 was a program that paid for me to resume at a different pre-school. This was a state-mandated program intended to serve children and youth three to twenty-two years of age receiving special education services which require mental health services (including attention to co-occurring substance use disorders).

Considering the thought that I was showing early signs of separation anxiety, the bill was a stepping stool. Towards the spring, she met with San Diego Unified School District (SDUSD) to discuss the safest school and when to begin. In that meeting, she expressed to the board members the dysfunctions I was showing at home and at San Miguel Daycare. Both my parents and the board members agreed that Alcott Elementary was my next destination.

Brand new beginnings, to say the least. My very first day was toward the end of the school year in May. Fortunately, I did just enough to pass me through at San Miguel, so I only needed to complete up until July. It was hard for anyone to fathom that only three more months of preschool were necessary, but it was what it was.

Things weren't easy during my days at San Miguel. Although Jhamir was a year older, we shared almost everything with each other. We didn't have much, so there were times when Jhamir and I shared a bowl of oatmeal and even the same underwear. After school, my mom would pick me up and take me to Rady Children's Hospital for my physical therapy appointments at least four days out of the week. This was a daily routine all the way through July until my mom discovered more news. She was pregnant for the fifth time with another boy.

2000

My youngest brother was born in the middle of the summer, on the 21st of July. Mike named him Jhaylen. I was officially the middle brother of the bunch. Donte was the oldest, followed by Jhamir, myself, Jhavari, and now Jhaylen. Mike and my mom ended up getting engaged and then married, so there were seven of us in a small three-bedroom apartment in the heart of La Mesa. My mom tended to us often, whether it would be with Donte's homework, feeding Jhamir, playing with Jhavari, napping with Jhaylen, or taking me to physical therapy appointments. She did it all, and she never showed a sign of quitting.

At Rady Children's Hospital, Dr. Wenger noticed the position of my knees and the direction they were growing in. I was growing quickly. On the charts, I was already taller than most four-year-old boys. Both of my medial collateral ligaments grew inward instead of narrow, which caused me to look knock-kneed. The only way to prevent future damage was again through another procedure. My mom was given available dates to select. From the looks of it, it was going to be a long summer.

The procedure was quite long, approximately three hours, but the longest process was getting admitted. This is the first procedure I remember vividly. The nurses had me change from my clothes to a hospital gown about an hour before start time. I sat with my mom between times, and we would look through magazines together and laugh at silly stuff. Toward the end of the hall, in the waiting room, was the huge indoor McDonald's that had a smell I loved.

Before every appointment, I anticipated getting fed if I was, to what my mom called, "good." Good meaning tough; she had always wanted me to be tough. I never really understood 'why' or 'how to be,' but before I could even catch my breath, one hour would go by, and I was given an option of either a bubble gum flavored gas mask or a strawberry flavored one. Spontaneously I chose bubblegum, which turned out to be a bad decision because it never did smell like bubblegum, yet it put me to sleep.

Slowly drifting away, I could see Dr. Wenger across the room, wearing a mask similar to mine, standing and talking next to a few doctors. The nurses wore masks on their faces as well. I wondered what their conversation consisted of because afterward, they walked over to me and asked me a bunch of questions. Their rapid ABC questions helped me fall asleep even faster. Dr. Wenger was ready and on deck. The mission was crystal clear: in order for him to correct my knocked knees, both my fibula and tibia needed to be altered inward so my knees would grow outward over time.

After the work was finished, I was placed in what the hospital called the "recovery area." There, my mom lay on the couch, waiting for me to wake up. She hated it because she said the let-out-couch was hard and felt like a rock. Night in and night out, she squirmed until it became comfortable and squirmed some more until it became uncomfortable. She hated it, but it was a sacrifice she was willing to endure for me. About an hour or so later, I woke up, and as soon as I did, the pain did as well. It felt as if the pain had met me and the nurses.

Once my eyes were opened, I heard, "Hey, Christopher, how are you feeling? Are you okay?" I was confused because all I remember was going to sleep to questions, and now, I was waking up to them. It was tough and even more challenging trying to describe how I felt by pointing at a laminated sheet of paper with facial expressions on them scaled 1-10. *Give me some space.* Nevertheless, I tried to see if my mom was next to me, and she was.

Eventually, I graduated from the recovery area to my own personal room, where I spent the time until I was clear to go home. My nursing team would awaken me to notify me that they were moving my bed and my belongings. As soon as I opened my eyes, right away, I could see my mom smiling. She and I stayed in the hospital for roughly two weeks until I recovered just enough to go home. Once I was stationed in my room, the very first thing I noticed was the smell of the anesthesia because it began to make me nauseous. I was not sure if it was the room or me, but either way, it somewhat stunk up the entire room.

Second, was the IV fluid shot in my inner arm. The nurses must have tightly wrapped a piece of tape over it to ensure I would not wiggle it loose because I was trying to move things without getting caught. It annoyed me. Everything became complex as if I had to start fresh.

My mom had a lot of downtime during this time. She would lay around watching the TV or talking on the hospital phone most of the time. Every thirty minutes or so, we would make eye contact, and sometimes that would be the sign that I had to use the restroom. So, she would pause her show, phone conversation, or her meal to come over and assist me. She never showed a glimpse of fatigue or despair, only enthusiasm to help me with whatever I may have needed. One week passed, and it was time to return home.

Dr. Wenger showed up towards the end of my stay. "How is he doing?" he asked. "Good. He is good," my mom replied. "Excellent," he paused. "He will remain in the individual cast for one month. We will need to see him back to finish physical therapy. Until then, no pressure on the lower body," he said. My mom smiled, "Okay, got it, will do," she said. He smirked at me while gripping his hand around my forearm and said, "Do not worry, you are going to be big and strong."

That was the first of many times he would say that to me, and each time, I didn't believe him. I was smart enough to know that he was just trying to make me feel good. I just stared back at him. He continued with more information before exiting the room. Our stay ended up being only one week and a few days before we departed. My mom could not be any happier.

The cast was tightly wrapped with a navy-blue coating. I could only see the tips of my toes from both feet branching out. I gazed at it; blue was appealing. First, I touched it and noticed how rock solid it was. Then, I gently pressed on it to see if it was breakable...*nope*. Lastly, I tried to lift my left leg, which was extremely hard. *Forget it.* I respected the cast. I understood that I was now physically limited, and because of it, crying became a consistent way of expression. Dr. Wenger had prescribed me medication, body crutches, and a comfortable wheelchair, which I spent most of my time in.

2001

Shortly after my 5th birthday, Dr. Wenger cleared me so that I could have my cast removed from both of my legs. During my appointment, I was scared, not of the results but of the idea of having a razor cut through the rock-solid cast. *Will it cut me?* I couldn't help but wonder. Luckily by closing my eyes while holding my mom's hand, I was able to make it through.

The nurses removed them one at a time, and each time, I stared at my legs and feet. I was stunned by the smell, complexion, and stitches that covered my scars. The nurses gently removed the extra pieces of cotton from my body. I looked over at the uncertainty on my mom's face. When she caught me, she smiled until I looked away. I was very confused by her reaction but said nothing in return. Looking back at my lower body, starting from my shins, I quickly noticed two identical parallel scars in the middle of both.

I was too afraid to move fast, so I did everything slowly. I turned my right leg inwardly and caught a glance of another scar on the right side of my shin bone. I could not believe what I was looking at. *This looks nasty.* The nurse who sawed my cast off was still a distance from me, so I continued to take advantage. I figured it would be wise to check out my left side as well, so I did. Aside from the huge scar on the front, I noticed the same one on the left side of my shin as I saw on my right. In addition, there was a sticky scar oozing with blood right above my Achilles tendon on my left leg. I was grossed out and a bit insecure. *Wooooooooooooooah.*

My mom grabbed my right foot and began removing the excess pieces of lingering cotton that stuck to me. I noticed my feet had twice the amount of stitched scars than my legs had. The nursing team returned to give my mom clear instructions on the dos and don'ts for the dissolvable stitches to heal correctly. The crutches were still necessary for about one month, but the wheelchair was not, which was great. It was a sigh of relief for her because I would now become less of a burden at home. I could apply pressure and walk with my crunches. Dr. Wenger preferred monthly check-up visits within the next few years to spot the development of my lower body. I did not feel confident in how my body looked or felt, but it was a step in the right direction.

As the summer transitioned into the fall, I was officially cleared from physical therapy after being diagnosed with Hypotonia, and school became a new topic. I continued my regular checkup appointments with Dr. Wenger to track the progress of the strength of my legs. I had made so much progress during the summer that by the first week of September, the walking crutches were no longer needed. Instead, I was given braces to wear. I was a happy kid. The most exciting part was being able to take showers instead of baths which I hated. The best part of all of the progress I made was the excitement for school that came along with it.

3

LABELED

Boone Elementary was the name of the school. Starting my first day of kindergarten was cool. Being out of school and in therapy for so long caused me to get comfortable. In fact, on my first day, I froze up. Seeing so many kids in one classroom made me a bit uncomfortable, and it shocked me. Her name was Ms. Baps, an extremely strict White woman. There were about twenty to thirty-five other kids in my class along with her. *Woah,* I was a rookie.

Intimidation grew quickly once I caught on to how advanced the other kids were compared to me. Playing catch up was hard, from finding my cubby, writing my name, reciting sayings, and even finding my assigned seat. It seemed like I did everything wrong while the other kids did everything right. The more intimidated I became, the more frustrated Ms. Baps became, making me even more insecure. *What am I doing wrong?* Boone was slowly running out of patience with me, so I acted out by doing what I wanted to do.

Like preschool, I found amusement in two things: books and

basketballs. Every chance I had, I scrambled through books: picture books, participation books, patterned concept books, predictable books, as well as wordless books. The text and illustrations in picture books caught my eye with their colorful stories. Its artwork showed a simple storyline that was so inciting. I was eager to finish them quicker than the previous one. I was trying to beat my personal best time in my head each time. I also did the same thing with a wordless book to speed through them. I never lacked the opportunity to grab one because my classmates found them amazingly easy, but I did not care because they were my cup of tea.

Every day Ms. Baps read a book to the entire class that required participation like clapping our hands, touching our toes, and sometimes even covering our eyes. In some of the stories, the book would have flaps, and she would flip them open and then close them as the story went along. These books excited me so much that she would have to warn me to calm down and, more than often, put me in time-out because I was not complying. I went overboard when the story promoted interaction with my classmates. My classmates did not respond well to my loud outbursts or bumping into them, which began to concern Ms. Baps.

I hated being broken up into small groups and individual reading because after that was nap time, and I knew what that meant. I would be the only kid who woke up with a wet spot underneath me. Some of my classmates recognized what was going on, and others did not; either way, it was embarrassing but nothing the staff could not handle. At times, Ms. Baps would separate the class into small groups and hand each group a relationship-themed book to read together. I didn't last long around my classmates because I would end up in a scrap. *Wait! It's mine! Stop!* I didn't play about my books.

Teacher! Ms. Baps! Teacher! I never failed to watch one of my classmates tell on me. *Tattle teller*, I'd scoff under my breath. Being separated from the group brought me joy because I never looked forward to reading with anyone anyways. I preferred reading solo. If the chance for me to get up and swap books were there, I took it. Sometimes I was successful. Other times, I was caught red-handed by Ms. Baps or a classmate. One day she mentioned the word "impulsive" while scolding me. I did not know the word's exact meaning at the time, but I knew it meant something along the lines of "I can't control you." That angered me. From that day forward, I didn't like her.

Fine, have the books. I found an alternative. Hoops. I was not as fast or quick as my classmates, but I genuinely enjoyed bouncing and throwing the ball around. Every day my options remained the same: football, jump rope, chalk, and a few others, but I just wanted basketball. When my classmates were not showing interest in me to share, I bounced it as far as I could and as high as I could. The rhythm at which it bounced kept me going. I tried to get as many bounces in as I could.

Once I got comfortable with that, I tried bouncing it through my legs like the pros. I could not, but I kept trying until the end of recess. Knowing how fast recess could fly by, day by day, I took complete advantage of utilizing the basketball so others would not have a chance to use it. "Christopher, come on in," Ms. Baps said. I flat-out ignored her. I could hear Ms. Baps from afar, but I ignored her because I knew I would be returning to hell if I followed her instructions. Heaven was on the outside, and that is where I wanted to be. The hassle to get me back in on time began to really boil Ms. Baps; one day, she made a concerning phone call home.

My mom answered and soaked the report all in but took it

with a grain of salt. I was just a kid being a kid in her eyes, so she threw the complaint out the window. Besides, my behavior at home, church, grocery stores, and even at therapy appointments did not match Ms. Baps' complaint. When my mom gave my brothers and me a command, we moved quickly. I feared her. I did not fear Ms. Baps. The only time it mattered was when our neighbors, who just so happened to be a deaf couple, secretly made one too many complaints about our noise level, so we were forced to find another place to live. Meadowbrook Apartments was the name, and it was in the Skyline region of district four.

2002

My mom could only ignore the frequent petty phone calls for so long. After a while, she began to wonder if I was just being a five-year-old boy or was there a serious issue going on at school. In fact, the times she made her rounds dropping my brothers and I off at school, she would drop me off last and stand near the door to see how I behaved from a distance. I never knew she was there.

Discreetly she watched how I acted with my classmates and with Ms. Baps. She picked up on my responses, but she said nothing. When coming to pick me up after school, I often looked up and noticed her and Ms. Baps conversing while looking at me. I could not tell what they were talking about, but I knew undoubtedly who they were talking about. *I gotta get out of here.* It was obvious that my mom got some sort of drop or report on what was going on in class. Out of frustration, I began to act out even more.

Overall, Ms. Baps treated me just like the rest of my classmates, but she knew I had a hard time mingling, fitting in, and obeying the classroom rules, so her patience began to run thin. I often wondered where her sense of patience in dealing with me came from, knowing how willing I was to do what I desired.

In the first week of March, I lost it. She was demanding that I come back inside with the rest of the students and even gave me quite a few 'pleases.' After a while, she figured I was intentionally ignoring her, so she went back inside. Eventually, she returned and again kindly asked me to put the basketball away and to come inside with the class.

Immediately, I turned toward her with built-up aggression and spoke, "No!!! Shut up before I get my gun out of the bushes and shoot you in the face!" She was shocked, appalled, and confused. Out of all the trouble I gave her, this was a bit over the top, but more importantly, it was definitely against Boone's policy. Of course, I did not have a gun, and I most certainly was not going to shoot anyone, even if I had one and knew how to use it, but what was said was said. I continued to play as I secretly watched her drift away into the classroom. She called my mom.

My mom came to pick me up. Still, she did not seem upset, but she looked a bit bothered by the report she received. Once at home, she heard the phone ringing. It was Ms. Baps again. She was explaining to my mom her thoughts on a board conference room to discuss my learning environment and how to better it. My mom knew what that meant, so she complied. The following day after dropping my brothers off at their schools, she and I showed up at the meeting.

There was Ms. Baps front and center, along with a few other staff members I recalled seeing around school from time to time. Ms. Baps got straight to the point, "I believe Christopher may need a different learning environment that is much more suitable for him." She began to inform my mom of all the previous behaviors leading up to yesterday's incident. I could see a confused look on her face, but she agreed.

The meeting lasted anywhere from thirty minutes to one hour, and all that needed to be said was said. Paperwork was filled out by everyone in attendance, agreeing that I would need to find a different school to finish kindergarten. Two days later, I was officially dismissed from Boone Elementary. Luckily, Harley E. Knox Elementary was willing to accept me and, in fact, was expecting me within a couple of days.

The 11th of March was my first day at Knox Elementary. It was just as big as Boone but more of a quiet setting and sat on the opposite side of town. Even still, I was the last brother to be dropped off at school in the morning. At times, I often wondered why. I started to believe that my mom may have intentionally done so, so she could be a fly on the wall for as long as she wanted.

I was right. After I walked into my classroom, looking back, I saw her hanging out as if she were anticipating something as she did at Boone. It became apparent to me that she and my teacher were aware of my shenanigans. I was right. They were fully aware of my impulsive behavior as well as my reading and writing levels. They wanted to "save me" to prevent me from having to repeat kindergarten, and that is exactly what they did. My classroom was practically the total opposite of what I was used to at Boone.

The number of classmates was few, and the number of staff was greater. The staff read emails from Ms. Baps that suggested that if they were to have me continue the following year at Boone to set up an IEP (Individualized Education Plan) as well as special education classes. Knox agreed but suggested that a fresh start elsewhere with special education classes set up would be doable.

I became accustomed to being limited in class because my

options were smaller. Instead of wobbling over to the bookshelf and throwing all the books around until I found the one I liked, I only saw a few available. Even during recess, there were not very many basketballs around and not as much ground to cover. It was even odder to me that my classmates did not see it as odd as I did.

By the time it was ninety-plus degrees during the summer, I hated Knox because of my peers. The fact that they were more apt to the environment than I was frustrated me. Sometimes, I would get into disputes. I got shoved and pushed a few times, but I did nothing in return. One day another Black kid punched me on the right side of my chin. It was not super hard, but I fell and stayed on the floor out of fear since my lower body was not strong enough to keep me up. I lay on that floor for about three minutes, waiting for my teacher to show up.

It was then that I knew I had low self-esteem and lacked confidence. I made a deal with myself to be as nice to the other kids as I possibly could so that everyone would like me. It did not work, but I did not end up in a fight. Soon my worries came to an end toward the second week of July. I made it through kindergarten, wondering what was next for me.

On September 3rd, I started my first day of school at Zamorano Elementary, and within the same week, my mom was referred to a local psychologist to help keep me afloat in class. Both my teacher Ms. Benbrook and my psychologist Dr. Desoto quickly became acquainted with my behavioral history at Knox Elementary. I had some good characteristics like compassion and helpfulness. I genuinely cared about my classmates. Whenever they were running low on supplies, I gave mine away to them. But some of the kids thought I was a bit crazy because I was known for writing "I'm going to be a pastor" on a blank sheet of paper over and over like a page of standards.

Wednesdays were "short days," so instead of school ending at 2 p.m., as it did on Monday, Tuesday, Thursday, and Friday, it ended at noon. It gave my mom the perfect opportunity to book my appointments weekly with Dr. Desoto since her and Mike's schedules were packed. And so, it was.

Throughout the first few weeks of school, I began to display some of the same previous classroom behaviors. The classroom was numerically similar to my stay at Knox, and Ms. Benbrook was about as strict as my previous teachers. She was White as well. Her patience grew thin. In fact, she expressed her consideration for my lack of direction and defiance during class with my mom. Hearing about my weekly visits with Dr. Desoto increased her confidence in my ability to be a better student, and her patience with me increased. As far as my mom was concerned, she wondered how long Ms. Benbrook would be able to keep up with me.

"I get to see my doctor today, right?" I asked excitedly. She knew exactly who I was talking about. I wished every day was Wednesday because Dr. Desoto showed me a lot of love. She was the first adult (outside of my mom) who I actually felt cared about me. She was a much older woman, a tall White lady with frizzy black hair and a friendly personality. She was genuinely nice to me, and quite frankly, I was more comfortable around her than my teachers.

Her kindness, mixed with the natural excitement in her voice, made me feel welcomed. It was a heartwarming feeling to hear her greet me. She met my mom and I in the lobby, where I eagerly released the Gala apple I brought into her hand. Gifting her, I let my mom's hand go and embraced her free hand. Every time I met with her, I brought her an apple. I asked my mom before we left if I could grab one out of the kitchen to bring it to her. I am not quite sure if she ate them, but all I knew was they were gone by the next time I met with her.

Dr. Desoto was given records from all my previous teachers, including Ms. Benbrook. They read: Failing to follow through on instructions and assignments, starts tasks but quickly loses focus and gets easily sidetracked, has problems organizing tasks and activities, cannot keep materials and belongings in order, cannot keep organized, and has trouble managing time, and meeting deadlines. He verbally dislikes tasks that require mental effort. He loses things necessary for tasks or activities, such as pencils, books, and paperwork.

It continued: Overall, he has become easily distracted by unrelated thoughts. He is forgetful in daily activities. He is unable to play or engage in hobbies quietly. He is constantly in motion or "on the go" or acting as if "driven by a motor." He talks nonstop. He blurts out an answer before a question has been completed. He finishes other people's sentences and speaks without waiting for a turn in conversation. He has trouble waiting his turn, so he interrupts and intrudes on others... That was from the school's point of view, but I did not feel guilty about such.

In response to the report, Dr. Desoto asked me hundreds of different friendly questions. She gave me cool activities, some lectures, some lengthy reading stories, and even normal one-on-one conversations to see if I had problems sustaining instructions. Sure, enough, I did. Many times, I unintentionally overlooked or missed common details, as well as made careless mistakes and outbursts. I did not listen when spoken to directly because I thought she would call my name for her attention plenty of times.

She turned to my mom for questioning, "At home, is he forgetful in daily activities, such as chores?" "Yes," my mom implied. "Hmm... what about fidgeting and squirming while seated or running or dashing around or climbing in situations where it is inappropriate?" "Yep, those as well," she implied again while slowly nodding her head. "Does he finish his chores in a timely manner?" "Sometimes," she implied.

"I believe we are experiencing Attention Deficit Hyperactivity Disorder (ADHD) and Manic Depression," Dr. Desoto said. "Manic depression? Huh?" my mom replied. "He is a Bipolar/ADHD patient. His birth record shows brain injuries, low birth weight, and even genetic factors that are usually leading causes," Dr. Desoto said. My mom stared back, waiting for the next statement. Dr. Desoto stared as well. The conversation continued.

Dr. Desoto and my mom continued conversing back and forth for another hour. She explained to my mom about genetic factors that my birth might have played their part in and how it works within my condition. My mom spoke little back in return but tuned in to every word. Dr. Desoto took a moment to comfort her, knowing the thoughts that tend to circle the mind of parents in frustrating moments like these. The two of them began going over treatment and the side effects, all while keeping an eye on my office adventures.

I was prescribed Ritalin, a stimulant for ADHD, hoping to decrease my behavior issues at home and school. Dr. Desoto, my mom, and the teaching staff were all hopeful about seeing changes with the help of my new medication. But there was a downside. I was ordered to take two tablets of Ritalin a day, although it was considered abnormal for a child my age to do so.

Dr. Desoto had four dosage options: 5 mg, round, yellow, flat (recommended for kids), 10 mg, round, pale green, 20 mg, round, pale yellow (recommended for adults), or the extended-release tablets 20 mg, white to off-white, round. She recommended the 20 mg, round, pale yellowish-looking pill, which my mom thought would be too much for me. It worried her, even more so after reading the side effects of rapid and irregular heartbeat, nervousness, anxiety, and loss of appetite. However, Ritalin was perceived to be the antidote to my behavior problems, so we were going to find out.

Nothing changed besides how I felt about myself. Taking Ritalin made me feel insecure about myself at home and at school. I just kept reading books at will. I managed to read at grade level from kindergarten and up, although my behavior was the focus. Reading was my strong suit. I enjoyed the colorful, picture-filled books to explore my mind in class and at home. It is what brought me joy as a boy on drugs.

Finishing my second semester of 1st grade was all the Zamorano staff thought about. If I finished well, Ms. Benbrook could sit us all down and discuss my further destination. She had high hopes that my medication and classroom adjustments would help subdue my behavior issues. Besides, I was not argumentative, so she believed I was trying my absolute best to comply with the rules. As for my mom, it was put up or shut up for me. Before sending me off into my classroom, she would squat down and look at me square in my glasses to prep me into doing the right thing, listening, and following instructions, and if I ever had to use the bathroom, let Ms. Benbrook know far ahead of time. I was offered rewards in advance. School was back underway.

Surely enough, I started off rocky, doing and going as I always went about things. It was as if the pep talks my mom gave me left my brain and flew right out the window. Ms. Benbrook made multiple attempts to grab my attention, and many times she stopped herself hopelessly. When she began teaching features of a sentence, such as first words, capitalization, and ending punctuation, I rudely interrupted her as if I knew what she was getting out. When she ignored me, I wandered off to anything that would engage with me: a classmate, a book, or even a basketball.

Ms. Benbrook continued to stretch the class' reading skills with a lot of teaching. Truly, this was the only time she would have my attention because I loved books. Our class did out-loud exercises like spelling and sounding out two letters representing one sound, such as *th, ch,* and *wh*. When she permitted us to yell them back to her in response, I yelled to the top of my lungs with pure excitement. When she gave us permission to slowly yell back broken up longer words into syllables for us to read, I yelled them back faster than the rest of my classmates. She kept teaching, although I was very distracting.

During storytime, I failed to sit still during much of the book, and when asked to appropriately read the text aloud with speed and expression, I went overboard. She kindly scolded me for it. I did not take it very well, so I got upset and ignored her for the rest of the story. I got up and walked over to other areas of the classroom to find some fun, and she yelled, "Return to your seat, Christopher!" She then finished her read-aloud and sped through the questions.

I struggled to emerge in writing and math. Ms. Benbrook was great at giving me a variety of texts, including opinion pieces, narratives, and explanatory/informational pieces to write about. Each time I started, I did not finish. My attention span was already so short; I was lucky to finish two paragraphs. As the weeks went by, it seemed like I was being assigned topics to write about more and more. Every time I turned them in, I showed little confidence. In fact, I felt so hopeless that I started comparing my praise to my classmate's praise. I was not the best, but I kept trying.

Right away, it was clear to me that math and I were not going to get along very well. Ms. Benbrook knew it too. She taught at a normal speed, but my ability to pick it up was terribly slow. Her curriculum was straightforward. My first task was to learn how to add and subtract numbers 1-20 and solve word problems using objects and drawings. *I got it!* As well as other simple stuff such as creating numbers using ten as a base. For example, twelve = one ten and two ones. After that, everything became a bit complex, and I started to hit a pit. She began teaching stuff like counting and writing the numbers 1 to 120, starting from any number less than 120. It all became a mental mess. I could not take it, but I felt too intimidated to speak out about it, so I just continued to act a fool. I found comfort in that, rather than solving math problems.

2003

After the winter break, the cycle continued. After my mom attempted to have our before class talk and slipped my medication in my mouth for the day, Ms. Benbrook told my mom that I was floating on thin ice after my behavior issues increased since learning social studies. As defiant as I was, I enjoyed social studies. It gave me lots of wiggle room, the upper hand, and increased my inner edge.

After instructing and teaching, she broke us into groups, where we could talk about our families, different types of families in the present, and our history. The intent was to develop communication and conversation skills, but every chance I got, I cut off my classmate from talking with an outburst or babbling past the time given to talk. When we used flashcards, I lost mine or stole my classmates so

I could have more than everyone. Ms. Benbrook threw in the towel and contacted my parents to have a parent-teacher conference.

My mom agreed. Monday, February 10th, class was over at 2 p.m. as usual. I stayed put until my parents arrived. I watched Ms. Benbrook set up a table and chairs, not knowing what exactly and who would be showing up. About five to ten minutes later, a crowd of folks walked into the room. I wobbled quickly over to my parents. Oddly, I was excited to see them, but they did not look too happy to see me. Sure enough, I realized it was a meeting about me, judging by the number of times everyone in the room glanced at me while talking. It was Ms. Benbrook, my grade counselor, the principal, the vice-principal, my parents, and I sectioned off in a portion of the classroom. I was not used to the room being so quiet, so I listened to see what was being said.

First Individualized Education Plan Meeting for Christopher Turner

Goal #1 Christopher will increase behavioral control for attention-seeking in a group setting as measured by teacher records and observations. Christopher will raise his hand before speaking and wait to be called on 5 out of 10 opportunities.

Goal #2 Christopher will increase behavioral control by decreasing inappropriate noise making by 90% in a group setting as measured by teacher records and observations.

Extended time for completing tests, oral tests, short-answer tests, extended time for completing

*shortened assignments, frequent breaks, reduced paper/
pencil tasks, and alternative materials.*

The school district was serious about me reaching my goals. In fact, if I did not, they suggested that I transfer to a different elementary school under special education. Academically, they were going to let me slide (which my mom thought was stupid) if I participated enough to get a good overall grade. It was behavioral issues that were completely under the radar, but my behavior was why I wasn't learning.

My parents and I also had a sit-down at home. Deep down inside, I was very afraid, but not because of the outcome. I did not know what to expect, but more so because of how serious everyone around me was. I did not think I was being a problem. To me, it was all good. I never saw a group of folks so serious about how I was acting before. It was new to me.

As I turned seven years old, my behavior was still a problem at school, of course, but Ms. Benbrook watched me more closely. Before my first IEP meeting, she let a lot slide, but as the school year came to an end, she was going to let up on me. My parents were more concerned than ever about their seven-year-old at home, school, and physical well-being.

Slow progress seemed to be the only thing I was good for, and I mean slow. Slow, but just enough to land me another IEP follow-up meeting to assess whether I met my goals or not. The outcome of the meeting not only determined whether I would be able to stay at Zamorano but advance to the 2nd grade. At just seven, everything looked like it was on the line.

On May 29th, the same group and I held my IEP follow-up meeting to evaluate where I was since the first meeting. This is what it read:

> *Mrs. Ransom and Ms. Benbrook discussed previous IEP goals. Chris has met all his goals. The team discussed new IEP goals. His behavior in class is great, except for inappropriate noises and raising his hand to get attention. This progress is discussed in present levels. The team feels Chris can be mainstreamed for one-half hour per day.*

I met their goals. As the year came to an end, Ms. Benbrook loosened up by letting the entire class roam free for the last few weeks of class. The majority of the time, I read books. Ms. Benbrook, knowing that's exactly what I would do during free time, referred my mom to the book club Zamorano held across campus for students who loved to read. With my inability to play like the other kids in the summer because of physical therapy, the book club would be better. The book club would also work in my favor because although I met my classroom goals, the chances of me staying at Zamorano were very slim.

I was on break for approximately two weeks before I went back to join the reading club. Within the last week of May, I started my first day in the Dragon Reading Club. The club accepted all ages and promoted reading across the entire school. One teacher was assigned as overseer of the club. Her name was Ms. Kitchen. She was a White lady with an average build but had crazy, colorful hair.

Unlike Ms. Benbrook, Ms. Kitchen was loud. From standing at the very front of the classroom, I could hear her. She was not a teacher I could ignore. I sat in the back on the first day because I was bemused and overtaken by her tone of voice. *Can she shut up?* I was just one of many students who joined the club. Some kids were in higher grades than I, some in the same grade, and a few were a tad bit younger. After settling in, came a lengthy introduction which I failed to sit still through because I was super anxious to grab a book.

Every book I touched, I read. In fact, I faded away. I grabbed a corner of the classroom and read until the end of the day. I did not know anyone at the club or make any friends, so I was all alone. I liked it that way. The club atmosphere felt much different compared to the school year's classroom taught by Ms. Benbrook. You could hear a pin drop in the room. I was so engaged in my book, and the other students were quiet, so it felt like no one was there.

Each time I finished a book, I started to rattle through stuff, which seemed to be the key for Ms. Kitchen to walk over to me. She leaned down with her glasses hanging off her face and softly asked did I need anything or did I look at the book I was reading. Each time I replied softly, "No, I'm okay." She smiled and nodded back, saying, "Okay, let me know if you need anything, I am here for you." She was overly sweet to me. Another time she came by to offer me a snack to eat, to which I obliged. By the end of the day, I had read about five books; that did not include those I sped through. Ms. Kitchen allowed all the club members to take as many books as we could return. I took full advantage.

Toward the middle of June, I was spending almost every day at the Dragon Reading Club. Ms. Kitchen and I formed some awkward yet cool bond with one other. She took some time to gather the club together to share what we had learned about the books we read. Each student went around and shared. I paid them no mind; instead, I twirled through pages. Once it was my turn, I did not have much to say, so I giggled. Ms. Kitchen giggled along with me as if I said a word or two. It was strange, but I guess it was just our thing. Eventually, she double-backed, and that is when I gave her a real answer. She applauded me; I felt accomplished.

In the middle of July, Ms. Kitchen reached out to my parents with high praise. My mom was surprised, but I felt like I was on top of the world. Enjoying reading and seeing my mom proud of me gave me an edge. For one of the first times, I felt supported by my world. My mom looked down at me with a grin each day she came to pick me up. So much so that I sometimes looked up at her, thinking, *Is this real? Is she as really proud of me as it looks?* Although the praise tickled my little heart, I still had my doubts about how much trouble I got myself into. I kept on reading because I guessed time would only tell.

July was ending, and I was one book away from reading a total of ten books in the club. I looked around and did not see other club members with the same number of tallies as me on the board. I was officially one of the top readers in the class. Well, a few of the older students had fifteen, twenty, and even more. I could tell they were much older than me, so it made me feel secure about my ranking. Ms. Kitchen awarded the top readers certificates of recognition, and I was one of the recipients. One of my very first color-coded awards; *royal blue!* A part of me thought *maybe I'm not used to this; maybe I'm not as dumb as I feel.*

That felt like my first win and arguably my last. I continued to go to my physical therapist to straighten my tibia and fibula and my psychologist. My mom continued to guide me through it all. At each appointment, she showed up with questions for my doctors and actively listened to anticipate what to look forward to. I was able to discern that she genuinely cared about me. She catered to me amazingly fast and aggressively for any needs that I had at home. She did not let up.

Although I made some minor progress, my chances of staying at Zamorano were slim to none. The school had enough of me, especially Ms. Benbrook. My behavior issues were still a bit much to move forward there, yet my academics improved after my time spent in the Dragon Reading Club. I completed just enough work to make it to the 2nd grade. However, 2nd grade was going to be a major shift and setting. The number of students the average teacher taught for 2nd grade Zamorano was far much more load management than other schools in the city. It was another hard pill to swallow for my mom, but like always, she buckled down and continued to push forward along with me.

The sun always shines hard in August, but that is when you know the summer is coming to an end. So, my mom reached out to Valencia Park Elementary to set up a meeting. The principal of Valencia Park complied, but first, she ran my academic and behavioral reports. Her name was Ms. Daniels, an elderly Black woman, who was plus-sized, wore a grayed afro, and walked slowly. It used to make me so mad to see her walking. After running my report, she was appalled but accepted me since Jhaylen and Jhavari would also be attending with me.

The conference meeting between my parents, Ms. Daniels, and my potential counselor went well. The school ended up accepting my brothers and I in the 2003 school year. It was a fresh start for me, a very fresh one. In fact, I was offered to stay in a general classroom size population under one condition, a teacher's aide had to be in attendance, so the option of who my teacher was going to be wasn't on the table. There were not too many main two teacher-filled classrooms, especially in the 2nd grade.

The teacher's name was Ms. Villery. She was my first Black teacher who had an extremely sweet voice. She met me for the first time a few days before the first day of school during preschool orientation for Jhaylen. Her hospitality toward my mom and I was heartwarming, and her smile was even better. There was no doubt in my mind that she and I would get along.

She took my mom and I on a classroom tour, so there were a few hours to spare while waiting. It was the very first building up the stairs away from the preschool section entering the elementary side; there was no way to get lost. The only difference was that this elementary's structure and setup were far bigger than any school I had attended.

Walking up the ramp with the two of them, I looked further and saw all the other classroom buildings aligned down the way. There were about four buildings connected to my potential classroom, and after that stood another building a little farther off that looked different. As we continued walking up the ramp holding hands and hopping around, I began to get excited about my new adventure.

Entering the classroom made my heart jump because of how breathtaking the view was. There were lots of rows of desks and chairs, far more than I had seen before. There was a huge whiteboard in the front of the classroom with lots of words written on it that I could not pronounce. Around the classroom were various books, notebooks, pencils, crayons, markers, and blocks, but not very many toys. I thumbed through books while my mom yelled, "Put that back, Christopher!" a few times until I did. After skimming through them, I went looking for a toy to throw around, but all I came across was a small squishy basketball; not much at all. I was confused.

After the classroom tour, the three of us headed down the ramp with a few more minutes to spare, and we continued down the campus. I overheard Ms. Villery covering the other buildings and which teacher taught in what classroom. Every so often, they would look down at me with grins on their faces as if they knew something that I did not. We started to reach the end of the campus where the lonely building was, which turned out to be the main bathroom for the 2nd through 5th graders. The building looked old and kind of creepy. At a glance, it looked like it was made of wood but not the same material as the classrooms.

I was released from crutches, yet my lower body strength was still extremely weak. My walk still looked very goofy, and my knee braces were still holding me up to par, so walking upstairs was going to be a real concern. In fact, they encouraged me to perform a test run to see how it felt for me. From the very first step, I was uncomfortable but not in pain. The pain grew once I held my right leg up to bring the left leg on the same level and vice versa.

The further I went up, the more uncomfortable my legs felt overall. I went up and down the stairs a few times to conclude that my bathroom breaks were going to need assistance just to be safe. As I began to walk back, Ms. Villery, in her sweet tone, asked me whether I liked the tour and if I had any questions. I was too shy to even think of any, and even worse, I thought I was a liability after walking up the stairs.

I woke up that morning filled with excitement. All I knew was I did not have a reputation at Valencia Park, so I was ready to set the tone. The school looked huge from the parking lot, even bigger than the first time I stared at it on my tour. *Maybe I'm just nervous and unsure what to expect; who knows.* I had the jitters, so I asked my mom a thousand questions on our way there. She answered them but in a very nonchalant manner while trying to make sure we were headed in the right direction.

The closer we approached, the more I noticed how empty the classroom was. All I could see was the back of Ms. Villery's head as she wrote on what looked like the whiteboard. We walked and stood at the door in silence until she noticed us at the door. She turned around urgently and greeted us with joy. I was the very first and only kid to class; we were exceedingly early. My mom and Ms. Villery chatted for a little bit. I could not comprehend what the two were conversing about, but I was certain that it was regarding my behavior.

Five minutes later, the conversation began to wind down. My mom walked over to where I was playing, leaned down, and kissed me on the forehead, "See you later, Chris, listen to Ms. Villery," she commanded. "Okay ... okay, mom," I replied. I watched her walk away, from the doorway to the very end of the ramp, until I could not see her anymore. I did not cry as I did previously because I trusted Ms. Villery. I expected a smooth day and an even better school year. Although nervous, I was completely hopeful with her in the driver's seat.

Christopher D. Turner. That was the very first time I recall seeing my name written out. She had already written my name on a name tag and securely taped it to the desk. It would have taken a lot of muscle work to remove the name tag with the amount of tape she used. She pulled my seat out, and I sat in it. I sat still. The room was so quiet that you could hear a pin drop. She proceeded back to the whiteboard to whatever she was writing out; I could not comprehend. I looked around at the many desks in the room, and from a distance, I tried my best to read the name tags at the edge of the desks ... "Bria... Willia... Di..." *Ugh, I am not close enough.* Sitting in the back of the class would be a challenge, but I was content.

Suddenly, I heard a pair of steps coming up the outside ramp, loud and slow. I waited to see if Ms. Villery would turn around because I would feel safer with her doing so, but she did not. Instead, I turned around, and it was a tall White man, slim and well dressed. As he made it to the door, he looked down at me and said in a very

calm voice, "Hey there, I am Mr. Duncan. What is your name?"
"Chr...is...topher," I said with a cracking shy voice.

"Christopher, Mr. Duncan will be co-teaching with me this year ... he will be with us," Ms. Villery said. Mr. Duncan removed his heavy business coat and propped it neatly on the back of his chair. I then realized that the desk I suspected to be odd was indeed where he would be stationed for the year. Ms. Villery and Mr. Duncan won me over with a smooth impression, so I had no idea what to expect next.

The first week was a complete blur. In the mornings, I took my meds with a nice glass of cold milk my mom poured for me, which surely backfired. In class, Ms. Villery kicked off the agenda with writing, but before the class could start diving into paragraphs, we began writing out our first and last names in cursive and introducing ourselves. I was shaking. My confidence was low, but I knew there was nowhere to run.

"Hey, everyone! Let us start by standing up and telling each other our first names and favorite colors. Let's start here! One at a time, and we will end up in the back," Ms. Villery exclaimed. She was excited, but I sure was not because I was in the back. *Ah, man!* About twenty voices later, it was my turn. My heart started beating super-fast, and I slowly stood up. "My name... is Chris..to..ph.. er.. and I like royal blue." I sat back down quickly. My heart was still beating, but even faster. I could not stop my voice from cracking, but I was glad it was over.

Eventually, we transitioned into sentences that would lead us into paragraphs. I could not focus. For practically the first half of the day, my mind wandered. I was not as talkative as usual; instead, I was incredibly quiet and unable to pay attention for anything longer than one minute. It was like I was in a continuous cycle of fading in and out of Ms. Villery's teaching. I gazed at the kids for minutes at a time: what they wore, how they sat, and even how they talked. I perceived them to be smarter than me, which only turned my shyness into intimidation.

I managed to snap back into focus when Ms. Villery began to teach something brand spanking new. I opened the blank notebook and grabbed the pencil as I was instructed. She kept it short and simple, "For today's class, we will start a journal. I would like you to write about someone in your life who is special to you. Write what you think about them. I will start the clock in one minute. I will give you ten minutes," she said. *Well, that's easy.*

My pencil was inches away from the page before writer's block slapped me upside my head. There I was once again daydreaming, looking at my classmate sitting next to me. She was so pretty, well dressed, calm, and noticeably quiet. She noticed me looking at her, so she looked up at me, but I quickly looked away right before she caught my eyes. I gazed at my classmate sitting in front of me; his backpack's design was dope. Just before I knew it, Mr. Duncan approached me from my right backside and said, "Can I help, Christopher?" My classmates lifted their heads and looked back in my direction. I was embarrassed. "Ummm... uh... no, I can do it," I said back. I could not focus and was afraid to ask for help.

I managed just a few sentences. *My mom is fun. My mom loves me. My mom is the same color as me.* Ms. Villery stopped the clock. She looked around to see who all had finished. Luckily, she did not look in my direction. I was hoping she did not ask me to share what I wrote in front of the class. Sure enough, she did not. I had the privilege of listening to my classmate's pieces, which turned out to agonize me because of my insecurity, first a boy, then a girl, another girl, a boy, and another girl after that. Not only did each of them sound brilliant but also confident. Their voices did not crack in front of the class like mine; instead, they were loud and fluent, and even more, they made everyone laugh. The feeling of infirmity set in within the first weeks of class.

It was odd. I was not as rowdy in Ms. Villery's class compared to the previous two years. Aside from wondering for more than half of the day, I only blurted out answers to get some attention or out of pure boredom and a lack of focus or care. I would try to stand up and roam the classroom if Mr. Duncan was not looking, but sadly he timed everything so he knew precisely when to catch me. Besides, Ms. Villery's vision practically covered the room.

The time she began a new lesson was when her tone of voice rose. She lectured first on opinion pieces. It was simple: state your opinion, provide reasons to support it, and close it with a conclusion. Second came narrative pieces: write about an event, describe actions, thoughts, and feelings, and provide a conclusion. Lastly, explanatory pieces: introduce a topic, use facts and definitions to develop points, and provide a conclusion. I could fathom the concepts at a decent speed, but my ability to produce ideas was an ongoing struggle during literature time.

Since my attention span sucked during math, too, I was having trouble learning how to solve math problems by using words and my memory. It was a total upgrade. The heat was on. I was no longer allowed to solve math problems by writing them down. Ms. Villery stood at the front of the class and used flashcards. She instructed the class to add and subtract numbers from 1 to 20 using mental strategies. Her hope was in our ability to add two one-digit numbers from memory by the end of the year. Luckily, Mr. Duncan's "no man left behind" mentality was keeping me afloat.

While Ms. Villery stood up front holding up '20 + 20', Mr.

Duncan gazed over at me trying to figure out the answer. My answer simultaneously stumbled out of my mouth as soon as she switched to a different set of cards. My classmates were wicked fast; they answered each card in a timely manner. At times I stopped trying and just tried to remember the answers given, but other times Mr. Duncan would casually make his way to my desk to ensure I snagged a few answers.

I had a few personal strengths during math. I picked up the difference between odd and even numbers. I mean, that was easy, all I had to do was remember the first one is odd, and the one after is even. I quickly raised it to 100. When it was time to compare numbers using the > < signs, I aced that too. *That was easy.* I broke down three-digit numbers into groups of hundreds, tens, and ones in a heartbeat. After that, I finished questionnaires regarding using analog and digital clocks; after all, I always anticipated recess and lunchtime.

During recess, hundreds of kids would flood the courts with balls: basketballs, soccer balls, footballs, and bouncy wall balls. There were also hula hoops, four square games, chalk content, and much more. For much of the time, I just roamed around the basketball court area and watched the older kids play. I did not have the guts to jump in and play or even ask to hop in, so I sat on the side and watched the fun take place. Deep down, I wanted to shoot some hoops too, but the fear of believing that I was different from the other kids overpowered the urge to play ball.

Occasionally, a ball would roll over in my direction. Instead of kicking or throwing it back to the area, I let it sit there until someone came and got it. I would gaze at the football and picture myself running up and down the field until someone came and retrieved it. After that, I would look over to watch the girls have a hula hoop contest; they were trying to see who could keep the hoop around their hips the longest, and the winner did not have to switch hoops. If the hula hoops were not in effect, I would check out the chalk drawings. Usually, the girls drew on the concrete. By the minute, recess felt like I was standing outside for years, but eventually, a teacher would come outside and blow a whistle that signaled us to return to our classrooms, and so I did.

Ms. Villery loved kicking off post recess with Science. She called it "warming our brains up," and I quickly realized what that meant. She taught the subject simple, I could grasp every word, but all I could seem to think was *why*. It all revolved around the human body, plants, the cycle of life, animals, and electricity, but that was all vague to me. I did not have enough courage to raise my hand and ask her where all these things came from, so instead, I pondered on other things and made my usual attempts to get up and walk around the classroom.

During "research time," she gave us books with pictures of humans and animals. They were super visual and candid. By the time I got the concept of science down, she had begun transitioning into projects that involved building structures which became the coolest part. Aside from the hands-on projects, I began to use Science as a time for wandering, catching sleep, or maybe drawing on a sheet of paper. I was not concerned with the human body very much.

Before I could leave the classroom for lunch with my classmates, I had to take my medication. Mr. Duncan received my mid-day dosage from the nurse's office, and if the nurse were not there on that day, he and I would walk over together to get it. He watched as I swallowed the two pills with a small cup of water and then led me on my way to the lunch area. Random students I had seen around campus sometimes sat at the same table with me during lunch. Though we never exchanged words, they were familiar with my face, so they sat at the table. Usually, I grabbed the edge of the table; that way, if necessary, only one person would sit beside me. Because I felt like an outcast, I did not want anyone near me. I became comfortable with sitting at the end of stranded tables alone. The grape jelly and smooth peanut butter sandwich was the best escape I had all day. *Mmhmm.* Not to mention my juice box and my sweet, glazed honey bun my mom packed me every day. Lunch was bittersweet.

Most of the kids finished their food quickly so they could be the first to grab a ball of their choice to play with. Me, I intentionally procrastinated. At least until the table was clear enough to act like I was going to go join a game. But deep down inside, I knew I was not going to. I had not made any friends, and I was way too shy to start any kind of conversation. Instead of trying to befriend anyone, I did the same exact thing I did during recess. The only downside was lunch lasted much longer than recess, so instead of looking like a complete idiot, I walked around a little. From the four-square games to the chalk area, the basketball courts, the football field, the soccer area, and even the tetherball poles. I was a legit loner with nothing but loud thoughts inside my head.

After lunch was the coolest part of the day; it was reading time. Ms. Villery encouraged and forced books, and I was excited about it. In fact, during her lectures, I blurted out random words and answers because I was so happy. On the board, she wrote complex words, such as two-syllable words, and instructed us to sound them out as a class. I wanted to steal the show. I wanted my time to shine. Sometimes she corrected me for speaking out, and other times she completely ignored me as if I were not there. During storytime, she read a book sitting in her chair at the front of the class; whether it was fiction, non-fiction, or poetry, I eagerly participated.

Mr. Duncan and Ms. Villery rarely got upset with how I

participated; they acknowledged me. She often asked me to read out loud to the class from my desk with a slow pace and a strong expression. I killed it. I felt a sense of accomplishment each time I was called upon to read a section of the story while the rest of the class listened to me. The more it happened, the more I grew an ego. During that time, the class was instructed to read solo. I sped over to the bookshelf to find the most intriguing non-fiction book.

I came across a cover with a basketball player on the front, Kobe Bryant. (After this day, I became a huge fan of Kobe Bryant). The purple and yellow cover caught my eyes instantly. As soon as I opened the book, I quickly noticed how large and complex the words were to pronounce, so I tossed it back on the shelves out of pure disappointment. Although Kobe was not the one for me, I kept searching, bobbing, and weaving around my classmates until I found something I could duck off in until Ms. Villery called the class back to attention. I had about thirty minutes. I settled for a Kobe Bryant picture book that I was able to enjoy.

For the very first time, I was given homework. I was stunned. I had no clue what homework was and how it worked. After she explained, I immediately had no interest in doing it. As the clock ticked closer to the end of the day, I was drained from reading my book of choice and physically from moving throughout the day.

Good thing it was Wednesday. Valencia Park also held Wednesdays as short days, so my appointments continued throughout the school year once school was out. By this time, I was just old enough to tell when I was due for a refill of medication because she would pull out of her desk a long yellow thin pad and rip out a sheet of paper for my mom to sign. I knew what was coming. Dr. Desoto and I's time together began to blossom as time went on. I really enjoyed our sessions filled with monster trucks and dinosaurs. It got to the point where my mom sometimes would hang in the lobby for the duration of my appointment.

My physical therapy appointments at Rady's Children's Hospital were not looking too good. Both my tibia and fibula were still brittle for my age. I was slowly growing into normal height for my age, but my strength never caught up. As I sat on the table swinging my legs, Dr. Wenger grabbed them one at a time and marked parts of my legs with a black sharpie pen while his assistant took photos with their cameras. I was clueless as to what was going on.

The keloid surgery scars on my shins always caught my attention; they stood out on my legs. The scars were so hard to miss. They were perfectly aligned diagonally on both of my legs. The longer I gazed at them, the longer they freaked me out, but I did not stop staring. Within the first thirty minutes of wandering mentally, I was now stumped by my own body. My thoughts grew. I began to think things like *Is this normal? Why do they never go away? What did he do for them to get there?* I was not sad, but I was afraid of being wrong, and more importantly, I wondered if I was normal like the other kids.

Towards the end of every visit, Dr. Wenger insisted and reminded my mom that my disease was not something he could kiss goodbye. Not knowing precisely whether or not my daily stretches were helping, Dr. Wenger still wanted me to do them and for my mom to help me with them. In addition to the stretches, he prescribed me a new prescription drug. The last thing my mom wanted was another set of pills added to my intake, but regardless of how she felt internally, she knew we had to do what we had to do.

"Back To School Night" sucked because I never liked the idea of my parents and teacher(s) in the same room. Plus, it was very boring. There were no books to read, no chairs to twirl in, and I could not get up and roam around my seat area like I usually did. It was packed. All my classmates brought their parents and some even an extra family member or two. Ms. Villery had all her work cut out for her. In the first five minutes, she broke down the agenda for the entire school year and what was to be expected. She even got to my mom's favorite part, classroom behaviors.

Thankfully, she did not single me or any other of my classmates out but rather generally spoke. Every five minutes or so, I could see my parents rotating from eye contact with Ms. Villery to their eyes on the handout, and lastly, down to me, all while nodding their heads. From the looks of it, it should have been named "Teachers vs. Students Night" because my parents were not happy with my lack of effort report from Ms. Villery.

On top of that, I had my first IEP, and the results were not helpful. In the beginning, they made plenty of attempts to make sure I sat still. They offered me snacks, toys, paper, and markers. None of it worked. I got what I wanted and went about my business. Each time was a clean escape, and when they politely asked me to come back to the table, I did until I made my move again. After the third or fourth try, they eventually let me go. Sure, enough, I looked back every so often to ensure my mom did not leave or was not coming after me.

Eight hours of class started to feel like fourteen; my interest in learning just was not there, and my medication kept me mellow and very reserved. I only paid attention when Ms. Villery popped in a VCR tape about the subject or when she kicked off a new project. I preferred the movie over working with others, of course, because I did not know anyone. I lacked a companion, and I began to compare myself to my classmates, who seemed to have already formed groups and alliances. Many of my classmates knew who I was because of my rebellious behavior, but they did not know much about me, and neither did I about them.

As a man, I often sit back and ask myself about my experience with Ms. Baps: *Had I been anything other than a Black kid, would I have been thrown into Special Education and labeled as bad, or would I just have been having a bad day*

4

HEAVEN & HELL

2004

Towards the end of the summer, my family and I moved once more. This time it was into an actual home back in district four. We moved to one of the most dangerous neighborhoods in the southeast of San Diego named O'Farrell. O'Farrell was next to Skyline. We lived on Amesbury Street, on the backside of a well-known street named Alderley, where a neighborhood gang resided. It was a huge sky-blue house that sat right in the middle of our street. The sidewalk was ground level, so to reach the level of the lawn, you had to walk up one set of five steps. The lawn was huge, and bricks bordered it. Adjacent to the lawn was a two-car garage and then, finally, the five-bedroom house. The inside was white, and behind it was a small backyard protected by side gates. As kids, it was huge to my brothers and I.

Everyone in the neighborhood knew each other. On the right of us was a Mexican family of maybe ten to twelve members who spoke predominantly Spanish and who we communicated with by hand signals. Our neighbor on the left was a quiet, elderly Black man named Mr. Nelson, who my brothers and I disrupted about a hundred times a day because of our outside play. My brothers and I were known as the kids everyone wanted to play with, especially since we were the only kids with a basketball hoop outside our house.

The only time we really saw Mr. Nelson was when he was leaving to go somewhere, which was not too often, but his daughter did come by all the time. Across the street was a Black family named the Bethune's. There were a few folks up and down the street we eventually got to know, but no one was too significant to us because we kept to ourselves.

For the rest of the summer, we thought of ways to have fun in our new home. We did all types of stuff other kids probably wouldn't have thought to do. Being the creative kid I was, I thought of the idea of using the garage for wrestling matches when our parents left. Donte introduced us to WWE. The five of us faithfully watched each WWE episode. Some of us liked Smackdown better than Raw, and the others preferred Raw over Smackdown, but we all had our favorites. Donte favored Stone Cold Steve Austin, Jhamir favored Booker T, Jhavari favored Rey Mysterio, Jhaylen favored Kane, and I favored Shawn Michaels.

We mimicked our favorite wrestlers' moves on each other. We had a spare mattress in the house, so when our parents weren't home, Donte dragged it into the garage so we could fight each other. Elbows, dropkicks, pins, arm bars, punches. Three versus two. One-on-one. Free for all. We beat the snot out of each other. It was painful, but it was fun. We'd go for hours, and then the only way it ended was when too many of us dropped out, or we broke something. That's how we enjoyed the remainder of the summer.

When the fun was over, I was back to reality: school. My lack of self-control and focus landed me a ticket to a different school; Ms. Villery could not handle me even though she liked me. She loved me as a boy (I could do no wrong in her eyes), but she didn't have the patience to handle a student like me. She left my mom enough time to apply at different elementary schools in the area that may accept my IEP and offer special education services.

Very few did, but since Jhamir went to a nearby elementary school in the neighborhood, it helped make September look promising. Jhamir was headed to the 4th grade at Nye Elementary, a few blocks away from Valencia Park and our home. My mom applied to Nye as the last option and got it. I was entering the 3rd grade but with my older brother this time. I felt a sense of security and confidence knowing Jhamir had a history there and was older than me.

My teacher's name was Ms. Yeldell, an elderly Black woman who seemed to have all the patience in the world and candy, too, making her my second Black teacher. I kept up my ways, but this year for some reason, there wasn't an assistant teacher in the classroom to help Ms. Yeldell if she needed it. As a result, Ms. Yeldell couldn't keep up with me. Often, she didn't even notice that I wasn't seated at my desk or doing the assessment. Afterwhile, I forgot there were rules to begin with.

Ms. Yeldell taught no faster than a turtle can walk a mile. It was that slow. Her patience was like something I had never seen. I took advantage most of the time, but I was able to tell when I needed to pay attention and when I could wing it. Besides, I still had zero friends. I did a few things well, like interpreting the difference between literal and non-literal text, expressing my own point of view about characters in the stories she read to the class, and 'comprehending what I read on my own. I had just enough discipline to know how and when to self-correct my mistakes before Ms. Yeldell got a hold of them.

I eagerly wrote my opinion pieces, introducing my opinion, noting its reason, and even providing my conclusion. My informative pieces were strong, too, because I loved non-fiction. True stories fascinated me. I had no problem expressing myself on paper for narrative pieces either. I would even use terms such as: because, since, for example, also, another, and but to elaborate on and make connections within my writing, but the remaining school subjects were a bunch of blah. Everything was horrible to me. My attention span was a problem, and the speed Ms. Yeldell spoke didn't help either. I could've cared a whole lot less about taking notes for research projects, digital tools, and other stuff she tried to convey during lecture time.

I finally made my first friend, and his name was Devante. He was much shorter than me but also more athletic. He was a math wizard, and he played in a football league for a team named the Valencia Park Hornets near my neighborhood. The two of us were Chargers fans, so that's all we really talked about. Every Monday was the opportunity to talk about Sunday's game. He talked about football and numbers so much that I became a little jealous, but he couldn't tell, and if he could, he wouldn't have cared. He was easy-going, funny, and friendly, which is why he easily befriended me. Plus, we were the only Black kids in Ms. Yeldell's class, so we connected very quickly.

My classmates were ahead of me at almost everything. My confidence in my mathematics skills was missing because Devante and the rest of my classmates were math wizards. Almost all of them knew how to do stuff like round numbers to the nearest ten or hundred and create graphs to represent data. I sunk into my thoughts of being inadequate and stayed there. Multiplying and dividing numbers up to a hundred and trying to understand the relationship between multiplication and division seemed like the most challenging stuff to comprehend. I was the last one to finish my multiplication chart (if I was able to) every Monday.

Multiplying 1's, 5's, 10's, and 11's were easiest. I attacked them first, but it didn't help me in the long run because I was horrible at the rest. Multiplying 3's, 4's, 6's, 7's, and almost every other number was a complete struggle. Time after time, chart after chart, I slowly began to give up in the classroom. My medication seemed only to keep me calm, just enough for Ms. Yeldell to teach. I was learning, but I wasn't reaching my full potential.

2005

My second semester at Nye was a bumpy one, in class, at home, in the neighborhood, and with the doctors. I was almost nine years old, still on tons of medication, and on the verge of needing another orthopedic surgery on both of my feet to ensure the bones grew correctly. I was an outcast on campus for many reasons as well. From some folks, I would receive extra attention, pity, and compassion, and from others, not so much. The number of school days I missed due to doctor appointments increased from three to four times a month to about six to seven times. Luckily, I passed the 3rd grade and was promised a seat for the 4th back at Nye Elementary. Thanks to Ms. Yeldell.

The summer of 2005 was life-changing as a kid but as a man,

today serves as trauma. My mom informed me that I was having my last name changed, but that isn't what actually happened. I knew my last name was Turner, and my brother's last name was Ransom (which was Mike's last name), but it didn't dawn on me that I was actually being adopted. I was too young to tell. At the time, I didn't know I wasn't biologically related to Mike. I didn't know that I was conceived by rape. I didn't think any of my brothers were half brothers (especially since it didn't feel like it). I didn't know what adoption was or what it meant in the long run. I didn't know the impact it would have on me and those around me. I was just a kid who thought my last name was going to match my brothers, and that, to me, was cool. Later on, I would understand what it meant.

It all happened quickly. I was standing in the middle of my parents. My mom was standing on my left, and Mike was standing on my right. Susan D. Hueguenor was the name of the judge that warm morning. I don't remember much else after that but the sound of the wooden gavel slamming. It startled me. Then came the round of applause that followed. I went from Christopher Dominique Turner to Christopher Dominique Ransom in the blink of an eye.

I entered the 4th grade at Nye Elementary with a new last name and a new teacher who was ready for me. My teacher's name was Mr. Penorando, a short Filipino man with a big attitude. I met my match. Mr. Penorando heard all about me and was ready to put an end to my ways. The important thing about Mr. Penorando was his military background. That was his teaching style and lifestyle. All he talked about was what he learned in the military; he even showed up to class wearing his all-black shades as if he were in the middle of Iraq, fighting in a war. He applied it to almost every example that he could. It got on my nerves. He was the opposite of Ms. Yeldell; he was strict and did everything by the book. *Who hired this nut?*

I never knew an angel and demon could teach in the same school, let alone the same bungalow buildings. From the first day of school to the last, I was afraid of him, but not enough to stop me from doing me. Every rule or command the school enforced, he reinforced. From standing on our markers on time, hanging our backpacks up correctly, pencil and marker placement, and all the way to walking in a straight line without slight errors. *This man is crazy.* I hated him.

My rebellious behavior and his military persona caused us to butt heads. He rarely repeated himself. I could tell, and he wasn't afraid to raise his voice at me either. I pushed his buttons just for the sake of knowing his perspective of me. In a sense, his style made it easier for me. He rarely called home or reported any of my behavioral issues to anyone. He just kept on teaching. He didn't care.

In his militant mind, telling my mom was a waste of his time. He didn't care whether I was learning or not. On one particular day, when I was doing my own thing, he embarrassed me in front of the entire class. I was talking under my breath while he stood at the front of the class and gave a lecture. Suddenly, he stopped and walked over to where I was sitting, pulled the chair from up under me, opened the door, and slammed my chair right outside of the door. "You're gonna sit there for the rest of class!" he yelled in my face while pointing his finger close to my nose. My knees were gushing in pain. After getting up from the floor, I sat outside for an hour while it rained. I cried outside that day.

My arrogance became my own kryptonite. I thought I didn't have to worry because, for the first time, I didn't have anyone breathing down my neck, but sadly that's what I needed. My classroom grade slipped fast. My reading fluency saved me. I was one of the best readers in the class. I was arrogant about it, too, because many of the other kids couldn't read as fast as I could or retain and apply the information they read. Just me, I could.

Socially, I was still in last place. There was no trace of Devante, I didn't make any new friends, and many of my classmates looked at me funny because I kept to myself. I think Mr. Penorando had a lot to do with it. (Most people don't understand: the teacher sets the tone on how much students will respect each other. Or at least that's just how I feel). When the teacher has made you out to be the bad kid, other kids will not want to hang with you because you have that reputation. That was me. No one wanted to come near me.

My personal shell was all I knew. During recess and lunch, I watched others most of the time, which is when I realized that Nye was remarkably diverse but separated. It almost felt like segregation. The Black kids hung with the Black kids, split into boys and girls. The same with the White kids, Mexican kids, Asian kids, and Pacific Islander kids. Seldom did I see an interracial group of kids kicking it. I learned a lot outside of class by just sitting back and watching my peers.

Yet a part of me just wanted to fit in anywhere at this point. The most painful part was knowing Devante was long gone and understanding that I had to make attempts to become a "cool Black kid." I hadn't seen him in class or around campus since the previous school year, so I didn't know how or what to do.

Since Jhamir went to Nye, my parents worked late hours, so we were enrolled in an activity program called 6 to 6. This 6 to 6 after-school program was funded by Nye and allowed kids to hang around in the auditorium until 6:00 p.m. when parents got off work. Although my mom wasn't technically working anymore, Mike was, so Jhamir and I were eligible for enrollment. I hated going to this program because of some of the kids who continually asked me why

I was much darker than Jhamir and had scars on my legs, which added to the feeling of being an outcast and low self-esteem.

Much of the program staff were Black women, one who I remember like no other was Ms. E. This woman, just like Mr. Penorando, hated me. She hated me to the core. Everyone knew the students she didn't like, and I was one of them. That's the perception I embraced because of how quickly she let me do my thing after telling me, "NO!" or catching me doing something I shouldn't be doing. If I refused to take my meds or follow a command, she turned away from me like she didn't care. I was still used to hearing three or four no's or "Stop!" as opposed to the one Mr. Penorando would give. It was safe to say that Nye knew what kind of kid I was before I had arrived, which was how I made it to a second year there.

I never fully accepted Ms. E coming down on me. Her voice escalated quickly, and her facial expressions made it worse. Every time she yelled at me, whether from a distance or up close, it startled me. Her face and voice never fully convinced me to change my behavioral patterns or take my medication. Instead, I would just be sneakier. I was afraid of that woman but not afraid enough to change my mind. Every day after school was a nightmare and another bad report to my mom.

While things were brewing on campus, so were things at the Children's Hospital. My tibias, fibulas, feet, and knees were still out of order, and it didn't help that I was growing rapidly. I was a lot taller than the average nine-year-old kid. The lack of growth direction and overall leg strength for my age needed serious attention. During the holiday times, it seemed like I was at Rady Children's Hospital more than in the classroom. My attendance was often excused for appointments and checkups.

It wasn't long until my procedure date was set and booked by Dr.

Wenger, his staff, and my parents. I was set to have surgery on my feet, tibia, and fibula to correct the growth and strength. From the marks Dr. Wenger was making on my legs with his sharpie, I could tell this was serious. Boy, I was in for one. He marked up specific areas on my feet to ensure my mom understood what correction was needed and why.

Dr. Wenger marked up the inside and outside of my left and right foot, as well as my inner tibia and fibula. Some of the marks he drew on me were long, some were short and swift, some high and some low. By the time my back-to-back appointments ended, I was zoned out because of the depth of his vocabulary.

2006

In the blink of an eye, I was waking up once again from another surgical procedure. "Chris ... Christopher ... How do you feel?" My mom was trying to wake me up. I was a deep sleeper. "I'm going downstairs to the cafeteria to get something to eat. You're doing well," she said. "Oo ... ooo ... okay, mom. Mom?" I thought of a question to ask, but she had already walked past the doors. Immediately I tried to turn my head to the left and right, wondering if anyone else in the family was in the room as well. This was the start of my new year.

My brain was hyperactive working even post-surgery. I couldn't move my entire body as fast as I wanted to. There was a sharp, throbbing pain coming from somewhere in my lower body that I couldn't identify. It caused me to grunt until I tried to say something, and that's when I realized my voice had changed. My voice was raspy. My mom returned, and the two of us slept in my room together.

The next day my mom stepped out again to head downstairs to show family members up to my room. I was in the room alone, again. These moments scared me. I started brainstorming about all the crazy stuff that could happen to me: *die, my legs fall off, a piece of equipment that was holding me together suddenly stopped, and nurses were nowhere to be found.* I was losing my mind. *How could all of this happen if they put me to sleep?* I didn't understand how my body was reacting to my recovery stage. My vision was blurry. I had an ongoing headache from the day before. I tried a few times to twitch any parts of my lower body but to no avail. The pain I was feeling from the waist down was overpowering any of my wishes.

"How's the pain on a scale of 1 through 10?" the nurse asked. I fell asleep again, and then I woke up gradually. It took about ten minutes to move my left arm at will, and once I did, I became stable and more alert. I started to twitch my fingers a little back and forth and move my elbow and my shoulder. *How on earth could my upper body be in so much pain after such a deep nap?* My vision was still blurry but a lot better than before my medication was applied. I soon realized that something was weighing me down from the waist, which was why everything felt so heavy. Instead of trying to lift my legs or turn over to the side, I tried tingling my toes just as I did with my fingers. I couldn't. I was one hour into twitching my toes from my big toe to my smallest one before picking up speed.

As soon as I mustered up enough energy to move my left leg about an inch above the bed, I felt a rush of something flow from my lower body to my brain. It shocked me and hurt all at once. My blood rushed from my feet to the top of my head, and I felt the quake of a huge headache. I scanned across the room in fear, dramatically, as if I had fallen off the bed. Before I had the chance to realize that my mom or a nurse wasn't in the room, my headache began to cease.

I figured I was back to normal. *Oh no, I'm not doing that again.* That was the first time I played with fire after having surgery and got burned. I never did that again.

My hospital stay lasted for about one week. The last three days were the most enjoyable because the pain subdued, and I was more aware that I was skipping school. Dr. Wenger came to see me on the second to last day. He encouraged my mom and explained to her what took place during the procedure and how much of a success it was. Plenty of side effects followed: dizziness, diarrhea, and nausea. My team of nurses brought a pair of crutches to the room and enthusiastically explained how they would become my best friends for the next month or so. That was just the beginning. After leaning the pair of crutches up against the wall, I spotted one of the nurses rolling in a chair. *What is that?*

I spent the last two hospital days learning how to position myself in a customized wheelchair, sit down, stand up, and even roll forward and backward if necessary. The plan was to have someone push me around without me needing to use my upper body strength. *But who's gonna push me?* I felt like I was learning how to write again. It was tough. I became anxious, scared, and worried. After a few hours is when I got the hang of it. Next came the crutches.

I was in no way buying the idea that these things would assist me, let alone for a long distance. As soon as my nurse placed them under my armpits, I was stuck. Although I was being instructed to lift my hand and crutch up to move it forward, I placed my foot on the ground. Like the day before, I felt the blood rush up to my brain. Feeling the cast touch the ground made me paranoid. *WOAH!* I was now overthinking. I stood there trying to soak in all the encouragement, hoping it would help convince me to move forward. Eventually, I got it, but that was just the beginning. Gaining rhythm and getting the flow was the next challenge. Everything was so dang complex, everything.

My wheelchair came in handy for birdbaths. *This is nasty. I hate this.* My mom sat on the toilet bathing me while I sat next to her in the wheelchair. She lifted each side of my body one at a time to get me clean. This task took about thirty to forty-five minutes, each time twice a day. For me, it was tiring, but my mom seemed to be cool with it.

After what seemed to be the slowest two weeks of my life, I finally returned to school. I wasn't aware of how complex things were going to be. My mom called up staff at Nye to confirm the services I would need around campus. Two minutes into the phone conversation, I could hear her yelling on the phone from across the house. At that moment, I knew it would be a long day. From the car to the school parking lot. From the parking lot to the campus. Everything looked brand new as if it were my first time seeing the campus. It turns out that I wasn't the only one serving strange looks. The minute the bell rang to get to class, my mom began rolling me towards my class, and everyone stopped and stared.

The further we went, the more awkward it became for me. I could barely keep my eyes open due to the heavy amounts of medication I was on. Kids slowed down their walk and stared at me as if they had spotted a car accident or like I was a new kid that they hadn't seen before. I wasn't used to receiving so much attention and compassion all at once. It was a weird feeling I didn't know how to respond to.

A few who had apparently known of me walked towards my chair as my mom and I were rolling along. "Say hi, Christopher ... he's okay. We just had another surgery, so he's taking a lot of medication right now," my mom assured the onlookers. They were confused, but they moved on. She dumbed it down for them. She was very polite but intentional about giving me space. I felt like a brand-new kid in a brand-new school. I was sad and frustrated.

Once we reached the nurse's office, my mom had a look of depletion on her face. She was dead tired. The weight of my wheelchair was heavier than she had thought. The challenge now was who would be the one to move me around and will they be strong enough to do so. Sure enough, the school nurse recommended a day-to-day rotation of aides who would assist. It worked, but it irritated me. *Man, hurry up!* I became accustomed to the ones who went faster than usual. Some days I went home with headaches, tears, or a sob story, if not all three. School went from having it my way to feeling imprisoned in a month's time.

Dr. Wenger set my follow-up MRI appointment a few weeks later, so the swelling was long gone. I was recovering well despite all the pain I was in. I was now expected to grow naturally. My next challenge was transitioning from being rolled around to becoming codependent on a pair of crutches. Fear was holding me captive. I depended on the wheelchair so much to the degree that I did not want to give it up. After being timid and mentally paralyzed for the first thirty minutes, I took flight. Dr. Wenger, a few nurses, and my mom stood at the beginning of the hall and watched me learn how to use the crutches step by step to the end of the hall.

I made it to the end of the hallway and back until I was instructed to stop. Each time I completed the distance, he told me to immediately turn around and come back, which was the hardest part. I caught a break after my first lap. Dr. Wenger whispered a few words to the nurses and mom as I watched. I couldn't make out what was being said, but I was more than glad to be at a standstill. The itchy burning sensation coming from the bottom of my armpits was decreasing as each second went by of me leaning on the crutches. I completed two more laps in the hallway as fast as I could to escape the burning feeling under my armpit. That was a mistake because it actually worsened the burn.

A few more weeks into recovery, I was completely miserable for two reasons: the pain I was enduring in my legs and my armpits. This was my first time ever using crutches, and it felt like I was learning how to walk again. I figured my team of nurses was right that day; the crutches were my best friends. I whined through some days, and on some, I cried. I even slept through some days as well due to how messed up my sleeping hours became. My mom attempted to self-diagnose me by upping my dosages of pain medications, but it didn't matter because the pain was gruesome. On many nights, I managed to pull in only four to five hours of sleep. The first thirty minutes were spent tossing and turning, trying to find the right angle that I thought would allow me to fall asleep.

On the flip side of things, the amount of time I was spending away from school was excessive. The shy kid in me loved it, but as far as my classroom grade, Mr. Penorando was holding me accountable. Although I was given a flexible fifteen-minute crutching headstart to and from class, sometimes I ended up being late because of how slow I was moving. In February, the rain poured on campus like no other month. The puddles on campus were deep and huge so finding a way around them was nearly impossible. By the time I made it to class, my cast was a little wet, my toes damp, and I was shivering, so the best way to avoid it was to complete my classwork and homework at home.

On March 3rd, I was back in the prepping room, being prepared to have surgery again. I was even more nervous than I was before. I was fearful, anxious, and worried. For the first hour or so, my feet went numb. The nurses could tell, so every thirty minutes, a nurse or two would wiggle my feet to keep my blood flowing and prevent me from going into shock. All I could think about was the pain I would wake up to again. Dr. Wenger went through a final breakdown of the purpose of the second procedure, what would be done, how long it would take, and what was to be expected.

Five hours later, I was woken up by my mom and my nurses. I was coming out of deep sleep while everyone seemed to be in an uproar. I got it. They were just trying to get me warm and energetic. It worked. Oddly enough, I wasn't in as much pain while recovering compared to the previous months before. My feet were numb, though. I felt a throbbing pain coming from inside of them. Then I realized that Dr. Wenger had stitched me back together.

From then on, all that was on my mind was being able to see them. I became fascinated by the scars. It was weird. Enthusiastically, I begged my nurses each time they walked in and out of the room to remove my cast so I could look at them. They chuckled and calmly said, "We will be able to review them soon, Christopher. Are you okay?" "Yes, I'm fine. I just wanna see them," I replied. What those nurses didn't know was that my scars, over time, though they made me feel insecure about myself, also made me feel innocent. And my innocence was all I had.

5

CHAOS

When I was able to leave the hospital, I made it home to chaos. I don't know what happened, but one day, I woke up, and Mike was packing his belongings. *What's going on?* My mom was yelling and throwing things with the hopes of speeding the process up. At that moment, I was confused until I found out there was an issue going on in the home. In four months, things went from okay to horrible. I couldn't get any answers from anyone, but I knew Mike was leaving and, from the looks of it, for good.

Child Protective Services (CPS) opened an investigation, and my life became one big cluster. While managing to get around in a wheelchair and walking cast, I met different social workers weekly. CPS workers showed up at the school campus to talk with me and to other campuses to talk to my brothers. I was puzzled, but because I was awfully familiar with meetings with counselors, therapists, and physiologists, I brushed it off and just went with it. I would frequently catch Mr. Penorando on the phone in the middle of class, and I knew why. The phone rang constantly.

"Christopher, head towards the main office," he demanded. About five times a week, he dismissed me to go to the main office to meet with a social worker. Once I arrived, usually, I would see Jhamir coming out of the same room I was walking into. We locked eyes but rarely said a word to each other. It got real weird real fast. Week after week, I wondered if he felt just as awkward as I did. I didn't know it then, but we were being told not to speak to each other.

I never thought I'd spend my 10th birthday with so much going on. I was coming in and out of Rady Children's Hospital for two reasons: x-rays and physical therapy. On top of that was more therapy regarding my parents' new divorce. I just rolled with it. So many questions, tasks, and exams were thrown at me that I didn't care if I answered them accurately. I started to see it as a time away from school. I spent more time at Rady Children's Hospital with doctors, nurses, and social workers, and it became my second home. My brothers and I had different social workers who were doing what I assumed was similar work with me. None of it made sense to me, but my brothers and I were requested to make regular trips to Rady Children's Hospital for one full year.

Back at home, Mike was long gone, and the atmosphere at home was awkward. I had to get used to going into my mom's room to see her just sitting there. Her posture was different, her attitude was different, her tone was different, the way she spent her time was different, and almost everything about her felt different. After the divorce, a cloud of depression hung over my mom, and because of it, my home felt like an abandoned building. Social workers frequently stopped by with food, warm games, and conversations for my brothers and me, and that's one of the only times my mom came out of her room. My family and I were going through very odd transitions.

I closed out the 4th grade, although it was a rough year. My attendance during the second semester was horrible, but I managed to be awarded a certificate for great reading fluency. *What? Foreal?* That was unexpected. I was a bit thrown off. I had read a lot of books during the school year (especially when I was away from the classroom), but I didn't see a certificate coming my way. I stood up on my crutches and made my way to the front of the class, which was awkward and made me nervous because that was the first time I stood in front of the class facing my classmates in the school year. It gave me a newfound appreciation for sitting in the back of the class. It turned out that I finished the 4th grade reading at the 5th grade level.

My mom picked up a new boyfriend named Chris during the summer, but she called him Big Chris to prevent any confusion in getting our attention. They had known each other for a while, but he was the complete opposite of Mike. Sure enough, he quickly befriended my brothers and me, so we began calling him Mr. Chris. He was a very energetic go-with-the-flow flashy pimp type of guy. He grew up in the streets of West Palm Beach, Florida, in a Piru neighborhood (so he said), so a lot of his clothing attire was red and of the latest trends. He always had a lot of money on him, and every time we crossed paths around the house, he was always sipping on an Ice House beer. He was almost always drunk, counting money and stealing my mom's car for his own personal missions.

Once Mr. Chris became the man of the house, the environment changed. We went from staying at home for the great majority of the day to shoplifting in different malls and stores across town. As a family, we plotted on stores and how to get away with it every single day. It was frightening, but I liked the adrenaline rush it provided. I was already impulsive, but this was different. This was ten times different. *I like this.* The thrill of knowing and trying to get away with the item was worth it. I rarely thought about the consequences because I always thought I could outsmart anyone. There were times when I suddenly remembered that what I was doing was wrong, but it didn't stop me. *I was supposed to pay for that stuff,* and I didn't.

We went to different grocery stores and clothing stores in different parts of the city. We were never caught. We laughed after every trip too. I got so good that I planned on getting a few of my classmates once I was back in class. This was the only time I was ready to go back to school because I contemplated the possibility of stealing from other kids. By no way did my mom encourage me to steal, but Mr. Chris was the leader who my brothers and I followed. It all seemed acceptable, fun, and rewarding.

I returned to Valencia Park, but Ms. Villery was nowhere to be found. My new 5th grade teacher on campus was Mr. Jones, and immediately I knew he had it out for me. A step above Mr. Penorando, he was my first Black male teacher, an older guy in his mid-forties that stood about six-foot-two-inches tall. He had an extremely fast walk and one gold cap on his front tooth, which he always put his finger over when he was listening to someone talking. The way he spoke to me was short, and his patience with me was thin in comparison to my other classmates. Mr. Jones, just like Mr. Penorando, didn't care about me, and like a boxing match, it appeared that he was well prepared.

It was almost like he read my behavior report and decided not to deal with me. On top of that, the classroom size was twice the size as the years before. More kids, which meant less time spent on subjects. My assigned seat was on the front row on the far left right next to the door. His eyes paced across the classroom during lecture time, but every five to ten seconds, I would catch a look from him that said, "I dare you. Do it?" *Is he watching me? Dang, he's watching me.*

I decided to turn it up a notch one day by making the impulsive decision to walk home with Jhaylen and Jhavari instead of waiting for my mom to pick us up. "Aye, let's just walk home." I abruptly said while looking Jhavari square in the eye. Jhavari and Jhaylen didn't say anything; instead, they followed me four blocks down the street. I felt a little guilty about it only because Jhaylen was only nine, and Jhavari was eight; we were little kids in a vulnerable situation. That was one of the worst decisions I felt I ever made because I knew then that I was dangerous and driven by my own will. It was going to be a long school year.

I didn't care that Mr. Jones was watching me because I just knew I could outsmart him. So I started stealing from kids as much as I could get away with. I brought my stealing habits into the classroom. Huge mistake. I stole from my classmates, the classroom, and even Mr. Jones. Money, books, pens, magazines, balls, or anything that raised my eyebrows. I was on another level, and it came back to bite me. Instead of pausing in the middle of speaking, he would just pick up the phone, call the counselor's office, and then send me on my way. The security pulled up, knocked on the door, and carted me to the main office. Sometimes this would take place within the first fifteen minutes of class.

My counselor's name was Ms. Leblanc, a short Black woman who went by the book. Every other day, if not every day, I sat in this small cubicle that faced a blank white wall until she felt like releasing me back to class. I couldn't blame her because I kept getting into something. On average, I sat there for about forty minutes. Within the first two months of the new school year, I was written up for theft or defiance eight to ten times and suspended three times since the school year started. I was headed down a very scary path.

I was making things harder for myself at school when things

were already difficult at home. My mom and Mike were officially divorced towards the end of October, and Mr. Chris was no longer around. I didn't realize how attached I was to the men at home until they weren't around anymore. It was confusing, but luckily my mom met and started dating someone else. His name was D-Ro; he was the guy who had been cutting the grass on our lawn since we moved in. D-Ro actually was the guy in the neighborhood who cut any and everyone's lawn for a fee. He was also one of the OGs from the neighborhood gang. About one month after he met my mom, he moved in.

D-Ro was older than my mom by eleven years, so he was more old school. He was a step above Mr. Chris. Mr. Chris was much younger and flashy like Rodney from the Hollywood film "Baby Boy." D-Ro, however, was more like Melvin, a laid-back OG who was both street and book smart with a lot of life as well as prison experience. Every day, he did three things: smoke, drink, and tell funny prison stories. His ability to capture the family with a story and make us laugh simultaneously was something we had never seen before, so my brothers and I would ask him questions just to hear a story. Every night he would invite my brothers and I into the bathroom with him while he shaved to have "man talk." He'd say a lot of funny, inappropriate stuff in that bathroom. A lot of what was said I can't repeat.

Everyone liked D-Ro, but I was starting to hate him because of the amount of domestic violence that quickly arose between him and my mom. I always assumed it was his fault, even though I didn't truly know. The cops were always at our house. Some arguments turned into harsh words, weed was thrown out, shelves pushed, and even a few fists were thrown. My mom fought this guy as if he wasn't strong enough to kill her. I hated witnessing these altercations.

One night in December, while my brothers and I were enjoying winter break, the two got into it again, but this time it woke me up out of my sleep, so I began to panic. I came into the hallway, where I met my brothers. From the living room window, I saw a police officer arresting D-Ro. My heart dropped when I looked on the ground and saw my secret Santa-gifted Barry Bonds orange painted baseball bat. That was the first gift I received from school, let alone from a classmate, and I was in love with it. I cried and begged my mom to ask the officer to give it back, but she couldn't retrieve it. It was used as a weapon, so there was nothing she could do. I didn't realize that the police considered it evidence. I loved that bat and knew I was going to miss it.

2007

Five days into the New Year, D-Ro's father bailed him out of jail, and he returned home; but in the middle of March, my mom and D-Ro got into another fistfight. This time D-Ro was sentenced to four months in a county jail for domestic violence. That felt like a long four months. He sent us drawings that he paid other cellmates to draw so that he could mail them to us. They were pretty dope. I used to take the drawing into my room and mock the exact piece of work. Once D-Ro was released from jail, things gradually got better at home. In fact, my mom and D-Ro ended up getting married, and instead of D-Ro, my brothers and I began to address him as "Pops."

A tough teacher, a broken home, and a new step-father made a confused boy.

6

CURIOSITY KILLED CHRIS/ TRYING TO FIT

I MADE A SAFE LANDING OUT OF THE 5TH GRADE AND STEPPED into the 6th. Since I was interested in arts and crafts, my mom figured the School of Creative and Performing Arts (SCPA) was the school for me. The only way anyone got into SCPA was by trying out. Any art was welcome: dance, music, crafts, etc., so I drew scenery in front of a panel of teachers. Weeks later, I received an SCPA acceptance letter. It was 6th grade through 12th grade, and it was a private school. The principal, vice-principal, and counselors were aware of my behavior history and made it clear to my mom that the zero-tolerance policy stood for everyone. I knew I could not uphold it, though.

The reality of going from one class to seven in one day was overwhelming. On the first day, my mom and Pops dropped me off in "The Circle," where schedules were handed out and yearly events were held. I maneuvered through kids that were twice my size just to make it to the "R" section. As soon as one of the campus counselors handed me my schedule, I was shocked. The classes and subjects puzzled me. I wanted to give up right there because I couldn't see myself managing seven classes, let alone pass them. I was blown away.

Semester 1 Classes
5015Q MUSIC 5th - 6th
1550 ENGL/LIT 6th
8035Q EXPL WHEEL 6th
4002 MATH 6th
5506 PHYS ED 6th - 8th
6006 SCIENCE 6th
6520 SOC STU 6th

It took me three weeks to memorize my routes to class and almost one month to remember I had seven minutes to get to my next class. I hated it. My teachers taught at a speed much faster than any of my previous ones. Adjusting and slowing my ears down just a tad was such a struggle that I slowly gave up towards the middle of class almost every day. I watched the clock until the bell rang. I lost a lot of classwork from having a messy backpack, and I rarely finished any homework. My focus was to just "make it through the day."

In addition, I was struggling with not receiving the same amount of attention I got in elementary school. I assumed that, to my teachers, I was just the new kid on medication with an intense, impulsive issue. By the middle of October, I was officially overwhelmed and completely stopped showing effort in my classes. I no longer wanted to raise my hand to answer questions, read aloud, or do my homework.

Since I didn't care, I became easily distracted and curious about everything else around me. One day while in my arts and crafts class, I picked up a huge knife and stabbed a big block of dough on my desk. All of the girls were scared, and one snitched on me, which led me to get suspended for two weeks. A few days after my return, I stole from a kid who sold Mexican candy, ate and sold some, but when he caught me, he beat me senseless. I was suspended for another week. I was testing the waters.

Before winter break, I was all signed up and paid to be sent off to 6th grade camp. I had two pieces of luggage that were probably twice my size. My mom was worried mainly because my older brother lost his virginity at 6th grade camp, so she gave me a long speech, then released me over to the staff who were loading the buses up. I was headed to Camp Palomar for one week. Far away from my family and around students who were strangers to me for the very first time. Absolutely no friends or family. A part of me was scared, and the other part was anxious and curious about what I could get into while away.

We arrived on a huge charter bus around noon. Everyone was exhausted, but not me. I was excited. Sitting still for two hours took a huge toll on me. My impulsiveness was spilling over, so I was ready to dive into whatever was available. There were approximately 5,000 6th grade students spread across cabins—girls on one side of the campus and boys on the other side.

The boys were broken up into two different cabins. My cabin, named Treehouse, had about fifty bunk beds sectioned and divided into names. My bunkbed section was titled Oaktree. I didn't listen to the cabin instructions and rules. Without choice, I received a top bunk, and I was bummed out about it because it was hard climbing the ladder to get in bed. Both the boys and the girls met in the cafeteria for dinner around 4 p.m. that evening, and everyone was in bed before 7 p.m. I slept for maybe four hours that night. I wasn't adapting to the new environment well, unlike my peers.

The next day was scheduled to be about campus lectures. Every student was to meet in the middle of the playground at 10 a.m. after breakfast. I sat while teachers yelled the instructions to follow through a speaker. They were strict and straightforward about the rules, dangerous spots, and areas that were completely off-limits. I didn't catch everything, but one thing I did remember was to "STAY AWAY FROM THE HUGE LOGS BEHIND THE BASKETBALL COURTS!" But of course, I didn't listen. In fact, it made me wonder what was behind the logs. Whenever someone told me not to do something, I became curious about why, so I did it anyway.

Everything that happened next plays in my memory like a movie.

We were dismissed to play after sitting and listening for almost one hour and a half. I wandered over to the basketball court to shoot some hoops because I felt like I naturally fit in there, so I causally caught a rebound and got some shots up. My peers were welcoming. I felt like I fit in on the court for the first time. It was such a heartwarming moment. Thirty minutes flew by, and I felt a massive wave of fatigue take over my body. I was well out of shape, but nevertheless, I kept going. That was the first mistake.

The second was costly. I tossed up an air-ball. (I was far off.) The boys around me giggled a little bit, and it killed my confidence. *Dang it.* Especially because my first crush was standing on the side watching along with a few of her friends. Once I spotted her giggling as well, I felt like I now had something to prove, so I did just that. *I have to go get it now. This is my moment.* I turned my head to check where the ball was bouncing. It finished bouncing over the first row of logs the teachers said were off-limits. *Wow.* I wasn't going to let this opportunity to prove myself fly by, so I went after the ball.

I would've gotten caught if I decided to walk around the log and get the ball, so instead of burning ten minutes of embarrassment,

I went after the ball head-on. I jogged slowly towards the first log the ball bounced over. The ball was completely hidden behind the logs, but I was certain it was behind the first one. The closer I got to the first log, the bigger the log appeared. The staff was right that the logs were half-human-sized. I sped up, and once I did, I noticed that the ball had landed a distance after the first log, so all I had to do was jump over the first log, and I was good to go.

Within ten yards, I shorted my stride so I could know when to spring upward. I took off with my dominant leg, which was my left. It felt as if I had cleared it with my left leg within the first two seconds. The second after that was the most frightening moment I had ever experienced. It felt as if someone snatched my right leg out of midair. My right foot didn't clear the log. I made it to the level of my shin, and that was all she wrote. I landed face-first on the wood chips on the other side of the log. I blacked out for about fifteen seconds. Lying there, I was shocked and confused. My classmates couldn't see me, and I wasn't scared... yet. I spit out a mouth full of wood chips and saliva. Then I got up slowly, got myself together, limped over to the ball, grabbed it, and walked back over to the rest of the boys. *I did it. I secured it.*

I felt like a hero until I checked myself out. Pain was coming from my lower body. My jeans were stained with dirt, and a new rip was showing near my left thigh area. My hoodie was filled with dirt, and I smelled like pinecones and wood. I started jogging back, and the closer I got to the court, I noticed other kids were staring at me. I figured it was just the dirt, they saw me trip and fall, or maybe both. I opened my mouth with a crooked smile to talk to my peers, and that's when I realized something was dripping from my mouth. It was blood.

The boys were waving me off to just hand them the ball and head to the nurse's office. They said it was best. We had only been there for half a day, so I had no clue where the office was located from where I was. Blood was dripping from my mouth by the second, so I had no choice but to find a staff member. No one in sight but children were staring at me. The only thing I saw worthy of walking towards was a building on top of the hill the court was sitting at the bottom of, so I began my mission. The hill was steep, but I kept one foot in front of the other. The closer I got, people began to appear who heard about what had happened. It turned out that I was indeed heading towards the right building. At this point, I was scared and wondering what was next for me.

This nurse was the most happy-go-lucky nurse I had come across so far. While everyone else seemed to be slightly freaked out by my accident, she treated it as if it was something she had already seen before. After she pampered me for thirty minutes, I explained what happened and where it happened. "You cut the inside of your lip pretty deep. But it's okay; we will just have to get you to the hospital. We are going to get you out of here and to the hospital, Christopher, don't worry," she said. I was going home for good.

That was the last thing I wanted. I lay down in one of the opening rooms for almost two hours in the dark until someone volunteered to drive me all the way back to San Diego because my mom refused to come to get me. No surprise, I just felt like a complete idiot for not even lasting a day at camp. I was even more afraid to see my mom's reaction to what happened earlier that day on the court. I laid on the cotton and thought deeply. I knew I had made a huge mistake by trying to fit in.

Since my mom was busy attending to one of my brothers and refused to come to get me, someone volunteered to take me back to San Diego, who was also headed in that direction. I spent almost three hours riding in the backseat of a White family of three's car. Three hours felt like ten. I took turns every ten minutes, switching from my left to my right hand, holding an ice pack pressed on the outside lip where my wound was inside. *I wanna go back.*

It was a mother and two daughters. The three of them talked, sang songs I had never heard before, and asked me a bunch of questions that I wasn't sure how to answer. I was so embarrassed and nervous that I preferred to be lost in my thoughts than to talk at all. It was the first time that I can recall being in such an environment that I was grateful to be in yet uncomfortable. I'm glad my mom didn't come and get me herself because that was a car ride I will never forget.

Once I walked through the living room door to head to my room, everyone was already staring at me as if they had already heard about what had happened. My entire day was filled with embarrassing, sad, and awkward moments. As soon as I hopped in the passenger seat of my mom's family truck, I realized that I was nervous for absolutely nothing; my mom didn't seem to be upset with the trouble I got myself into like the previous times before. It threw me off, but it gave me a sigh of relief, so I rolled with it. This was one of the first times in my life when I reflected on what I'd done. *How did I end up here?*

I ended my first semester at SCPA known as the reckless class clown, who was always in the principal's or nurse's office, not the cool kid I wanted to be. My teachers were slowly losing their grip on me. Their patience was wearing thin. I was aware that my grades were slipping, but I was in denial, so in my mind, I believed everything was going to be fine.

2008

Semester 1 Report Card
5015Q MUSIC 5th - 6th – grade received B

1550 ENGL/LIT 6th – grade received F (2 semester)
8035Q EXPL WHEEL 6th – grade received D (1 semester)
4002 MATH 6th – grade received D (2 semester)
5506 PHYS ED 6th - 8th – grade received C (2 semester)
6006 SCIENCE 6th – grade received C (2 semester)
6520 SOC STU 6th – grade received D (2 semester)
Semester 2 Classes
0104Q ARTS 5th - 6th
1550 ENGL/LIT 6th
4002 MATH 6th
5506 PHYS ED 6th - 8th
6006 SCIENCE 6th
6520 SOC STU 6th
1439Q THEATRE WHEEL 6th - 8th

With tutoring, counseling, and focusing for all of about ten minutes in class, I was able to pull in grades good enough for me to stay admitted and not be kicked out. Good thing I had another semester to get it right in class. The only downside was being put on academic watch. I was to check in with my teachers every other class day to discuss areas of improvement. My mom was aware, but like always, she didn't come off as bothered or worried. I was given a list of options for short-term goals and long-term goals to choose from. My answer to each one was, "I don't know." It frustrated the mess out of my teachers. All of them seemed to care more than I was willing and able to work. They wanted more out of me.

I hated Physical Education (P.E.) more than any other class. I wasn't fast, strong, or quick. The idea of preparing to feel the pain in my lower body during class was enough for me to think of enough excuses to get out of class. When I did go, I didn't really try.

I cut corners during laps, couldn't complete a pull-up, and skipped numbers while counting push-ups and sit-ups. Instead of taking P.E. seriously, I searched for bunnies in the field and chased them around the field. However, it was difficult because the bunnies were fast, so I had to move quickly while trying not to get caught myself.

I became good at watching others watch me so I could get away with my desires. One day the security guard left his golf cart in isolation and parked. I saw this as an opportunity to joyride. I was curious about how it felt to be behind the wheel, and by getting others' attention, I'd finally be cool. I noticed that he didn't turn the cart off completely, so I crept up to the abandoned cart, stole, and drove it a few yards down. Someone must've been praying for me because although I had a need for speed, I forgot that I didn't know how to park it myself, so I just hopped out and let it roll down the grassy plains. I was suspended for a week and a half. That was probably the most spontaneous decision I ever made. It was dumb, fun, and worth it.

I spent more time at home with my classwork than actually in the classroom with my classmates. From what I was hearing, a seat at SCPA the following year wasn't promising. SCPA wasn't putting up with me anymore. I was too much for mainstream classes to handle.

Semester 2 Report Card
0104Q ARTS 5th - 6th – grade received A
1550 ENGL/LIT 6th – grade received F
4002 MATH 6th – grade received D
5506 PHYS ED 6th - 8th – grade received C
6006 SCIENCE 6th – grade received C
6520 SOC STU 6th – grade received D
1439Q THEATRE WHEEL 6th - 8th – grade received C

7

IDENTITY CRISIS

In July, I was accepted by Alexander Graham Bell Middle School. However, I was under three conditions: to be bused there and back, enroll in all special education classes, and begin sessions with the on-campus therapist. The worst petition of them all was the school required uniforms. According to my mom, it was a great offer, so I didn't have a choice.

For the next year, I had to wear navy blue or maroon collared shirts that had "Alexander Graham Bell" printed on the right of my chest, tan khakis, a black belt, and all-black shoes. It put a hole in my mom's wallet, but she felt like it was worth it—a total of ten outfits to shuffle week in and week out. I was nervous and anxious all over again. I had never ridden a school bus before, so I wasn't sure what to expect. My mom dropped me off at my designated stop on September 4th, the first day of school.

I had seen the average size of a school bus rolling down streets before, but it didn't dawn on me that the one I was riding wasn't the typical size of a school bus. I put two and two together and realized the term "short yellow bus" wasn't just a term; it was reality. I was assigned to be picked up and dropped off on a short yellow bus for the entire school year. The number of kids and the way they were seated seemed a bit different as well.

There were about seven kids on the bus total, and the first half of it wasn't full of rows of seats but shackles, straps, and buckles. The first half of the bus was reserved for students who were disabled. There were six rows of seats in the back, three on each side. Seldom did those rows get full; there might've been a student in each row. Since I was taller than most kids, I sat far away every day and stretched my legs across the seat. I was embarrassed when I exited the bus. The last thing I wanted was for anyone to look me in my eyes when I got off, so I stared at the ground each time.

I had a feeling about how the school year would go, and fortunately, I was right. This was special education like I had never seen before. The campus was just as huge as SCPA's, but most of my classes were located in the back of the school, called the "bungalows." There were ramps instead of stairs, and teachers' assistants were assigned to each classroom. Already, I hated it. The worst feeling was knowing I was one of the few Black kids in each of my classes.

Bell had a high population of Black kids, but very few of them were in special education. On campus, other Black kids would see me and stare as if they hadn't seen me before. *They know I'm different. I don't belong here.* I quickly became insecure about myself. *They must know I'm in special ed.* Then to make myself feel better, I shifted my thoughts to *Nah, they just know you're new probably* and went on about my day.

Semester 1 & 2 Classes
8027 ADVISORY
7323 APPL SC/HLT 7th - 8th
0101 ART 7th 1
7710 ENGLISH 7th
7950 MLT ST SKLS 7th
7744 PRE-ALGEBRA 7th
7750 WD HST/GEOG 7th

    I met my on-campus therapist within the first week. Mr. Heather was a young, short White lady who was so soft-spoken that I assumed she was new to her job. I was wrong. She had a way of getting into my mind. I avoided making eye contact as much as possible because I already wasn't comfortable admitting my mistakes, but she never broke eye contact with me regardless of how I felt. She stayed on top of me: my classes, homework, classwork, trips out of class, detentions, suspension, etc. Towards the end of week one, she gave me a squishy toy ball to keep and carry with me to class. I was supposed to use it when I became anxious or curious to prevent bad decisions.

    Another purpose the toy served was to prevent my outbursts by squeezing it before I felt the urge to disrupt my teachers. She also gave me a rubber band to keep around my wrist to pull away from my skin and release to pop my skin whenever I felt the urge to blurt out an answer. (The irony of the rubber band represented street and or hustler affiliation to other Black kids on campus.) With both objectives, I had more losses than wins, so we brainstormed with other tools to keep me present in class, not in the principal's office or at home on suspension. She and I got off to a smooth start. She even kept in close contact with my favorite teacher during the semester, who was Ms. Cornell.

Ms. Cornell was a middle-aged White lady who had the sweetest voice that made my heart tingle whenever she bent over to whisper in my ear. She was my advisory teacher, and I had the biggest crush on her. At first, I was confused by the purpose of the class, but I came around to understanding it. Ms. Heather and Ms. Cornell worked together to ensure I was on top of my game. It was working. I was doing better than ever before because my progress report had A's and B's on it for the first time across the board. Although it wasn't a report card, I was comfortable and happy.

For the first time, I felt like I was worthy of being taught. Sometimes I would hear through the grapevine that I had one of the best grades in the class, if not the best grade. My teachers started showing me a favor that I wasn't used to receiving. Sometimes I caught myself daydreaming in class, thinking to myself, *this is what it's like to be a good student?* While I was winning in the classroom, I was still losing socially amongst my peers like never before. This time, I made it harder on myself by concluding that I was unworthy of being cool like all other Blacks. Almost every Black kid on campus belonged to a group: some gang members, some athletes, and some had all the girls. Me? I was just Chris.

I observed how other black teenage boys styled their uniforms. Their pants were sagging; they didn't tuck in their shorts, so they wore basketball shorts under their sagging khaki shorts. They didn't button up their shirts all the way like my mom made sure I did. I pulled my tube socks up to my shins, but they wore theirs near their ankles. I laced my all-black K-Swiss to the top, but they wore all-black Converse and kept the strings loose. I realized that what I wore was a part of why I was so insecure.

Sometimes I believed many of them had a lot of girls, whether they were in a gang or not. If I happened to walk by, I would hear them saying things to each other like, "You ain't got no b****es" or "Yeah, that's my b****, we be f***in!" I was shocked because Lord knows my mom would've killed me if she caught me using words like that or desiring a girl like that. Plus, I was way too shy to even look a girl in the eyes.

I had already built the habit of walking around campus with my head down, so I kept doing it until I made it past the groups I was intimidated by and was safe in class. Those moments were the hardest because if I kept my head down for too long, I'd spot torn condom packages on the ground, but If I looked up at the wrong one, I'd make casual eye contact with a girl that belonged to a gang member. Both times made me nervous.

Other Black dudes on campus used slang so often and so fluently that it sounded like a coded language. It was easy to spot who was in a gang and who wasn't by their accessories. If he was affiliated with a Crip gang, he kept a pair of baseball gloves in the back left side of his khaki pants pocket, and their hair was long and curly. For a member of the Bloods, the gloves were on the right side, and they wore the same identical rubber band on the wrist as I did. The gloves turned out to be used during a fight that I knew nothing about.

If someone wanted to "catch the fade," they were to strap on their gloves and fight. I surely knew these guys didn't play baseball by now. The bold ones even wore colored bandanas instead of baseball gloves to symbolize their affiliation. I made sure not to become acquainted with any of them. That was until I was changing for P.E. one time.

His name was Diamond. We saw each other in passing many times before. He and I met while we were changing before I was switched in and then out of my P.E. class. "Was hannin, bro? I'm

Diamond. What's your name? Where are you from?" I was so nervous that my voice began to crack during my response.

"I'm not from nowhere.......but my name is Chris." He laughed, "I'm just messing with you, bro. Nice to meet you, Rel. I'm from 59 Brims. Let me know if you need anything from around here." I didn't know what to say, so I just said, "Yeah..." We shook hands. *What the hell is "Rel"*? I didn't grip his hand as strongly as I should've. His was more of a firm slap and grab. He kept eye contact as I looked away. So many thoughts were running through my mind that I couldn't focus for the rest of the day. I was hoping I didn't come across him again or get myself into any trouble.

2009

Math was officially my weakness, but by the time the semester ended, I was doing better academically than I ever had before. My teachers had a soft spot for me, my therapist was proud of me, and my mom gave me what felt like the tightest hug I ever felt. She squeezed my ribs so hard. My mom had her hands full, so she pressed my therapist to be very persistent with me. Ms. Heather and I met every Wednesday (short days). The goal was to win in each category, and I was only winning in the classroom. She believed I could get my F up to at least a C in math by the end of the year since I had another semester in that subject. She also figured I would make a few friends.

I wasn't as confident about my goals as she was. Since I was afraid she would disapprove of Diamond, I didn't bother to mention him. I didn't want my mom to find out about him either. The daily dose of medication and my fidget ball and the rubber band were supposed to simmer down bipolar, ADHD, depression, and schizophrenia. Still, it didn't seem to be the resolution. It was clear that I needed more willpower to get this done. I was still suffering massively, and it showed in many notes and failed quizzes. I couldn't wait for June.

I was ready for the 8th grade already. I had completely tapped out. I thought getting a few good grades would do justice, but it seemed to do the total opposite. My supporting system wanted me to go harder. Instead of making a report of classmates I socialized with every week, I just filled out names and made it look believable.

Often, Ms. Heather fell for it (or at least I think she did). I explained to Ms. Heather that these were the things I'd have to possess before making friends, but she disagreed. It was frustrating because I couldn't convey to her that her method won't work simply because she wasn't Black, she didn't grow up in Black culture, and I didn't think she understood Black culture. My words were falling on deaf ears. It made me appreciate Diamond a little more but not enough to step outside of my comfort zone to try to be like him because I knew I couldn't be him no matter how hard I tried.

It didn't matter what secluded areas I found around campus to hide from everyone so I could stare off into space in peace and eat my lunch; Diamond always found me. Every time I looked up and saw him coming, I would say to myself, *Aww, dang, man.* I became a professional introvert, so I'd get upset whenever my thoughts couldn't entertain me. Instead of speaking up about my space, as Ms. Heather suggested, I kept quiet out of fear of letting others down and just suffered.

For a gang member, Diamond never stopped smiling. He would walk up to me with his confident limp in his walk, smile, and make eye contact. "Aye, bro, where you get your rubber band from, that's hard." I couldn't tell him where I got it, and I for sure wasn't going to tell him that I had a therapist, so I just looked away, cracked a fake smile, and said, "Oh... I'ont know, bro. I found it." I wanted to be cool so bad; it was killing me on the inside. I needed another outlet besides drawing all day.

Before the school year ended, my mom and landlord agreed that things had changed, so it was time for us to move away. She didn't fully agree, but eventually, she came around to it. After looking around months before my birthday, she had found a house in district four in Paradise Hills, not far from schools and stores. I didn't mind because I was used to new beginnings. I'd just get annoyed when I failed to remember the ways of the new area, rules, routes, distances, and people in the neighborhood. This was by far the biggest move.

Semester 1 & 2 Report Card
8027 ADVISORY – grade received NG
7323 APPL SC/HLT 7th- 8th – grade received A
0101 ART 7th 1 – grade received B
7710 ENGLISH 7th – grade received B
7950 MLT ST SKLS 7th – grade received A
7744 PRE-ALGEBRA 1 7th – grade received F
7750 WD HST/GEOG 7th – grade received A

In September, I got dressed on the first day of the new school year, filled with fear again. Although I had a good 7th grade year in special education classes, I still suffered from ongoing issues. I had been seeing counselors, therapists, and a physiologist for Bipolar, ADHD, and Schizophrenia. One part of me felt hopeless. The other part wasn't sure if I even knew what hope was. I was a mess.

Semester 1 Classes
4080 ALG READINESS MS
1520 ENGLISH 8th
7951 MLT ST SKLS 8
5502 PHYS ED 8th
6005 SCIENCE 8th
6551 US HIST & GEO 8

I was drugged with medication to keep me quiet in class. I also still had squishy balls, rubber bands, and an isolated desk to prevent me from being distracted. That was how the year began. Since I ended 7th grade with an F in Pre-Algebra, I was placed in an Algebra readiness class so I could learn the basics I failed to learn last year. I was the only 8th grader in that class. It was embarrassing. The rest of my classes were at the 8th grade level. In fact, the classes didn't seem so modified to the special education level.

I kept seeing Diamond, and it was never a dull moment around him. I grew into actually listening to the stories he would tell me – someone he beat up, someone's girl he took, a shooting, or high school options. We'd talk about it all. This year he didn't hold back with questions. It seemed like he wanted me to have a girl, join his gang, and play ball with him. He'd say things like, "Aye, Brim (referring to 59 Brims), when you gon get you one (referring to a girl), bro?"

Most of the time, I'd laugh, hoping he would jump to a different question I was comfortable enough to answer, but he didn't. He waited for me to answer while staring me in the eyes. "I will, bro, uh, I got one already." That's how I usually replied, and he bought into it without any further questions. I didn't have the courage to stand by what I said, so sometimes, I made promises and answered questions so we could part ways quicker and head to our own classes. Then one day, he brought up the idea of joining the school basketball team.

I had seen the coach around a few times, so I knew who he was, but I had never thought of joining the basketball team. Sometimes, I shot the basketball around by myself during P.E., but I never played against or with anyone, so I knew joining was a huge step. It was almost wintertime, and I formed a liking for basketball after watching Kobe Bryant on TV nearly every other night, although I wasn't physically athletic or skilled. I also didn't know anyone, so I wasn't certain what the future held. Ms. Heather agreed that it would be a huge step for me, and my mom seemed happy that I was deciding to try. I had a little support system, and my grades were decent, so I was motivated to do it.

However, I ran into a brick wall when Diamond dragged me into practicing on the courts with him. *What courts!?* was my first initial thought. I was hoping he wasn't talking about where I thought he was talking about. Now I had walked past the basketball courts, the only basketball courts located at the back of campus where all of the Black kids hung out. Walking toward the courts for the first time during lunch was one of the scariest moments.

Diamond was pumping my head up. *I don't know why this guy believes me. He doesn't know me.* I kept saying to myself as we walked to the courts. The outside courts were where the gang members and street dudes played while the girls stood around watching. By the time we made it to the back, I had sweat dripping from my butt to my ankles. My hands were shaking, and I could barely hold eye contact with anyone. *Just leave.*

It was Monday, so I was feeling a little optimistic. At a glance, it was nothing like I was used to. I started trying to piece it all together, so I didn't embarrass myself. This was nothing like structured basketball; it was streetball. Watching the Lakers play on TV compared to what I was watching puzzled me. The game was being run like a circus. I could tell that some of the rules were made by them: no out of bounds, guys were traveling, fights were breaking out. The current game was ending, so Diamond gave me a look that basically said, *get ready; we're up next.* My hands were shaking so much that it took me a few minutes to tie up my shoelaces on my K-Swiss.

I'm panicking. I'm thinking of everything that could possibly go wrong. Diamond was standing on the sideline waiting to be selected, and by this time, he was pumped. I just stood there with a blank stare. He was picked second by one of the two team captains, then another went and another and another until it was down to me and two other heavy-set kids who had been in the previous games.

And just like I predicted, I didn't get picked. I was embarrassed. The captain glanced at me, walked away, and in-bounded the ball. The game started, and Diamond drifted away. I'm not sure that he realized I didn't get selected on either team. I came by during lunch for the rest of the week just to get my heart crushed over and over again. By the following Monday, I was heartbroken and unsure about joining the school team. I didn't know what to do next.

From that day forward, I believed sports weren't my niche. I never expressed my feelings to Diamond or anyone at all. Instead, I bottled them. I still went on to try out for the school basketball team with Diamond because I wanted to keep my word. It was a three-day try-out. I did horrible on all three days. The worst part was realizing my competition wasn't the cool kids who were balling on the blacktop. It was a bunch of guys with little to no experience like myself. Those three days of tryouts went by slowly. Each day I sat in class waiting for practice to start, and once I was there, I couldn't wait for it to end. I was too afraid to back out because the little pride

I did have was a delusion that made me believe that I was going to be a factor on the team. Boy, was I wrong.

The following week Diamond and I walked up to the list of players who made the team hanging on the outside of the gym. We made it. I stared at the dangling piece of paper, trying to determine if the meaning behind my name sitting in second to last and Diamond's in first defined our skill level. I was too afraid to ask, so I drew the conclusion. Week after week, practice after practice, game after game, I sat on the bench. I was who I thought I was going to be. The coach wasn't willing to waste any time with me because he was all about winning, and I couldn't blame him.

Two months or so in, I still didn't get off the bench, so I never asked why my mom didn't show up to any of the games. Even worse, after timeouts, Diamond would come to sit next to me at the end of the bench and blab on and on about how good he was doing. It was odd, but those were my favorite moments of the games. I always looked forward to it happening because it made me laugh. Overall, we were a horrible team with a horrible record, but it kept Diamond out of the streets and me occupied. That was the best way I could end the year 2009.

2010

Semester 2 Report Card
4080 ALG READINESS MS – grade received C
1520 ENGLISH 8th – grade received B
7951 MLT ST SKLS 8 – grade received A
5502 PHYS ED 8th – grade received B
6005 SCIENCE 8th – grade received B
6551 US HIST & GEO 8 – grade received C

Not bad for a kid who barely paid attention and sat in the back of class sketching Lil Wayne all class long. I pulled off another decent semester at school. Whether the squishy ball was working or my teachers were patient with me. I was still standing; either way I cut it. I could've been doing better in US History and Algebra Readiness if I wasn't too busy daydreaming about meaningless stuff like having sex for the first time and falling asleep in class during lectures. My attention span hadn't grown since elementary school, but I made it happen since that was the goal. So on to the next, the quest for high school options.

Before any of the high school talks could take place, I had to first graduate, which I didn't do. I passed on, but I didn't get to participate in the walking ceremony because I decided to test my fate with just a few weeks left of middle school. Towards the end of the year, substitute teachers became the norm at Bell. Maybe because the actual teachers were over it or because there was nothing much else for them to teach, but I loved it because it gave me the opportunity to exercise my curiosity.

I had a substitute teacher for my US History class which was the last class of the day. We watched movies all day for the last few weeks of school, so the classroom lights were off, and it was super loud because the substitute teacher preferred turning the audio of the movie all the way up. I sat in the back of the classroom near one of the teacher's aid's desks. She was never near her desk, but her purse was. *Jackpot.* I had a game plan. I knew exactly what I was going to do and how I would do it.

Without thinking twice, I made my move and came upon a handful of twenty-dollar bills, fifty-dollar bills, and one ten-dollar bill. I had no clue how much it was or what I would do with it, but I knew I came up, because I had never had that much money to myself before. After strategically stealing from her, I snuck off to the bathroom across campus to try to figure out where to stash my wad of cash. *Right here? Uh. Uh. Dang!* I was panicking because the print in my khaki pants was too visible, but the print in my socks was even more visible, so I split it evenly. I placed half of the cash in my pockets and the other half inside my left and right socks. Back to class I went.

As I was walking back to class, I spotted the inside lights were on, so I knew something was up. Security was standing in the middle of the classroom along with both teachers. They asked us all to empty ourselves, and when I did, I tried to frame one of my classmates by planting the cash in his belongings. My classmate was highly upset, my teachers were upset, and the security was glad he found out who it was. Thirty minutes later, I found myself in Mr. Donaldson's office. Mr. Donaldson was the meanest principal in the world. "This was your last straw. You ruined it. You will not be participating in the graduation ceremony," he said. I thought the punishment was stupid because I was already on my way out, but it was what it was.

8

SUMMER OF SUFFERING

MIDDLE SCHOOL WAS OVER. MY MOM AND THE REST OF MY family didn't get to see me walk across the stage during the graduation ceremony. Instead, my certificate was mailed home. Bipolar, ADHD, Schizophrenia, and now puberty; it wasn't a good mix. This was the beginning of a summer that changed my life.

My mom was getting fed up with me, so she called up Ms. Heather to see if she was able to do in-home therapy sessions, which were even more embarrassing. Unfortunately, Ms. Heather's time was up with me, so it wasn't long before I was seeing someone else. I would've been a fool to believe I was off the hook. Dr. Heidenfelder, a psychiatrist located in the downtown district, was recommended. I had an appointment once a week. We always found a parking spot within decent walking distance, and our wait in the lobby usually wasn't long.

My mind was racing. His office was boxed off by a blurry wall-like curtain. Oddly enough, it was the coolest thing I ever saw. You couldn't see from the outside in, but you could see from the inside out. Since I couldn't see him, I couldn't tell when he was going to come out and call my name. Dr. Heidenfelder was incredibly quiet, patient, and soft-spoken, just like Ms. Heather. He and I had talked for almost an hour. Most of that time, I felt as if I was making it harder for me to help him because of how many times he repeated and rephrased questions he had already asked.

*I don't understand what the f*** you're asking me.* The sessions were weird and awkward because he asked a bunch of questions that were way over my head. I grew angry. It felt like I was in a crime investigation room because of the amount of tension and pressure in the room. When he lifted his head back up, I assumed another question was on the way, so I braced for it, but to my surprise, he looked over at my mom, and I was relieved.

Towards the end of my appointment, the conversation had shifted. I was no longer answering questions. Dr. Heidenfelder was drawing his conclusions and setting up my next steps. I could hear him telling my mom more stuff like, "He scored a 129 on his IQ test, which puts him in the category of very smart people, but there's a huge discrepancy between his IQ and his behavior. He's struggling with anxiety, depression, and schizophrenia. Also, at his current ability to use the information immediately after learning it, he may struggle severely at the high school level." Then he'd prescribe me a new or high dosage of medication. *I guess.*

I didn't think I had depression or anxiety—hell, I didn't even have those words in my vocabulary yet. Either way, I had no choice. The prescription paper was a small, yellow six by six sized sheet he ripped off and gave to my mom to fill at the pharmacy, just like Dr. Desoto used to do. If she didn't have the transportation, we set up for delivery, but most of the time, we headed to the clinic after our appointments to get what I needed.

By the middle of July, I was taking a pill named Abilify twice a day to treat schizophrenia, bipolar disorder, anxiety, and depression. The side effects were hitting me hard. My vision blurred in and out. My appetite changed rapidly. On some weeks, I rarely ate, and on other weeks, I was overeating. The worst side effect of them all was paranoia. So, on my next visit, Dr. Heidenfelder took me off Abilify and switched me to Geodon. Geodon was similar to Abilify, but it was lighter on side effects, except for the drowsiness. I fell asleep much quicker.

Playing football outside of my home with my brothers was something I enjoyed doing on the weekends to avoid falling asleep so fast, until one day, my hip gave out on me. No warning. No pre-existing pain. Nothing. Absolutely nothing. Just a popping sound in my hip that left me in complete shock.

My brothers and I met some random people in the neighborhood to play a game of two-hand touch football on a Saturday afternoon. One of them was running the quarterback position. Jhaylen was playing running back; Jhamir, Jhavari, and I were lined up at wide receiver. We were having a hard time trying to score. At the end of each play, I felt like I heard, "3rd down! 3rd down again, bro!" To make matters worse, the heat was scorching, so sweat was leaking to my ankles, and my hands were extremely sticky. I was hoping Jhamir or Jhavari would make it happen for us because I was thinking, *man, please don't throw me the ball.*

On the very next play, I lined up on the far left at wide receiver as I did many plays before. The only difference was that this was a much-needed down. As soon as I heard "HIKE!" I heard something snap in my lower body, but I wasn't sure what it was. I continued through the play. A post corner route was the one I had in mind, but with each step, the pain increased, so I didn't want to take the risk of cutting inside, so I just faded away.

For whatever reason, the quarterback decided to throw me the ball; I was covered by two but seeing the ball fade over my head pushed me to run even harder, but I missed it. *If I was just a little faster... I would've had it.* The defenders let the ball bounce down the street, and they were excited because it was now turned over on downs. I jogged the rest of the way to grab the ball. I had no clue where I was hurting, but I was eager to win the game and curious to see who was going to score the game-winning touchdown. *It's gotta be me.*

I don't remember how the game ended, but shortly after the game was over, and the sun was almost going down, the adrenaline I previously had left my body, and that's when it hit me—*my hip*. I was confused and scared. I never had any problems with my hips before. I stood up and tried to pace back and forth in my room, and it was difficult. Every time I took a step with my right foot, it felt as if my bones were rubbing together in my hip area. I kept walking around, delusional, hoping it would go away or that I was just overthinking. I was wrong. When my mom peeked in my room to tell me goodnight, I stopped her before closing my door and said, "Mom... My hip hurts. It's kind of hard to walk." "Boy! Goodnight," she replied and slammed the door.

I hiked my hip up whenever I was walking for almost one week until my mom realized I wasn't exaggerating. She kept telling me to fix my walk and that it looked stupid, "Boy, why are you walking like you have a problem! Stop." She wasn't buying into what was going on, and it began to frustrate me. If I can't get her to take me to the ER, then who will? The more I complained, the more she began to become concerned. A sigh of relief came when she glanced over at me one day and said, "Chris, go put on your shoes... Let's go to the hospital. I'm tired of you walking like that."

I was very afraid of going to the hospital because I knew it was something bad. As the minutes went by, waiting for a nurse to come out and call my number, the pain on the right side of my body was gruesome. I wanted to cry, but for some odd reason, I couldn't. I shuffled in and out of positions for almost two hours. One minute, I was sitting on my left side, hoping that would take the pressure off my right side, but it actually did the total opposite. I started to feel a bone or two sink towards my left side. It was the scariest thing I had experienced in my life.

My name was eventually called, and my mom let me lean on her as we made it to the x-ray lobby room. We picked another number and waited for our time. Almost three hours had gone by, and I could tell that she was just as frustrated as I was. I started to feel guilty and afraid. As soon as it was our turn to get x-rays, my mom rushed over to the nurses on call and explained what was going on with my hip, so they brought me a wheelchair so I wouldn't have to walk. They took my x-rays faster than I had ever seen them before.

Once I was done with my x-rays, my mom rolled me back into the x-ray lobby. A few minutes later, I saw one of the nurses who was in the room jogging back into the lobby, "Hey, Mom... you guys will be stationed in room number five!" Almost four hours since our arrival, we were ready to receive what we had driven thirty minutes for.

Dr. Wenger was already in the room, along with the four other teams of doctors he had walked around with. Never have I ever seen him in the room before us. Usually, it was the nurse, my mom, and I, and then after waiting for Dr. Wenger to gather his information, he walked in. At this point, I figured I had hurt myself badly that day in the street playing football with my brothers because of the look on the nurses' faces.

One of Dr. Wenger's colleagues slowly looked over at my mom and said, "Ma'am, I am glad you brought him in. He needs to have emergency hip surgery. Had you brought him in any later, he would've needed hip replacement surgery." It was as serious as we all anticipated it to be. I needed to have surgery on the same exact day because my Greater Trochanter (the ball joint of my femur) slipped out of the hip socket of my hip. After hearing that, I tried to piece everything together. The snap sound, the pain of sitting down, the hip hiking walk. I still didn't want to believe it, but I had no choice. My mom was in disbelief as well. Five hours later, I was changing into a gown and rolled into the waiting room again.

The procedure took two hours to complete. It was the longest procedure I had had so far. Dr. Wenger stopped by to follow up with the specifics, and then I was an in-patient for one day and released to go home. I was sent home with Oxycontin, which didn't help ease the pain. When the pain was too much to bear, I just cried. That was the only fitting expression.

I tossed and turned all throughout each night – at one, two, sometimes three in the morning while no one else was awake. The blazing summer room temperature was over-piling my room while trying to find the right comfortable spot that didn't force me to turn was hard. Sometimes I got tired of trying, so I just sat at the tip of bed, lost in thought, until I cried myself back to sleep. In my mind, I was hoping the summer would come to a fast end.

After I finished my bottle of Oxycontin, I moved on to Ibuprofen, which didn't do much either. Although I was in less pain than when I was first released from the hospital, the Ibuprofen didn't have what it took. I continued to fight through it. By this time, I was able to put pressure on my right side when using my crutches instead of keeping my right foot in the air. It was like learning how to walk all over again.

With each step, I could feel the screw shut up in my pelvis. I was shocked because it was the first time I could actually feel something installed on the inside of my body. I spent most of my days scared to walk. Instead of doing the little things, I'd ask my brothers to hand me stuff. My mom hated it and encouraged me to do it on my own, because I wouldn't get back to one hundred percent by asking other people. I didn't listen. A lot of the time, I spent the rest of the summer days sleeping, which was unlike me because I never took naps. This was also the beginning of lifelong overbite in my walk pattern due to the screw in my pelvis.

Two different pills, for two different reasons, for one entire summer, all while learning how to walk again. So many things were thrown at me. August 2010 was easily the most problematic month of my life. I was learning how to balance my walk, prepare for high school, and cope with the news of unlearning who my biological father was. The night my mom explained to me that Mike wasn't my biological father was the day I questioned if life was worth living still. *If she was raped, then...technically...I'm not supposed to even be here...right?*

This was the summer where life opened up my eyes by the overwhelming feelings of therapy, a physical pain I had never felt before, and a new level of insecurity and uncertainty from a teenage boy who had just found out he was an accident. I could've been the fly guy who hit the mall with a few friends, spent some money, and bagged a few girls, but instead, I fell asleep every night early high off pain pills. I should've been someone cool, popular, and social, but I was the complete opposite. I should've been picking from the many high schools that wanted me to go to their school because I was such a stellar scholar, but I was wrong, dead wrong. I was basically...nothing.

9

MARCY DAY

There wasn't a single high school in San Diego that wanted me on their campus because I was considered a tyrant. Not being accepted to any high school in the district due to my behavioral history and low academics sucked. My mom submitted applications to schools that offered special education and support for IEPs like Mission Bay, Serra, Sweetwater, Hoover, Morse, Lincoln, Mount Miguel, and Helix High School (in that order). Mission Bay High School was the first to say "no," followed by Morse, Helix, and the rest. Even in a ten-student to a two-teacher ratio classroom setting, I was considered impossible to teach. Although I had a decent 7th and 8th grade year run, the damage had already been done. My needs were just too large to be met at the high school level.

The only school willing to accept me was Marcy Day Treatment Program. It was a ridiculously small school that wasn't well known. Marcy was a school for kids who were considered helpless and hopeless. Let's just say it was a pipeline to prison. Kids from different walks of life went there. It was said that most kids didn't make it out of Marcy, and little to none graduated from there. Some dropped out in their early 20's and even late 20's. Some had tattoos and even babies. Once it was described to me, I knew I wouldn't like it. To attend, I had to be bused from outside of my home to the front of the school every day. It was good to hear about how hard it was to get suspended and attractive to know there wasn't much homework offered.

The school bus was shorter than the average size, just like the one at Bell Middle, so when it pulled up to the curb of my house, I was nervous. For weeks I had no idea what to expect from the other students. When the bus driver stopped and pulled the emergency brake, I felt my knees shake. "You need some help?" the driver asked. I was on crutches. "No, I can just hop on one leg up to the top," I replied. I really needed help, but I didn't want anyone to help me. I got on and hopped my way to the back seat near another Black student.

Curtis was his name. I sized him up while he wasn't looking – he was Black, but the total opposite in height. He was about 5'6, while I was nearly 6'3. I stared at the amount of green he was wearing, jewelry, and his sagging pants. I started to wonder if he was from a gang, and sure enough, he was. I tried to look away in time so he wouldn't catch eye contact with me, but he caught me. "Curt. Was hannin?" he said. "I'm Chris," I replied. I was hoping he didn't want to befriend me.

Before I knew it, I felt the bus slowing down, followed by the emergency brake sounding off. It was a short fifteen-minute ride. I let everyone else get off before me because the last thing I wanted was to be in anyone's way. I was one of the last kids to crutch my way off the bus, slowly making it down the steps.

In the distance, I could see a staff member near the entrance with a huge smile on his face as if he were happy to see me. Outside was a silver fence at least ten feet from the ground and guarded around the school. I figured that was designed to keep us locked in. I kept crutching through the entrance, where I was greeted by the happy-go-lucky White middle-aged man who turned out to be one of the two staff members in my classroom, named Mr. Colin.

By this time, I had only seen about ten kids on campus. I was shocked. Within the first thirty seconds, Marcy resembled what I heard about in Juvenile Hall. Not knowing what to expect gave me no expectations, but I wasn't ready for this. I was one of the first kids in class. There was a seat already assigned with my name on it. I sat there and slowly let my eyes dance around the classroom, trying to figure the place out. I didn't like it; I didn't like it at all. *This is going to be a very long year.*

I felt like I was starting all over again, but this time even worse. I was sad for the first two weeks of school because I felt like a prisoner. Every class had two staff members stationed inside monitoring all the students, and I wasn't used to it. I was used to getting it done my way and getting away with things here and there. No more random drawings, no more random side conversations, no more getting up and walking around in the back of the class, no more pulling out random magazines and books to keep myself occupied. The only thing I could get away with here and there was daydreaming, but even then, Mr. Colin and other class staff members caught me.

I became familiar with my on-campus therapist named Ms. Stephanie. It blew me away when she and I met because she seemed to believe me. I wasn't expecting any of that because, in the past, I felt misunderstood by Ms. Heather and Dr. Heidenfelder. Ms. Stephanie, on the other hand, treated me with compassion. I also had to interact with Ms. Ashley; she was my on-campus nurse who fed me my medication every day. She was cool too. Ms. Ashley would always say, "I've heard very good things from Ms. Stephanie about you." *Whatever that means.*

Semester 1 Classes
1540 ENGLISH 1 college prep
0191 ART1 college prep
4041 ALGEBRA 1 college prep
6023 EARTH SCI 1 college prep
5503 PHYS ED 1

The classwork wasn't hard at all, but I could not pay attention long enough to learn anything due to how uncomfortable I was. I also didn't feel comfortable trying to make any friends because of how much of a misfit I felt like I already was. A lot of the other kids came from rougher upbringings than I did: homelessness, gang banging, street violence, drugs, fights, street tagging, and even identity theft. To me, these kids were reckless, and I often felt like my behavioral issues were not on the same level.

I also noticed how the majority of the kids carried themselves. It looked like some of them didn't have much compared to me. For the first time in my life, I recognized how well my mom was keeping me. I never had hygiene problems, I never had to recycle an outfit, went without a haircut, or even dress in mismatched attire, but some of the other kids did. It was heartbreaking and humbling at the same time to witness.

The one thing we all had in common was our academic struggles. Some of us struggled more than others, but nevertheless, we were all behind. English started to become my strength. I was confident in my English class, and I was never afraid to express myself on paper or read a book with really great fluency. I loved it. My art classes were just as easy, too, if not easier than English, because of how much I loved freedom, expression, and creating.

My Earth Science class was boring. I hated every second of it. I barely paid attention because it was the class I had after lunch which meant I just took medication that put me to sleep. *Stay up. Stay up.* I tried my best to keep my eyes open, but sometimes I gave in and slowly laid my head down on the desk for as long as I could. Then I placed my head in between my folded arms until one of the staff members in that class startled me, "Aye, Chris, Chris. You cannot sleep in here. Get up. You hear me!? Get up. Thank you." *Dang man.*

I earned an "A" in my P.E. class for the first time because I played basketball by myself for an hour. However, I struggled badly in my Algebra one class because I didn't learn anything in Algebra readiness at Bell Middle School. My Algebra teacher's name was Ms. Salsa, a middle-aged White lady who wasn't as attractive as Ms. Cornell and seemed to be more concerned with bragging about how much she knew about mathematics rather than teaching us, or at least that's how I felt. She was so arrogant that it got to the point where whenever I felt like I didn't know or wanted her to repeat something, I didn't ask her because I feared being belittled. I prepared for failure long before the semester was over.

My days at Marcy in the first semester were long, and they went by extremely slowly—because of how high I was in class. I wasn't learning much, and whatever I did learn, I forgot. I slept, daydreamed, slept, daydreamed until one day I looked up, and it was almost January. Just right before winter break, I was handed my report card by Mr. Colin. I lifted my head off the desk, scraped the dried-up drool on my face, and immediately flipped it over. It read:

Semester 1 Report Card
1540 ENGLISH 1 college prep – grade received A
0191 ART 1 college prep – grade received B
4041 ALGEBRA 1 college prep – grade received D
6023 EARTH SCI 1 college prep – grade received C
5503 PHYS ED 1 – grade received A

2011

Semester 1 Classes
1541 ENGLISH 2 college prep
0192 ART 2 college prep
4042 ALGEBRA 1 college prep (repeated course)
6024 EARTH SCI 2 college prep
5504 PHYS ED 2

After so many pep talks, medication switching, and physical therapy for my hip, I was back on Marcy's campus and off crutches. Ms. Stephaine believed that if I practiced the steps she taught me, I'd be cleared to become dually enrolled in a high school for at least one semester. She couldn't make any promises, but I was glad to hear it. The goal was to transition entirely into a mainstream setting eventually. Although Mission Bay denied me the first time around, there was a possibility that I would be able to attend Mission Bay and play a sport because Jhamir attended. If it weren't for Jhamir, I probably would've been stuck in Marcy and graduated from there (I'm assuming so).

I thought that was a good thing to think about, but it actually became harder for me to focus because I kept thinking about

Mission Bay. *How would I make any friends?* There was no way that I could picture myself on a high school campus playing football or any other sport alongside Jhamir. Marcy had become a crutch for me. I knew I wouldn't get the same treatment I was getting once I left. I couldn't get my mind together, and it showed up in my grades at the end of the school year.

Semester 2 Report Card
1541 ENGLISH 2 college prep – grade received D
0192 ART 2 college prep – grade received A
4042 ALGEBRA 1 college prep (repeated course) – grade received F
6024 EARTH SCI 2 college prep – grade received D
5504 PHYS ED 2 – grade received B

I was kissing my dual enrollment goodbye after seeing an "F" in math on my report card. I really didn't want to go to a regular high school at that point because I knew the classes were going to get harder. If I couldn't pass Algebra 1 at an adolescent day school, I knew I was in trouble.

Ms. Stephanie didn't see it that way, so I was offered a deal. The "F" in Algebra 1 could be fixed if I took and passed two weighted college classes (1570 ENGLISH 3 college prep & 1169 CARE LIFE MGMT) and started my first semester back at Marcy for my sophomore year. That was the last thing I wanted to do, but I didn't have much choice, so I accepted the offer.

June 13th was the last day of school, and I was scheduled to start summer school on the 27th. I only had one week and a few days to kick my feet up. Those days went by so quickly that I barely felt like I got to see my eyelids. I wasn't mentally prepared to step foot back on Marcy's campus again because the first year was already too much.

I was wrong. It turned out that summer school was only a few hours of the day. After completing classwork, I went on field trips and enjoyed those moments. Plus, it was easier for me to at least try to focus, knowing that I'd be free by noon. Instead of counting the time, I counted the classes. *Just two.* I enjoyed English, so it was a piece of cake, and my Care Life Management class was basically a waste of time. I did so well that I caught one of the staff member's attention.

His name was Mr. L., and he was someone who had always stood out to me from the day we met on campus because he and I were the only tall Black men on campus. We mirrored each other. During the summer, he became a mentor to me. Since there was a possibility that I was going to be moving on, our relationship became personal quickly. He opened up and shared stories with me that would help me in the real world as a young Black male. He would code switch often; one moment, he was a friend, and the next, he was Mr. L. The more we hung around each other, he became someone I looked up to.

He always had a story, but since my attention span was short, it only allowed me to focus for a few minutes. *Man, where's mom? This dude is talking too much.* I tried my best to listen to him because he would kill me if he knew I wasn't listening. Until one day, he shared something with me that was thought-provoking. It was about his time as a UNLV football student. The two of us were waiting for my mom to pick me up. We sat on the table while staring at the empty streets through the fence, and he started talking.

"Boy yo momma be on you boy! You know she called the office four times while we were out." *shakes head* "You have a good momma, man, and that's what will carry you. Mines didn't play just like yours doesn't," he said. He then removed his shades from over his eyes and looked me square in the eye. I knew he was about to get even more serious. Whenever he removed his shades from his face, I paid attention because I knew he was getting ready to drop a gem.

"Bro, I was a college student, a grown man, when my momma found out I was cutting up in class. You know what she did? She drove up to the school and came into my class and sat next to me until I got my act together, and then she told me, 'boy don't you dare disrespect me like this. I worked too hard to pay for your black a** to go to college.'" At first, I laughed in my head. *Who in the world lets their mom embarrass them like that as a man, and why would a mother want to do that? Stupid.* Looking back, I didn't understand what Mr. L meant by that because I was too immature to understand the meaning behind that story. He highlighted points in his life to show me what was important in mine. I'll always appreciate that.

When my report card displayed an "A" in both English 3 and Care Life Management, that's when I knew things might be changing for me next year. I was anxious to know what was next. Since the summer was over, I had one week left to get back into the groove for my sophomore year at Marcy.

On September 11th, four days after the first day of school, Ms. Stephanie walked into my class along with the other on-campus therapists to present awards. I had no idea that on one of those pieces of thin, white paper lay my name and a "Most Improved" title above it. I was surprised. For the first time since my freshman year, I felt like I had accomplished something. I didn't think I deserved it, but I was glad to be recognized.

In the middle of November, I heard Ms. Stephanie calling for my name through one of the walkie-talkie radios of the classroom staff members. I was asked to go to her office like times before, but for some reason, I felt like this time was a tad bit different. I was feeling lucky.

She was smiling from ear to ear when I walked in. "Christopher!" she said and then paused. I had a blank stare on my face. "You have been accepted into Mission Bay High School! You will be with your brother soon." We hugged, and she gave me a folder of papers to take home to have my mom sign.

Although I was happy about leaving Marcy, I was also afraid of transitioning to a huge high school, but I didn't really express it. When I was at home, I didn't say much. At school, I was quieter than usual, and whenever I was out with my family, I held very minimal conversations. I couldn't get outside of my head. *I didn't even change. It's probably just puberty. I won't last at Mission Bay High.* All I could think about was how much of a misfit I was socially and how big I assumed Mission Bay was. I didn't feel like I was ready, even though I was being coached as such by those around me, so I shut down. I stayed in my room all day because I felt safe there. I didn't have to deal with the world that way.

10

MISSION BAY

It was Wednesday, November 30th. It was the day that, for the first time, I would be sitting in a high school classroom with thirty-plus kids. I remember getting five hours of sleep that night because of how nervous I was for the next day. The morning felt even longer than the night.

I arrived at Marcy and went to my first three classes like always, but I couldn't help but watch the clock minute by minute. By the time I got to my third class, I was overthinking so much that when my teacher called on me to answer questions, I simply replied, "Uh... I'm not sure where we are. Can you show me?" Then I would get coached for not participating. "Hey man, that's not going to work on a high school campus. I'm just letting you know right now," Mr. Edgar would say.

After class was over, I walked to the front of the school and through the tall fences, where a short yellow bus was waiting for me to hop on it and drop me off in front of Mission Bay. It was just me and the bus driver on board, literally. Oddly enough, I was cheered up by the view on the way. It was my first time seeing this part of San Diego at fifteen.

The ride was long, and the 5 North highway seemed to be never-ending, but I could see a beach in the distance and airplanes landing at the airport. It was my first time witnessing a beautiful scenic view. *Woah. Wow.*

We exited the freeway. A twenty-minute ride, not bad, but not what I thought it would be. At a stoplight, I looked to the left and saw "Mission Bay High School" painted in large font on a building, and next to it was an electronic board with announcements on it that shuffled through information. Then it hit me... this is it. *This s*** is huge. What the f***.* I was shocked. From the front three buildings attached, I figured the campus was huge. It was bigger than SCPA and Bell. We made a left at the light onto the campus. The bus driver drove all the way to the end so he could turn in the roundabout and drop me off in a direction that would allow him to leave soon after.

By this time, my heart was beating extremely fast. I stepped off the bus and looked back at the student parking lot. I was in awe of the nearly one hundred cars. I wondered if the cars belonged to students or teachers because they looked fairly new. It was November, not September, and not Marcy, so I didn't have anyone at the entrance greeting me, so when the bus took off, I was lost.

It took me almost ten minutes to find anyone on campus to help me find the main office to get my schedule. Jhamir and I didn't have cell phones back then, so I had no way of knowing where he was. I finally came across a teacher coming out of her class, and she gladly showed me. "Back from being sick?" she asked. "Um, oh... no," I replied. She smiled, and I kept moving. As soon as I arrived inside the main office, I started talking to a lady I saw sitting at the front desk. She quickly cut me off and said, "Um, excuse me, sir, you must sign in first." She showed me where to sign in, and I did. I then took a seat and said to myself, *I have a long way to go.* I felt like I was in a foreign country.

An hour after being dropped off, I took a picture for my student ID card and then received it in the main office. "05269611," it read. The lady gave me clear instructions for it. It was for library use, and whenever a staff member or a teacher asked for it. Then, she gave me my lunch number to dial in once I became a full-time student. I was to remember and to hold on to everything she said. *What if I forget?* That was my first time processing more than one instruction at one time; I was a bit overwhelmed.

Before leaving the office, I was introduced to the principal, Mr. Hilgers, and the vice-principal, Mr. Michaelian. It was probably my first time ever seeing two older White men well dressed because I couldn't stop staring at their perfectly tied ties. They shook my hand firmly and asked for my name, but something told me the two of them already knew who I was, so I just said, "Chris." Mr. Michaelian went on about his business, but Mr. Hilgers stood there. Without asking, he leaned in towards me to look at my piece of paper with my one class on it and asked where I was headed. "Um, it says..." I had no clue what I was looking at, and he couldn't see it, so he grabbed the sheet and said, "Oh! Ms. Davenpourt. Follow me."

Ms. Davenpourt's 6111 Biology
1 college prep

I followed his lead. He was a heavier set man. The two of us were silent while walking. *Dang, this place is huge.* I stayed a few feet behind him near his hip area so I could look around and walk at the same time without being noticed. There were two main halls, and both were long. The halls traveled from the football field, baseball field, gym, and all the way to the front sidewalk where students were picked up. As we passed the cafeteria area, my eyebrows raised, and my jaw slowly dropped the closer I got to the football field... *that's the field?!* I only got a glimpse. We swung left, and there was Ms. Davenpourt's door.

He walked me into Ms. Davenpourt's class, and he pulled her to the side to introduce the two of us. We shook hands, and she pointed me to my assigned seat. As soon as I turned my head, I saw what looked like thirty students staring at me. *Oh, s***.* Immediately, I put my head down and looked at the floor. I took my seat and pulled out my binder to get caught up because the class had already started twenty minutes ago. Ms. Davenpourt continued to teach. *Great, this woman has a Russian accent, and I'm late. I'm not going to do good here.* Over time I gained a reputation for being a mild-mannered, shy, and timid guy in her classroom. I didn't talk at all.

I stuck with this biology class until the end of the semester. I was surprised at myself for making it through because I didn't learn a dang thing. I was always on time after my first day. Ms. Davenpourt and I spoke to each other every day but nothing further than a simple "hello" or "Hi." She was kind and unbelievably detailed. Her classroom was full of items that related to biology. Since I sat in the middle row of the class and the seats were high stools, I looked forward and never thought about stealing anything from anyone.

I was one of thirty-two teenagers. Everything felt extremely different. All of it was Greek to me. On day two, she gave the class a homework assignment and didn't exclude me from it. I was angry because I still felt entitled not to have any homework. Instead of letting me off the hook, she pointed out where in the textbook to read from to gather all of the information needed to help me answer the questions. It was fifteen questions. *Mannn.* I thought about the assignment all the way home.

I never thought that one class would be so hard to process. During the morning, I could get away with not paying attention and blurting out stuff whenever, but I had to switch gears once I stepped off of the bus to walk to Ms. Davenpourt's class. The atmosphere in her class was mature. There weren't voices speaking while she taught; it was just hers, and everyone else was listening quietly. When she gave out instructions, no one asked her to repeat them. Sometimes I didn't ask her to repeat it because I didn't want to be embarrassed for being the only one, so if I didn't get it, I let it go. I would rather fail the assignment than speak up. It was my first time ever being in a classroom setting with such large numbers.

These kids were smart, ten times smarter than me, or at least I believed so. I was an abstract thinker, so my thoughts didn't come to me in chronological order like most of my classmates. When Ms. Davenpourt asked for participation, I never raised my hand or even made a facial expression that said I possibly knew the answer. I was intimidated by the number of juniors in the class and even more so by the freshman. I was one of the few sophomores in the class, and because of that, I became insecure. Without asking to find out, I jumped to the conclusion that I was dumb since I was in the class, so I didn't put my best foot forward. Ms. Davenpourt was giving me the benefit of the doubt every step of the way, which helped me pass the first quarter of her class.

2012

On January 27th, I graduated from Marcy, officially. There wasn't a ceremony or anything like that, just a certificate and a picture with the principal, Ms. Ortega. My support system was super excited to know I was moving on from Marcy, but I wasn't. Ms. Stephanie was overjoyed, and so was Mr. L. The more I came across anyone congratulating me, the more I was sucked into the pessimistic mental state I was already in. *How could they possibly be proud of me? I'm behind. Do they not know?*

For the first time in my life, I rode a school bus that wasn't short. Jhamir and I hopped on, and he went straight to the back, and I wiggled my way around to find an open seat. Once the bus took off, I looked around as I did the first week in Ms. Davenpourt's class because I was surprised to see so many students on the bus. The crazy part to me was noticing there were open seats still available. We stopped at another neighborhood to pick up more students before making it to Mission Bay High, and during the bus ride, I got punked for my g-shock. Once we made it, we hopped off one by one. I took a deep breath and headed to the main office to get my updated schedule. By this time, Jhamir was already gone, long gone.

Monday Tuesday Thursday Friday
Period 1/5 - 7:30am – 8:59am
Period 2/6 - 9:04am – 10:33am
Period 3/7 - 10:38am – 12:06pm
Lunch - 12:06pm – 12:45pm
Period 4/8 - 12:46pm – 2:14pm

Wednesday (Minimum Days)
Period 2/6 - 8:41am – 9:47am
Period 3/7 - 9:52am – 10:58am
Lunch - 11:03am – 11:33am
Period 4/8 - 11:38am – 12:44pm

Semester 2 Classes
4041 ALGEBRA 1 college prep
6112 BIOLOGY 2 college prep
8026 ADVISORY CR9-12
4088 MATH CAHSEE SUP

Algebra? As if I didn't take Algebra in the 8th grade, here I am, taking it again as a sophomore in high school. Ms. Davenpourt's compassion for me landed me another seat back for the second semester. The first two classes weren't on my mind as much, but I was curious about what advisory in high school was going to be like. I looked at the bottom of my schedule, and that's when I saw "Math CAHSEE Sup" and then thought to myself, *what now*. I had a huge fear of math.

Mr. Mesa's class sat near the rear of the campus, which was close to the fields. Walking into his class felt much different than Ms. Davenpourt's because he was going to be my first male teacher, and it was Algebra. He gave his intro, "I go by Mr. Mesa. I'm a New York native. I have a military background. I grew up loving sports. I played football and wrestling, and I also participated in the shot put in the track and field events. I love coaching, but more importantly, my heart is near to my young athletes. I take their success seriously."

After he broke the ice, the rest of the class had to do the same. I'm glad I decided to sit jam smack in the back of the class because it gave me some time to think of something to say. "Hi, my name is Christopher, and I like the Los Angeles Lakers," I said while staring at the whiteboard, trying not to make eye contact with anyone. That was the slowest five seconds in my entire life that made me feel like thousands of people were staring at me when in reality, it was only thirty-two.

Advisory was my last class before lunchtime, and I loved it. I did absolutely nothing. It was a class that was intentionally used to catch up on mainstream classes, but since I didn't care much if I was passing or not, I used it to take naps, surf the web, or ask to go to the restroom to walk around. I mean, I figured that I wasn't failing. As long as I could assume that I had a "C," then studying or reviewing work wasn't more important than watching Kobe Bryant's highlights. Ms. Labe didn't mind. Usually, she asked me, "Are you all caught up in your classes?" Of course, I said yes. Free access for one hour and a half to do whatever I wanted.

I made my first friend at Mission Bay in Advisory. It was pretty awkward for me but also a huge break. He was White and the quarterback of the varsity football team, and from what I could tell, he was cool with practically everyone. On this day, he sat across from me and looked me square in the eye, and said, "What's up, bro? I'm Nick. I think I've seen you around before. What's your name?" A wave of nervousness crashed over me.

Before I could answer, he asked a question. "Is your last name Ransom?" he asked. "Yeah," I replied. He squinted his eyes and centered his body towards me. "Are you Jhamir's little brother?" he asked. "Yeah. I'm Chris," I replied. "That's cool, bro. I heard about you. I'm the quarterback on the football team here. You are new, right?" he said. "Yeah," I replied. "Man, that's so cool. Nice to meet you, bro," he said, attempting to continue the conversation. I just nodded my head and said back, "Yeah... same." He turned away to answer someone across the class who was calling his name, so I sat and observed the room. The first and most charismatic person I had seen on campus so far.

During lunch, I never saw Nick. I grabbed lunch and slowly walked around campus. The good thing was I was still learning the campus, so everything looked dope to me. I knew I wasn't fooling anyone though, because everyone, for the most part, could tell I was the new kid. Whenever I felt like someone was looking at me for too long, I acted as if I were looking for someone. I was working hard to avoid anyone or anything that made me nervous. Good thing I had food to eat because that was my only real distraction.

Sometimes I got desperate, and usually, I got lucky and stumbled across Jhamir and his friends goofing around campus. Jhamir was a pretty popular junior and one of the hardest-hitting strong safeties on the varsity football team. His friends, Rodney and Donshay, were really popular varsity players as well. I wanted to hang out with them so bad, but they weren't my friends, and I figured they had no interest in befriending me, let alone hanging out with me. So instead, I trailed them, hoping they didn't catch me.

The end of the school day would drag. I should've been paying attention in this Math CAHSEE Sup class more. If for nothing else, the tools I was being given were tools that were going to get me through my Algebra 1 class for the first time and prepare me for the CAHSEE test. Apparently, the CAHSEE test was a California-mandated test required to receive a high school diploma. It was prep, but it was taken seriously enough to be an actual math class. I didn't care. The last thing I wanted to hear was that I needed more math problems to solve. I hated it so much, but the only thing that kept me afloat was knowing that it was my last class of the day.

A lot was going on in my life as a sophomore in high school. I was depressed, trying to balance the effort of being accepted, passing my classes, and taking my medication on time. I didn't have a therapist, and my mom and I parted ways with Dr. Heidenfelder because our insurance wasn't covering the cost anymore.

Semester 2 Report Card
4041 ALGEBRA 1 college prep – grade received C
6112 BIOLOGY 2 college prep – grade received C
8026 ADVISORY CR9-12 – grade received NG (Not graded)
4088 MATH CAHSEE SUP – grade received C

I wasn't expecting that, but it was what it was, as *long as I passed.* Ms. Labe didn't see it that way. She felt compelled to reach out to my mom to have a conference meeting and discuss what may be necessary for my IEP. The two of them thought it would be a great idea to assign me a therapist because my behavior issues were starting to creep up again, and they didn't want me to go back to Marcy.

11

BALL PLAYER?

During the summer, I was projected to have a sixth surgery procedure done on my lower body to prevent my height from reaching 6 foot 5 inches too fast. Dr. Wenger requested closing my growth plates in both knees to prevent issues later in life. I was filled with fear all over again when Dr. Wenger officially set up a surgery date, but this time I was ten times more anxious than the rest.

Since I thought of trying out for the junior varsity football team, I was hoping for a speedy recovery to give myself a shot. Towards the end of July, I was right back in that same wheelchair, being prepared for another procedure. Yep, no football for me. The goal was to close both growth plates on both lateral sides of my knees and shut them completely so the rest of my body could play "catch up." Before being wheeled back into the operation room, I listened to Dr. Wenger's same old speech phrase for the last time, "You're going to be strong."

About one hour and some change later, I woke up—just me. My mom wasn't there this time. I reminisced as a kid, remembering how the pain brought so much discomfort, tears, and complaints. I thought about it so much that I had an adrenaline rush, and I wasn't feeling the actual pain. My mind was all over the place, but I was trying to remain calm. Almost an hour post-surgery, I haven't dialed for a nurse or even opened my mouth. I finally turned my head to the right, and for the first time, I had a window to look out of. It was an ocean view of San Diego, enough to take my mind off of post-surgery thoughts. *I can't wait to get on that field.*

The pressure and pain I was feeling on the inside of my knees grew deeper and deeper. I couldn't take it, so I slowly turned over to reach for the remote to dial for my nurse. While reaching for it, I saw my mom and nurse walking through the hall towards me. *Thank God.* Tons of questions and statements were thrown at me, and I was so high off of the medication that I couldn't process any answers. All I could feel was painful pressure on my knees as if someone had gripped and locked them tight with a screwdriver so I couldn't move.

The last thing I needed was more medication prescriptions. I was given ibuprofen and four refills of it. It was a lot, but I figured something would have to keep me afloat. I was going to be in bed for at least another month. That was the worst news Dr. Wenger had ever given me. My heart was crushed. Football tryouts were kicking off in a few weeks, and he suggested I take the season off, but I chose not to be cautious and limit my physical contact until the middle of August. As my mom and I parted ways from Dr. Wenger, she rolled me downstairs, and I pulled my hoodie over my head and let tears roll down my eyes. *I just want a chance.*

I never wanted anyone to see me cry. If anyone were going to, it would've been her, but I wasn't comfortable enough for her to see it this time. It was an uncontrollable moment. I kept my head slouched over so no one could see my face. I stared at the thick bandages over both of my knees that covered above my kneecaps to my shins. I couldn't believe that I had to keep them wrapped up for a long time. I rode home with my hood on and the window rolled up, looking out on the highway, staring at the unending beach skyline, letting my mind race.

I had one six-inch metal screw in my hip, a fractured pubic bone, and now my growth plates were closed. Since, for me, sports was a potential social avenue that would give me a name at Mission Bay, the healing process was that much harder. *I can't believe this.* The bigger thoughts enlarged. *What's the point of this surgery stuff? What's the purpose? Why me? When will this be over?* I had questions and no answers. I returned to Rady Children's Hospital about two weeks later, two weeks before a full one month for a checkup. Dr. Wenger walked in and greeted me along with his group of doctors.

He gave me the good and bad news. He was always straightforward, but it was a bit different this time. "Because of the closing of your growth plates, you now have entry-level osteoarthritis. You'll be fine. You will definitely have to limit the use of your knees in sports and in the years beyond. It was a successful procedure. You will continue to grow congruently now. From this day forever, you will be fine, just in pain from time to time. Make sure you stretch."

I recapped and second-guessed what he just said, hoping I heard wrong; *Arthritis, arthritis? Like the stuff older people have. Granny has that. Huh?* He removed the bandages and peeled off the gauze on my knees, and I saw two ugly fleshy scars oozing fluids through dry blood. He grabbed both of my knees, wiggled, and bent them over and over and over. He was checking my mobility and talking to my mom at the same time. So I wouldn't get caught, I took a mental count of all the scars from the waist lower without moving my head. A total of sixteen hypertrophic scars. *Dang.*

I was cleared, but not for physical contact. I still went for it. My high expectations came back to bite me. I assumed since I was a soon-to-be junior and Jhamir had the utmost respect as a varsity athlete on campus, that I was going to be on the varsity team as well. I was wrong. The head coach of the varsity team was named Matson. Coach Matson. A hard nose. Most players had to earn his respect, and to some, he showed favoritism. He also had a temper and wasn't afraid of yelling at anyone. His plan was always to play the strong and bench the weak, so he had no issue with handing me my gear and signing me up for the junior varsity football team instead. *A junior on junior varsity, wow.*

Jhamir was a favored strong safety who, being the oldest brother on campus, was identified by coaches and players as "Ransom." Jhavari, being the fastest of us all, was a highly promising freshman for the junior varsity team, who was also identified as "Ransom" or "Lil Ransom." And then there was me, "Ransom." I've always felt some type of way when coaches used "Ransom" to get my attention because it didn't feel like the name belonged to me, nor was it my identity or what I was. I remember correcting a senior, "Don't call me that." He turned to me and said, "Everyone is identified by their last name. Get used to it."

At the same time, what made things worse was that my older and younger brother were overshadowing me. It was a hard pill to swallow because I was itching to be someone of importance. Being identified as "Ransom" or Jhamir's younger brother didn't help either. I made the junior varsity team, but since I was still on crutches, I sat on the bleachers every day and watched Jhavari and the rest of the team practice. I had one assignment: give the players water after drills. The waterboy...I was basically the waterboy.

It got boring, and at times while I was off on that island by myself, I sat around and thought to myself, *why am I doing this?* Whenever I felt blood rushing down from my knees to my ankles, I stood up on my crutches and walked around until the numb feeling went away. I wandered away to the varsity field and watched Jhamir and the rest of the team practice. I tried being discreet to avoid getting caught by any of the players.

On August 30th, we had our home opener vs. Orange Glen. I hadn't practiced for two seconds, but I was strapped and fully geared up from head to toe as if I were going to get playtime. Once the game started, I forgot that I was even on the sideline because it was the closest I had ever been to a live football game. *This is dope.* Everything was in high definition, and I had a front-row seat. The tackles, jukes, slips, drops, all the way down to our head coach, Coach Farrar, who called the plays the team had practiced over and over. We lost badly. 36-6 in our home stadium and in front of the varsity team, and it wouldn't be the last time either. On the other hand, Jhavari had a breakout game, which was his first of many.

On September 4th, I returned as a junior at Mission Bay High. The most boring year of high school. I sat around in class doing nothing and daydreaming, anything to make time pass. American Literature didn't have any spice, and neither did Ms. Romero. I never knew a teacher at her age could be so boring. She had the appeal of a young and vibrant White woman but taught the way a dry, older White woman would. She either lectured for the entire class or sat and let us write about whatever she lectured about the day before. My medication was no match for my short-term memory. I was lucky if I could remember to write my first and last name on the top of my paper without her having to remind me. It was bad.

Semester 1 Classes
1583 AM LIT 1 college prep
1960 JOURNALISM 1 college prep
6211 CHEMISTRY 1 college prep
5703 PHYS ED 5

American Literature was boring, but Journalism was the most boring class I had by far. Almost three hours of reading and writing from both of my teachers. Mr. Kreamer's voice didn't help either. A White man in his sixties, but you could have mistaken him for someone in their seventies if you talked to him over the phone. Between every word was a two-second pause, and almost everyone talked over him. *Can you hurry up? Dang man.* I established myself as the class clown and embraced it because I couldn't stand to hear him talk. I sat in the front row but on the far right of the class, which was on the opposite side of the exit.

After Journalism, I walked across campus to Mr. Corbin's class. Mr. Corbin had a twin brother on campus who also taught, but I hadn't met him yet. Mr. Corbin and I got along pretty well because he wasn't strict. He didn't care that I was a class clown or barely paid attention. Chemistry itself was my least favorite subject, and I think he could tell.

I failed all of my quizzes and tests but did well on my classroom assignments because I figured out who was the smartest in the class and sat next to them. Even when our assigned seats were changed for stationary purposes, whoever I thought was the genius of the bunch, I made sure to rush to the open seat next to them. I never got caught cheating by any of my classmates or Mr. Corbin because we often worked in groups, but I never participated. I couldn't embarrass myself like that. I left all of that molecule and nuclear stuff alone. *Y'all can handle it. I'm not answering any of these questions.*

By the start of November, the football team had two wins and three losses, and I contributed to none. Riding the bench, that's all I was good for. I didn't expect to play, but the joint pain I felt during up-downs, blocking drills, and tackle drills were worth it if I could get other Black kids to accept me. I was willing to put my body through some of the worst pain to earn a name on campus. Since I wasn't smart and didn't show any evidence of other talents, football had to be the only option, and so far, it was working.

I had all C's and one A. The one A was in P.E., which was handed to me because I was on the football team. When I handed my mom my progress report, she looked at it and gave it back to me. "Good job," she said. It was dry, but she and I knew that was all I was good for, so she didn't mean anything by it. That was my expectation, C's. I was the son who brought home the C's.

Someone must've been praying for me because I was making it through the first semester of my junior year in the classroom and the football facility. I gained a lot of weight from post-surgery, which wasn't beneficial on the field or in the weight room, so I was nearly 230 pounds full of body fat. Luckily I was close to 6'4. If I weren't, I would have appeared to be fatter. All of the other defensive linemen could bench press and squat almost twice their body weight, both junior varsity and varsity. Whenever it was time to lift weights, I was nowhere to be found, and no one went looking for me. I was amazed at how many workouts I could skip without a coach noticing and survive each day at practice. I started to regret it once we ended the season with two wins and eight losses.

I tried out for the basketball team one week later, hoping to make the varsity squad. I thought my height alone would wow the coaches enough, but I was wrong. After meeting the coaching staff after the first day of tryouts, I was discouraged. Coach OJ was his name. He was the junior varsity coach and the first Black coach I met on campus. He was a heavy-set man who had a southern accent, but I couldn't figure out where down south he was from. He was also a bike rider who had an old-school feel for the game of basketball. He approached me to let me know that I would be practicing with the junior varsity squad for the rest of the week of tryouts. At that very moment, I knew that respect and positions were earned on campus regardless of grade level.

I, along with the rest of the players, ran all week; we barely touched a ball. I was out of breath within the first thirty minutes of tryout practice, and from that point on, I contemplated quitting. *Just walk out, e*specially when Coach OJ became blunt. It seemed like every five minutes, I was being called a "Slow a**" or being told to "move my slow a**." I was giving it all I could, too, but it wasn't enough for the coach. My knees were sore, and I didn't feel like I had much mobility. Every cut, drive, pivot, and switch move was slow, and it took a lot of brainpower. Coach OJ was right, but I was bothered since it was the first time hearing strong criticism. I never hated running and basketball coaches as much as I did during tryouts.

On Friday, after practice, he gave us a speech. It was about twenty-plus potential players, and my head was filled with doubt. I knew I didn't have a chance. "Great job from a lot of y'all. Y'all worked hard. I was surprised. Some of y'all could've worked much harder. I was disappointed in many of you. We are going to have to pick up on the drills much quicker. We are going to have to learn how to hold on to the ball. We are going to have to learn the basics before we can fly. The results will be posted on the door of the locker room," he went on and on. He repeated himself and looked us all in the eye while doing so. I caught the late bus home and hung my head down low. I knew it was going to be a long weekend.

I returned to campus on Monday, and in between my classes, I intentionally took the longer routes to make my rounds around the basketball locker room. *Dang, nothing so far.* For four periods straight, I didn't see a thing posted. *Maybe it flew away. Maybe he's unsure yet. Maybe he's editing the list... and adding my name to it.* I was saying anything to myself that would make me feel good and keep me from thinking negatively, and it was working. During P.E., in the distance, I saw someone who looked the complete opposite of Coach OJ posting what I believed to be the results on the door. I slipped away secretly to avoid getting caught and walked towards the door.

It was the varsity basketball team coach posting up both lists. His name was Coach Kane. I think he knew someone was walking up. He taped it on the door and walked away. My full name stood out at the very bottom of the list, just as it did at Bell. I felt the weight leave my shoulders when I saw it on the paper. I even stared at the page for a few minutes in disbelief. I pronounced my first and last name five times under my breath and looked at each letter to make sure they didn't make a mistake. *Yep, that's me.*

I made the team, but tryouts were the easiest part. I was in for one. In fact, I was still out of shape. All of my teammates were fast. I finished every defensive drill, fast-break drill, and rebounding drill in last place. It was horrible and embarrassing. Every so often, I would get called a slow m*****f***** by Coach OJ. When I pushed the last ounce of energy I had to finish, I would still hear remarks like, "You need to pick your d*** knees up, Ransom." I was looking for him to ease up, but he never did.

I went home discouraged every day, but I preferred that because it gave me a certain level of clout on campus. Sometimes it made me the laughingstock because I was a junior playing on the junior varsity team and not the varsity team. I laughed with guys who I thought were laughing with me when in reality, they were secretly laughing at me. I could see it in their eyes, and in those moments, anger brewed on the inside. The discouragement made for an awfully long winter that was just getting started.

On December 1st, we played in our first tournament, and I didn't play a single minute. Coach OJ said he wasn't going to tell us who the starters were until it was time to go out for the tip, but I was no fool; I knew exactly where I would be. We won our first game, 45-42, against Christian High. It felt like I was watching a movie. The referees, the supporters, and even both teams felt surreal to watch. I had never seen anything like it before, but I had time to get used to it because my only job was to sit down when the ball was inbound and stand up during timeouts and at the end of every quarter.

We played in our second and final tournament before the regular season. We lost to a school from Highland Salt Lake City, Utah, who looked and played like a varsity team. A few guys were dunking during warmups, which made me glad that I wasn't going to see any floor time because all I could picture was seeing myself getting dunked on. I guess it worked out in our favor because we lost 64-31. Both tournaments exposed our weaknesses as a team: rebounding, size, attitude, strength, and teamwork. I thought it would be a long season, just as Coach OJ said it would, but it wasn't. In the blink of an eye, basketball ended, and we didn't win a single game.

12

SENIOR YEAR

2013

Right before the spring ended and the summer of my senior year was on the way, I made two new friends who became like brothers, Andre (who went by "Dré") and Derrell. These two were the first Black kids to introduce themselves to me. Each encounter threw me off because I wasn't expecting it, but I loved the fact that they wanted to befriend me. I met Dré and Derrell roaming in the halls at different moments, but when we crossed paths, they gave me a warm handshake and said, "What's up, bro?" and asked me for my name. It turned out that Dré and Derrell had been best friends since the sandbox and groomed themselves into sharp athletes who also grew up in the southeast. I clicked with the two instantly.

Derrell was a big personality on campus who everyone loved. He had a sense of magnetism about him that drew people near him. To this very day, I've never heard anyone say anything bad about him.

He was always laughing and cracking jokes, but he was even more known for the cornerback position on the varsity football team. Football was one of his talents, and his IQ as a football player was higher than most high school players because of the amount of experience he gained during his pop warner football days.

Dré was everything I dreamed of being in high school when I was in elementary school, but since I knew I could never obtain it, I admired him. He had it all on and off the football field: dog, finesse, and aura. He was the guy practically everyone knew on campus. Whenever he and I hung out, I was around his pre-existing friends, who mirrored some of the same traits he had. I met his friends too at different times: James, Lamarriel (who went by LT for short), Airric, Frankyln, Deion, Isaiah, Alex, and Justin.

Some of those guys were football players, some were basketball players, and a few played both. I even reunited with Devante (from the 3rd grade), who had known Dré since they were kids. It was a wonderful feeling to become friends with those guys. I looked up to all of them, and I learned a lot from them in a short time. I smoked weed, drank alcohol, and occasionally ditched school with a few of those guys. Don't get me wrong; I wouldn't say these were bad guys or a bad influence; they just showed me a side of the teenage life I had not experienced yet, and I loved every second of it.

Dré and Derrell, along with the rest of the guys, actually grew up with their fathers and had relationships with them. Oftentimes, I think that's why they believed in themselves so much. It kind of rubbed off on me. I listened and learned from them, especially when it was time to leave campus. I didn't drive or have a car as they did, but they didn't mind letting me ride with them when we hit the road. While I was stepping on the bus to take the long ride back home, they were pushing the gas themselves.

Dré and I continued to grow closer as friends through good times and laughter. We acted a complete fool in Mr. Corbin's Design & Mix Media class because Mr. Corbin was a former NFL quarterback for the San Diego Chargers who was super laid back and didn't like to micro-manage his students. Knowing that Dré and I were ballplayers, he cut us slack, so we took full advantage. Most of the time, we had our software tools loaded up on our desktop for our classwork, but we couldn't stop cracking jokes and talking about music and sports long enough to complete our work.

We sat off on an island in the back of the class, wayyyy off in the corner. Nobody could see what we were doing, plus it was only a two-seater desk. We searched music websites like datpiff.com and traded our favorite tracks when Mr. Corbin wasn't monitoring our screens. Dré and I had similar music tastes: Wiz Khalifa, Kendrick Lamar, Jay Rock, ScHoolboy Q, Juicy J, and Mac Miller. Whenever Mr. Corbin switched his screen to check everyone's screen, we minimized our tab so we wouldn't get caught. It was hilarious because he tried so hard to catch us, but we were just too fast. We got a good laugh out of it. I wouldn't trade the fun Dré and I had in Mr. Corbin's class for nothing.

Well, there was one difference in that class, Dré finished his work, but I didn't. Mr. Corbin did things the simple way: he gave us the assignment at the beginning of class and then left us be. The assignments were simple too, but I preferred procrastinating and copying off of Dré towards the end of the class. The problem was since it was a graphic design class, my finished product was supposed to look different than his. However, my work looked a little too similar to Dré's. Starting off my day in Mr. Corbin's class was probably the best thing for me because my freedom wasn't chained. I had a sense of free will, and I loved it, although my class grade wasn't looking too sweet.

I enjoyed my long walk across campus to Ms. Andrews' History class because she was an easy-going teacher. She knew who I was because she already knew Dré and Derrell, and I was a new student-athlete, and she was an advocate for student-athletes. She knew all of the coaches on campus, and every teacher who was connected with coaches didn't want the student to fail. My introverted side kicked up in this class because I didn't have Dré or anyone else to talk to, so I sat in the back and watched time pass. I listened just enough to remember what to do but not to actually learn anything, and I kept my mouth shut so I could answer the questions when asked.

Semester 2 Report Card
0245 DES MIX MED college prep – grade received C
6702 US HST/GEO college prep – grade received C
4142 GEOMETRY college prep – grade received C
7953 MLT ST SKL 10-12 – grade received A
8027 ADVISORY – grade received NG

It felt like time was just passing me by. After witnessing how fast my junior year went by, I wondered how concerned I should be for life after high school. All of my friends always talked about how badly they wanted to play division one football or basketball. But as for me, I knew better. I knew sports weren't for me, but I didn't know what was for me.

Time forced me to think hastily. *Should I just go ahead and play varsity football?*

I blinked, and then I was inside the varsity football locker room, picking out my locker. I was able to choose from the top row of lockers since I was a senior. After choosing a top locker, I sat around for a moment and soaked it all in. I couldn't believe it. I was humbled by knowing that, by default, I had to play on the varsity team because I was a senior. I walked out of the locker room looking forward to being on the same field with Jhavari, Dré, Derrell, Airric, and the rest of the guys.

We had "two-a-days," also known as "hell week," which was basically two practices in one day with an hour break in the middle. It felt more like hell than anything, so I called it hell week. On the first day of practice, I got a taste of varsity football. I was winded within the first twenty minutes. I was in the middle of bear crawl drills with the rest of the offensive lineman when one of them messed up, and before you knew it, we were all doing up-downs for five minutes straight. Three minutes into it, I felt like I was going to die. I started to think about how out of shape I was. Since I wasn't used to being held accountable, I figured it was best to walk on thin ice with my o-line coach.

I was weak, not only for an o-lineman but for any position. I wasn't benching or squatting nearly as much as the other lineman, and it showed in the weight room and on the field. I was getting put on my butt nearly every other drill. It was embarrassing, but I held my own. I contemplated quitting every day during that summer. It was too hot, the days felt long, and I assumed I wasn't going to play much, but I didn't give up. And then I met my coach.

"My name is Coach Roman, a former Rugby player at Humboldt State University. Nice to meet you, Ransom," he said. He was the team's offensive and defensive line coach. Then there was Coach Carp who specialized in the running backs and receivers. Coach Washington, a former NFL middle linebacker and super bowl champion for the Washington Redskins coached our linebackers. Coach Galley was our free safety, strong safety, and overall defensive coordinator. Coach Peterson (the funny one) controlled our entire special teams group. Last but not least, our head coach, running back, and quarterback coach was Coach Matson.

Coach Matson looked, dressed, and acted just like John Gruden, the former Oakland Raiders coach. From head to toe, he could've been mistaken as John Gruden, from the visor, shorts, t-shirt tucked in, ankle socks, and running shoes. Plus, he was crazy like him too.

Our first game occurred before school started and showed just how good our coaching staff and my teammates were. We traveled by bus up north to play Orange Glen. Everyone was nervous, but we knew how hard we worked and what we were capable of doing. Plus, we were like the underdogs of our division. No one in San Diego county expected much from us, so we had something to prove.

That night we proved ourselves. We beat Orange Glen, 41-3. They knew they didn't have a chance by halftime, but they played their hearts out. Walking away with our first win was a good feeling because I shifted my thinking; *well, if I don't play, at least we will be a winning team.*

The following week was the week school started. There was an unspoken rule at Mission Bay: "take it easy on the seniors." So, I only had a few challenging classes, Stocks and Management, Statistics, and English. I expected it to be an easy ride, but it wasn't. Thankfully, I had an amazing counselor who was incredibly supportive by the name of Ms. Schwartz. She had heard all about me, and her motto that applied to me applied to all of the seniors: "I want to make sure that all of you graduate on time." Her actions matched her words.

Miss Heather was still willing to drop by once a week and have sessions with me. However, she didn't know that I was getting burnt out on therapy. It wasn't because of her or anything she was doing; it was more so because of me. I didn't think I needed it anymore, and I didn't want any of my new friends to know I had a therapist. That would've been beyond embarrassing for me.

She dropped by the same class at the same time on the same day, Tuesday mornings, in Coach Frink's English 3 class. See, the thing about it is Coach Frink didn't teach as a traditional teacher would. He was a baseball and football coach, so his style was different. His voice was more demanding, louder, and encouraging. So, whenever anyone knocked at the door to pull someone out of class, he paused from teaching, and that ultimately shifted the attention to me. It sucked. "Ransom, door," he said while shrugging his shoulders bluntly.

I never had the guts to tell her, so instead, I showed up and did what I had to do. After a while, Miss Heather wasn't working with me; she was working with a liar. I lied to practically all of the questions she asked me and made-up conversations just to make time pass. It's one of those things that if I could go back and do it differently, I would because I didn't know how beneficial therapy was. Nonetheless, Miss Heather and I were falling off slowly.

On the Friday of that first week back to school, we beat a faith-based school named Horizon Christian Academy, this time, 41-0. Our defense shut down their offenses from gaining any yardage. Derrell caught an interception that he almost returned for six points. I enjoyed watching Derrell and Dré succeed on the field. It was honestly pretty embarrassing to watch the other team lose from the sideline; that's how bad of a loss it was for them. I looked forward to games every Friday because I knew my friends would handle business, although I wasn't getting any burn.

After Horizon Christian Academy, we played Patrick Henry High on our home field and beat them 35-22. That was such an exciting game. It was the first one that made my heart race, and I loved that feeling because sitting on the sidelines started to become more boring than I thought it would, so the only thrill I got out of the game was watching a close battle.

That following Monday, I was thrown into the first team practice squad. I made sure that I was on my P's and Q's during practice: clearing out blocks, and pancakes, playing until the whistle sounded, and no false starts. That week went by fast. I blinked, and it was Friday, 7 p.m., at Claremont High School. I was going to get my first start in my first high school football game against one of Mission Bay's historical rival schools.

We had a few rival teams: Madison, La Jolla, and Claremont. There was one known rule for seniors on the football team: we don't lose to Claremont, EVER. Claremont High School was like our little brothers. They weren't considerably on our level. That night I found out that it wasn't some closet rule; it was true (we won….). I didn't play how I envisioned I would, but I played well for someone who had never played one down in an organized tackle football game. For the first time in a long time, I was proud of myself. It was hard not to smile while walking up to my mom after the game.

I sat on the bench against Christian High (who we beat 24-21) and Madison High (who beat us, 42-7), but I was right back at it versus Kearny High, Senior Night. This time I played even better. When I was in the huddle and heard Nick call "gold," I would get excited because I knew that meant the play was going in my direction. Since the colors of our uniforms were black and gold, black meant the play was going in the left direction and gold in the right direction. I lived for the moment Nick aggressively whispered "gold" in the huddle because I knew at any moment Coach Matson could've pulled me out of the game.

I played the next two games as well versus La Jolla (who we beat

48-17) and Point Loma (who we also beat 26-22). My favorite game of the season was versus Point Loma because Dré saved us by turning a wide-receiver screen into a fifty-yard plus touchdown that was called to the "gold side." If it wasn't for the block I secured, I don't think he would've made it to the end zone. I remember looking up as the play transcended down the field. *Man, this dude is fast.*

The last game of the season was versus Coronado High, and on that day, I received my first and only reality check. SOMEONE PUT ME ON MY A**. After playing quite a bit, I got comfortable, which was a huge mistake. It was the foggiest game of the year, and as a team, our minds were set on the playoffs. I'm assuming the fog was heavy because the elevation in the city of Coronado was an island that sat on a lower level than the rest of San Diego. (To get to Coronado High, you had to cross a long bridge.) I guess the fog stole my attention, I don't recall, but I do recall being on the floor, looking up at the fog.

Coach Peterson asked me to fill in on the kickoff return team for the last few games of the season. I enjoyed it more than actually playing in the trenches because I had more room to roam around like a defensive back, safety, or running back, you know, the positions everyone dreams of playing but doesn't have the skill level to actually play. I was on the front line on the far right, so I was always close to my team's sideline. My job was simple: pedal backward in the direction the ball was kicked. If Dré gets it and decides to take the ball to the right side, block the kill man in front of me; if not, let him be.

The ball landed deep on the far left end of the field. Dré picked it up and ran down the left sideline. I left the kill man alone because he had no chance of catching Dré. Before I could actually get to the left side of the field, the kill man charged straight at me and blindsided me. *OH S***. I didn't see him coming.* It was the first time I experienced being hit so hard by another body in my life.

When I raised up from the turf, I noticed he was a lot smaller than me, but he knew I didn't see or feel him coming, so he hit me hard, just enough that I would fly back a few feet. As the game went on, I was glad it happened because it drove me to vengeance. *I'm not going out like that.* I was looking for that guy for the rest of the night but couldn't find him, so I ended up taking it out on one of the defensive linemen who I injured in the fourth quarter. Despite this change of events, we won 49-13 and were headed to the CIF Playoffs.

Although I only played a few snaps versus Brawley in that first CIF playoff game, I was content as long as we won. We ended up smoking Brawley 41-16 and prepared to go to the next CIF level against Madison, who embarrassed us during the regular season.

It was raining hard the night we played at Madison's house. It was like something you'd see in a football movie. Madison was tough, but we were tougher. Dré caught a game-winning catch that helped us beat Madison 21-18. That following week, LT picked apart Rancho Buena Vista High defensive backs with his route running ability, and it gave the team the burst it needed to carry on all game long. Their cornerbacks couldn't handle our receiver core. LT was like Vince Carter, Dré was like Tracy McGrady, and Nick threw for 200 plus yards, leading us to beat Rancho Buena Vista High 56-49. I enjoyed watching that game more than any other game.

One more game, just one more. One more game, and we were CIF champions. Although some of my teammates' parents didn't agree, Coach Matson demanded we practice during Thanksgiving break. A lot of our key guys were injured yet still playing. Even though the playoff battles took a toll on some of my teammates' bodies, they were able to get enough rest for our last opponent, Saint Augustine.

Saint Augustine had been dominating all season long, so we weren't surprised when we heard that they, too, were advancing to the championship. They say defense wins championships, and Saint Augustine proved it. We didn't look like the team that murdered Claremont, La Jolla, and Coronado. Instead, we looked like Claremont, La Jolla, and Coronado. I can count on two hands how many first downs we earned. Our running backs couldn't get out of the backfield long enough to move the chains. Nick didn't have enough time to get the ball to Dré or LT. Their defense killed us, and that's what stopped us from being crowned as champs.

August
at Orange Glen (Escondido, Ca) (W 41-3)

September
at Horizon Christian Academy (W 41-0)
vs Patrick Henry High (W 35-22)
at Claremont High (W 41-0)

October
vs Christian High (W 24-21)
vs Madison High (L 42-7)
vs Kearny High (W 42-28)
at La Jolla High (W 48-17)

November
at Point Loma High (W 26-22)
at Coronado High (W 49-13)

CIF Playoffs
vs Brawley High (W 41-16)
at Madison High (W 21 - 18)
at Rancho Buena Vista High (Vista, Ca) (W 56-48)

CIF Championship
at Saint Augustine (Qualcomm Stadium) (L 49-0)

    I saw my friends cry for the first time. A lot of teammates were sad for a few weeks, but the entire school spirit was crushed. There wasn't much school spirit for a while. It was a turning point for a lot of my friends, who focused on the next important thing. For some of them, it was college, track & field in the spring, or getting high and going to class. As teammates, we were hurt, but the relationships we built would transcend forever. As for Dré, LT, and I, we wanted to finish out the senior year strong by playing varsity basketball (that's what I had been waiting on).

    We had only one week to rest before tryouts began, so we didn't really have much time to grieve over the loss against Saint Augustine. Both Dré and LT accepted football scholarships to Texas Christian University and the University of Massachusetts, respectively, so realistically speaking, they didn't need to play basketball; they just wanted to. I briefly asked LT if he was going to play, and he looked at me and said, "Ya, I'mma ball." Though his answer was clear, his facial expression didn't look convincing. I took his word for it and expected to see him at tryouts. I didn't ask Dré because I knew he was one of those freakish athletes that not only could play any sport but was going to. I felt more confident knowing I was going to walk in with those two.

    Coach Kane (the varsity basketball coach) was a hard case,

harder than Coach Matson. He was like the male version of the late great Pat Summit. Everyone on campus knew him to be the coach not to play with. I never had a class with him, but I found the rumors about him to be true. He didn't play any games. I thought Coach Matson was crazy, but in reality, Coach Kane was insane, and I was soon to experience his insanity.

He drove the same car every day (an all-black BMW) and parked in the same spot near the basketball gym. He kept the same gym bag of basketballs in his office and brought them out to the gym every day before practice. He did everything in the same manner and the same routine, over and over and over. He was like a robot because he rarely smiled or changed his everyday routine.

During tryouts, I was wishing that I hadn't joined because of how tired I was after practice. After the first few days, I knew I was the sorriest player on the team. My game was weak, no left-handed layups, no left-handed crossover, no speed, nor endurance, no bounce, no court vision, and no basketball IQ in comparison to the guys out there. My jump shot and defense were my only two decent attributes, but I didn't think that was enough.

I think the worst part about it all was I constantly compared my game to the other players who were trying out. Sometimes I would sit out during drills because I didn't know what to do, and no one had the time to teach me. (I don't blame anyone, though, because I wouldn't have taught me either). Watching other players effortlessly do reverse layups, dunks, no-look passes, knock-down shots, and lockdown each other made me question whether I belonged. *Don't quit. Keep going.*

To top it all off, Coach Kane ran us until we couldn't run anymore for all of the team and individual errors made during practice. I puked a few times, but I jugged some water after and got back out there. We ran every day at the end of practice because I was bound to screw up. We ran sprints, and there was a certain way he wanted us to run as a punishment.

Full court. There and back is counted as one rep. One must be completed within ten seconds. There and back twice is two reps. Two must be completed within twenty seconds, and so on and so forth. Once we made it to the end of the court, we had to start all over from the top if we didn't touch the line with our foot or hand. Most of the time, we ran what he called five in fifty-five, which meant five sprints in fifty-five seconds. If one of us didn't make it, we all had to do it again, and you can guess who didn't make it almost every time. Towards the end of tryouts, I altered my assumptions about him because of how many passes he gave me. He wasn't the worst guy on campus. He was just about business.

I didn't think I was going to make the team. I was still in football shape, but not basketball shape. The worst part about that was that Dré and LT weren't either; however, they were naturals, so all of the drills weren't a problem for them. Since I didn't have much ball skills, I was running the five in every scrimmage. Good idea for Coach Kane to throw me in at the five, but it didn't serve me well because I didn't have the skill set necessary to play the five either. I was just out there taking up space.

After the days of tryouts were over, Coach Kane told us that he'd have the results within one week. He kept his word. One day, during lunch, as I was headed to one of my classes to turn in a late assignment, LT informed me that the results were posted on the boys' basketball locker room door. Once I got to the door, no one was there. The paper was taped to the door with one piece of scotch tape. The wind was close to blowing it away, so I grabbed the paper and held it down. There in alphabetical order, it read: *Christopher*

Ransom. I didn't think I would make the team, but I did, and it was like a dream come true. *Came a long way from those days on the blacktop at Bell.*

My mom showed up to a few of my games, but since her lower back couldn't handle the rock-solid bleachers, I relied on one person to take me home, Dré. It wasn't much for him since we lived about ten minutes away from each other. Dré, along with practically the rest of my teammates, either knew how to drive or had their license and a car. Dré had his license and his own car. I had never been behind the wheel before. Thankfully, Dré and I were pretty close because he was always willing to take me home as long as I'd give him a little gas money here and there.

That was a good feeling because I knew then that he was not only an enjoyable friend but someone I could potentially trust if I needed help, but I didn't want to use him just when I needed help. I looked forward to those rides home more than the scrimmages and games themselves. Unfortunately, since I knew I wouldn't play often, sometimes that's all I would think about before the tipoff.

See, Mission Bay was a pretty big school. The population was high, so maybe I shouldn't say that Dré was the most popular guy. Maybe he was just popular to me. I don't recall what type of car he drove. All I remember was that it was burgundy. Not too old, not too new. I just knew where to find it, although he never parked in the same spot because it was one of those cars that was easy to spot. (Not many cars are painted burgundy).

Dré and I had some of the best car rides together when the night was over. Around 9 p.m., it was a guarantee that we were on the freeway flying and bumping music through the sound system of his car. Since I didn't have a cell phone of my own at the time, and he did, he shuffled through some songs we knew just as we did as juniors in Mr. Corbin's class.

Then he'd turned the music down to talk. "Bro, I think it's weak that Coach Kane doesn't give you much burn. Like dang, n**** put the homie in the game."

I laughed. It was never a dull moment with Dré. He kept his window rolled up, but I liked mine cracked a little so that I could feel the night's cool breeze. Just like it was the day I first arrived at Mission Bay, I witnessed the skyline view with the passing of landing airplanes on the 5 highway heading south. It was also one of the only times I got to see downtown San Diego fully lit up at night. It was pretty cool.

2014

It was almost as if Dré spoke it into existence because Coach Kane subbed me in a game a few games later. It was random, I didn't expect it, and I didn't think I was ready. Coach rarely sent for anyone, and rarely did he get up to see who was on the bench. As he was coaching those on the floor from his seat, he'd just yell your name. We (us players) had to listen for the call, so when I heard my name, it woke me up. My teammates were so accustomed to it that we knew when he was calling for someone. "Chris... go in for Slim!" *Oh, shoot.*

There were about five minutes left in the fourth quarter, and Scripps Ranch High called a timeout. I had been squatting down after checking in at the scores table before the timeout, which was killing my knees. After the timeout, I stood up, tucked my jersey in, and boldly walked on the court. *This is my opportunity.* I was asked to help on defense at the five.

One of my teammates launched a three on the first position, and it bounced off of the rim and backboard and landed in my hands. I kissed it off the glass, and a referee blew the whistle before it fell through the net. I was fouled, although I didn't feel it. *And one.* As I turned around to walk to the free-throw line, I thought to myself, *I really just made that.*

Senior night was another game I played vs. Cathedral Catholic High. It was the game that acknowledged the seniors' last year as student-athletes. The night didn't go as expected because we were getting blown out, and I hadn't seen the floor until the fourth quarter. The funny thing about it was that it was more embarrassing to get subbed in during those last five minutes than not to play. It wasn't like no one knew that I was a senior because I was already introduced as one. At this point, there was nothing I could do but show up and give everything I had for the last five minutes. I didn't do much, and the clock ran out to sound the game buzzer.

I didn't play a single minute during the playoffs. I'm glad I didn't get checked in because the intensity was too high for me, and I think the coach knew that. There were times during the playoffs when we looked like we were going to lose, but I was hopeful. Sometimes we were down ten points, and then there were times when we were up five points with momentum on our side. The crowds were louder, and the teams were tougher. I was proud of my teammates because they were playing hard, really hard. We were able to beat Castle Park High by scrambling for a few loose balls that put us ahead when we most needed it.

During the semi-finals, weeks' worth of practice, the coach expressed dearly how much of a shooting team San Marcos was, and the only way to get to Morse was through them. "They live by the three! Understood!?" Coach Kane yelled. "Not any of those mid-range jump shots but deep balls!" He told us over and over and over again that if we could contest and defend the three, we could easily win and give ourselves a chance at the championship. He didn't talk much about playing in the CIF championship because he wanted us to focus on San Marcos High first. *Live by the three, die by the three.*

After the tip ball, it was like all hell had broken loose. San Marcos started firing from all cylinders like the Golden State Warriors. They had two players who could shoot from literally anywhere on the floor (just like Klay Thompson and Stephen Curry), and though they made it look simple, we couldn't stop them. They had two shooters that would come off of a pick and land in the deep corner pockets of the court. This team was shooting at a collegiate level.

We played some really good shooting teams throughout the season, but nothing like what we were experiencing. I remember sitting on the bench thinking to myself, *Well, this is over.* And it was only the end of the second quarter. There was a lot of silence in the locker room, and my teammates looked defeated. For the first time during the season, I felt sorry for them. I remember seeing everyone's head down. We all knew it was over.

By the time the fourth quarter had eight minutes left, Coach had subbed me in. Coach Kane never checked me in before the five-minute mark, so I knew then that he was throwing in the towel. The season was over. I remember hearing some of the players on the San Marcos team talking trash directly to our faces. I had never experienced trash talk like that before, upfront and in my face. It felt weird, but there was nothing I could say back.

I was only in the game for three minutes, and I felt the feeling of defeat for the first time. It was then that I was grateful that I didn't get any playing time during the CIF football championship. It was then that I slowly started to understand why my former football teammates were crying that day and sad for weeks. The last thirty seconds were the worst because the stands were almost empty, and my teammates had taken off their warm-ups and headed towards the exit. That was the last basketball season I ever played.

Kiwanis Tournament
vs. Helix High (W 65-53)
vs. Morse High (L 68-67)
vs. Mount Miguel (W 74-44)

Surf n Slam Hoops Classic
vs. Potomac School (McLean, Va) (W 61-60)
vs. Woodcreek High (Roseville, Ca) (L 63-43)
vs. Cedar Park Christian High (Bothell, Wa) (W 52-26)

League
vs. Scripps Ranch (W 52-26)
vs. Lincoln (W 80-51)
at La Jolla (W 54-40)
vs. Mater Dei Catholic (L 49-35)
vs. University City (W 54-39)
at St. Augustine (L 59-51)
vs. Cathedral Catholic (L 61-34)
at Scripps Ranch (W 57-32)

vs. Bishop's High (W 63-47)
vs. La Jolla High (W 63-47)
@ Lincoln High (W 52-29)
vs. St. Augustine High (L 54-53)
@ University City High (L 66-39)
@ Cathedral Catholic High (W 54-40)

Playoffs
vs. Castle Park High (W 66-58)
vs. University City High (W 53-48)
Semi-Finals
Vs. San Marcos High (L 66- 50)

Overall 15-8 League 9-5

    I practiced in the discus track and field team, but the season went by fast, and I didn't perform well. After the track and field season was over, there wasn't another reason for me to go to school every day, but I had to get on the bus. My teachers were off my back, Miss Heather was off my back, and my mom wasn't checking in or checking for me. No assignments, no frustrations, and no one expecting anything out of me. I remember getting my last progress report, and it had one B, but the rest were C's.

    The last thing I had to do was find a prom date, which wouldn't be easy because I didn't know very many girls, let alone talk to any. All of my friends were talking about it. Prom was a big deal at The Bay. It was in all of the school announcements, and fliers were posted in nearly every hallway. A few of my friends had girlfriends, so they already had a date. It seemed like every time we hung out or caught each other walking through the halls, that was the start and end of our conversations. I never ran from those conversations because I knew I would find someone that would go with me, or so I thought.

    For the first time, I found myself searching for a girl who I thought might've had an interest in me. Although I had been shy around girls all of my life, I had to think hard and fast if I wanted to pull off walking in with a date on prom night. I stayed up all night thinking and thinking. I went to school every day plotting and scheming for a girl to ask. And then it hit me. There was one classmate who I met in Mr. Auer's statistics class. Her name was Ailed.

Ailed was a student-athlete who didn't associate herself with many people. She was a junior who played on the varsity soccer team, but other than that, I knew her as a classmate. Ailed was a very pretty Mexican girl who stood about 5'5. She was really cool to be around in class. For some reason, we bonded as classmates, and we always sat by each other. If I needed to borrow anything, she would give it to me and likewise. She even let me cheat off her work on a couple of tests a few times. It never went beyond that, so the thought of asking her out to prom instantly made me nervous. My palms started sweating. I knew she was the only chance I had, so I went for it.

One day after class, I just walked up to her and asked her. She responded how I envisioned it, "Awwwww... really... Are you serious, Chris? Yes, of course, I'd like to go with you to your prom." I was surprised, but at the same time, I wasn't. The sleepless nights were worth it. All I could think about was how I didn't have to worry about being one of the only student-athletes without a date. Ailed, in some sort of way, saved me.

From that point on, we started messaging each other through social media about prom ideas. Problem number one: I didn't have a plan. She explained to me that she had already had the perfect dress. It was one she had worn before, purple and white with dashes of silver. She sent me a few pictures of it, and I liked it. "That's cool. We can do purple," I replied.

I didn't have purple in mind, but at the time, I felt like she was doing me a favor by going to my prom with me, so I didn't waste any time trying to debate a second color. Problem number two: I still didn't have a license, car, or a way to get us to and from prom. But Dré offered the back seats of a Bentley to Ailed and me. My respect for Dré grew after that because his date and mine had a blast that night.

Ailed and I had a good time at prom, just like the rest of my teammates and classmates. The entire day was another one of those memories I knew I would stash away for generations to come. Following were Grad Night, Senior Ditch Day, and Senior Brunch. I had an encounter during Senior Brunch that made me think with a sense of urgency. I remember sitting at the table across from Derrell and a few other guys who were discussing the next steps for college. I had nothing to add to the conversation, and for the first time, it made me think about life after high school. *What am I going to do?* I hadn't had this conversation with myself and surely not anyone else. I guess we can say I was just living in the moment.

Only a few guys were headed to division one universities like Dré, LT, Devante, and a few other athletes I was acquainted with. However, hearing Derrell talk about how eager he was to go to JUCO made me think. Airric, who was also ready to take the JUCO path, said the same thing. *I need to come up with a plan.* I wasn't thinking about the military because I wasn't confident in my physical ability to pass boot camp, and I definitely wasn't going to try to go to a university. *Man, I'm in trouble.* I began to realize that I should've been thinking about college a long time ago.

On June 16th, I graduated from Mission Bay High with a 2.7 GPA. I didn't care what my GPA said because I was just happy I made it. I was happy to be a part of the seven seniors to walk across the stage that day because, truthfully, I knew I wasn't projected to graduate. Out of everyone, I could hear my mom yelling my name through all of the loud claps and cheers in the audience. What was considered out of reach for me was my reality, and I couldn't believe it. That was the end of a chapter and the beginning of another.

13

G-HOUSE

I REMEMBER WAKING UP THE NEXT DAY AND DOING ABSOLUTELY nothing. It felt weird because I realized Mission Bay held me accountable. By law, I had to go to school, but now, no one was holding me accountable, not even the law. Oddly enough, it wasn't a good feeling, so I did some soul searching. I got used to it after a few weeks, but that same feeling as to what was next kept taunting me. Dré was long gone, and so was LT and everyone else. So, I reached out to Derrell for advice.

I had my own cell now, so I was able to call him and discuss the idea of going to Grossmont College. He explained to me that after he realized that he didn't want to take any of the football scholarship offers to the schools that offered him, he figured Grossmont would be the best option. His goal was to still make it to a D1 university for football. He told me that he, Airric, and a few other well-known football players around San Diego were considering the same idea. He strongly suggested that I continue the same route with football rather than basketball, and since I had no sense of direction for myself, I felt like he was right. It wasn't bad advice by him; it was bad planning by me.

A few more days went by, and I was still hanging around the house thinking, overthinking, and thinking some more. He reached out to me again through text, "Yo bro, what's the move? Tryouts started." I didn't reply. The next day I called him, acted as if I wasn't hip, and asked a ton of questions. "Yeah, bro, stop playing. Come on out, let's get it, hahaha." *Here we go again*, I said to myself. I knew exactly what I was getting myself into this time. There were no secrets. I didn't know what I wanted out of football, so I was lost. I needed a path, or maybe I needed to find my path. I was crossing my fingers with hopes that I was headed down the right one.

It turns out that Derrell and Airric had mentioned my name a bit. They needed more defensive lineman, so Derrell threw my name in the bucket, which was kind of dope because he knew how much I wanted to play defensive line in high school but never had the opportunity. *This is my opportunity.* He knew I hated playing offensive line. That was a great move by him because I'm not sure what position or where I would've ended up playing if it wasn't for the word he put in. I still had one huge problem: I wasn't strong enough to play on the defensive line and didn't plan to lift weights.

Grossmont College was a huge jungle. I had never felt so small on a campus before like I did at Grossmont. See, I downgraded the thought of junior college. It was only just a step above high school, but I wasn't expecting the level of maturity I witnessed from day one. For some reason, in my head, I thought it was going to be just like high school. But it wasn't. This was a bigger pond with bigger fish. Things were different. The players were more alert, advanced, smart, skilled, and had a higher IQ of the game of football. It was only tryouts, but these guys could really play, and it was a whole lot more trash-talking going on.

It was my first time being on a team with so much diversity, both culturally and racially. Most players were a lot older than me and were dying to make it to the next level, so they practiced with a chip on their shoulders. Some players were in their early and mid-twenties, and some were even in their late twenties. A few players had kids. It was shocking to me. What I didn't realize was junior college enabled guys to come and play from all over the country.

The defensive line group was filled with players from the south. The rest of the team was from other states, such as Georgia and Texas, and a few guys were from Arizona. Throughout practice, I could hear different types of slang and coded languages being used all across the field. It was strange, but it made me pay attention. What was only a game to me was the ticket to the next level for them. It was just Grossmont Football to me, but to the rest of them, it was "G-House"!

My defensive line coach was named Coach Bullard. Coach Bullard was from Killeen, Texas, had a very country accent, played defensive end at Grossmont (back in the day), and later transferred to UTEP (University of Texas at El Paso). From day one, the only way he liked to get my attention was by yelling, "Big Ransom!" He called my name at least twenty times a day during practice for different reasons. Most importantly, he was serious about me perfecting my craft for the next level. That's all he talked about. That's all I kept hearing was the next level. If I weren't being chewed out because of my weaknesses, I would be laughing at Quan.

Quan was probably the only defensive lineman I was cool with on and off the field. Quan was from South Florida. He was shorter than me but a lot bigger, stronger, and a whole lot faster than me. He got off the line extremely quickly! Off the field, he was a super funny guy, but on the field, he was vicious. He was good, really good. He'd catch me stalling during drills and look over at me in his South Florida accent and say, "See, Ransom, that's why you need to work out!" Everyone laughed, including me. Each time he said it was funnier than the last.

I learned more about my teammates off the field. A lot of the players either previously had offers to different division one football teams or came from a division one football team. It seemed like as every day went by, I was learning something new. I was learning how life worked for some athletes. I was hanging around young men, not boys anymore. It was all still too new for me, and I knew it. I tried to listen more than talk, even during the not-so-serious moments. Life just started to look too real, too intense, and less freelance. Football wasn't adding any spice to my life like it was in high school. In fact, it was taking away the fun of it.

I made the team. Someone must've been praying for me because I'm not exactly sure how I made the cut. I made the team as a defensive end, was offered a revolution speed helmet, and I was able to pick a better-looking number, *57*. I liked the way it looked on me, even in practice.

Whoever was praying for me must've stopped because the rain was back the next day. School was about to start back up, and I didn't know what I wanted to major in. I still liked art, so I figured I'd be better off taking my general education courses and figuring the rest out later. That wasn't a smart idea. I filled out my schedule with fifteen units – full of writing, reading, and a few other literature courses. I wasn't sure what I was doing, and I was too afraid to ask for help, although resources were there. I didn't pick according to plan or to what was needed in the long run. I should've asked for help, but I was in too deep. *It is what it is.*

On top of that, I didn't have a ride to school every day because I didn't have a license or a vehicle of my own. School was set to start on September 6th, so I only had a few more days to figure things out. My mom suggested I get an MTS membership pass so I could ride the bus and trolley whenever and wherever. She figured it was time I got around on my own. She was right, but I didn't really want to do that. I bought one anyway. Derrell, just like Dré did in high school after those basketball games, offered to take me to and from school as long as it was on the same day that I had a way to his house in the morning. Like Dré, Derrell had always looked out for me, and I never forgot.

My first class of the day was English, and I started it at 7 a.m., which was a whole lot earlier than when Derrell's first class started. English was a course I was taking three days a week. So that meant Monday, Tuesday, and Wednesday, I had to rely on public transportation to get me to and from Grossmont College. It sucked. It went a little something like this: I caught the city bus on a street named Woodman, a few blocks away from my house. The bus took me to the nearest trolley stop on a street named 62nd, where I hopped off. Then I hopped on the Orange line, one of the many-colored trolleys that ran throughout San Diego. I'd let four stops pass before it was my time to get off. Those four stops were named Massachusetts Ave., Lemon Grove Dpt, Spring St., and La Mesa Blvd.

I hopped off the Orange line at a station named Grossmont Transit Center. It was right next to a mall, and it looked completely different from all the other previous stops, so it was really hard to miss. Most of the time, I had my earphones plugged into my ears to make the time go by faster. From there, I hopped on the nearby city bus that went straight to Grossmont College. It was me and tons of other students who rode that same city bus every day. It was always crowded, and I never understood why. There was no real purpose as to why I was going to school because every day, I felt like I was going through the motions just to do what I thought I should be doing rather than searching to find out.

Class ended for me around 3 p.m., just before practice. After practice was over, which was around 5:30 p.m., or sometimes 5 p.m., I took the same routine back home. The city bus, all the way to the Grossmont Transit Center, passed La Mesa Blvd., passed Spring St., passed Lemon Grove Dpt, past Massachusetts Ave., and hopped off at 62nd St. I waited for the city bus to show up, which usually took a few minutes because it was the last one of the day. I hopped off at Woodman St. and walked home. From 6 a.m. all the way to 7:30 p.m. I was away from home for the first time without accountability and supervision. My days were long, and during that time, I did a lot of thinking

I wasn't getting any playing time on the field, but I wasn't bothered by it because I knew I wasn't the best man for the position. I was practicing with the third-string defensive line group, so it would've been a long time for me to see the field. Quan filled in the starting slot. I'd be lying if I said I didn't enjoy watching him play (he was that good to me). We played our first game at Southwestern College, which was considered one of our longtime rival schools. We lost to them by a lot. The score was 35-6. The following week was a home game, but this time we won, 17-14. It was a close one.

The following week we played the best junior college in California at the time, named Riverside City College. Over half of their roster had players who came from division one football teams or were headed to one. A guy in particular who ended up going to USC and then playing for the Oakland Raiders was a wide receiver named Isaac. Isaac was a monster that year, but our defense contained him the day he traveled to Grossmont. We pulled out an upset on our home field. It was such a big upset that it made the newspaper. 38-28. No one expected that to happen.

That same Saturday night, Derrell called me and asked me if I wanted to go with him to a kickback party to celebrate. I texted him back, "Yeah, what time do I need to get ready?" I'm not sure who invited him or who was the host of the party, but all I remember was being drunk and high. I was the highest I had ever been. Derrell and I had always had fun on Friday and Saturday nights, but I was too far gone on that night. That was the moment when I realized I didn't care about tomorrow or value the current day. After kicking back for about four hours, a fight broke out, and the police were called. After that, all I remember was Derrell and I running down the street to shake the scene. Things could've ended pretty bad that night, but they didn't. Instead, they ended badly for me the next day.

14

JAIL

This was one of the turning points in my life. I got arrested. All of the stealing I was doing from the school's bookstore and cafeteria had caught up with me. I'm not sure if someone was watching me that day or always had been. I'm not sure if someone snitched on me. I'm not sure if someone was on duty watching the cameras in the back, but I had a strong feeling that someone saw me. I don't know how but I was mad that I had been caught, arrested, and humiliated in front of the entire campus.

As many student-athletes did, I started taking a few things from the bookstore here and there. You know, snacks, candy, utensils for school, or maybe a shirt or two. (I wouldn't five-finger these items in one visit. I accumulated them over time). I wasn't super reckless, but I was out of control. I knew when to do it and how-to but also when not to. I wasn't a rookie at taking stuff, so I was on my toes at all times.

On the day I was arrested, it wasn't the bookstore; it was the cafeteria I went into. The difference between the bookstore and the cafeteria is I wasn't the only one who stole from the cafeteria, just the bookstore. I knew plenty of players on the team who went into the cafeteria to do their rounds and walked right out. So, it gave me even more confidence to do my thing.

It was the afternoon, maybe twelve or one o'clock, when I walked into the Grossmont cafeteria that served everything you could think of. I always walked in when I felt like it was packed. It was easier to camouflage with the kids who looked rich. The food was good too, plus I was hungry. My mom broke me off in the morning like she always did, so I had money. I wanted to save it too, like always, so instead of planning to purchase, I planned to steal. "One breakfast burrito, with everything on it, please," I ordered the same thing every time. It took a few minutes for the cooks to make it. After the cook handed it to me, I grabbed it, slid it in my jacket pocket, and stalled as if I were going to head to the cash register. Instead, I walked straight out. *I done did it again.*

I messed up by not sticking to the script. I saw a few of our teammates sitting outside near a pair of huge boulders that we used as our seats. I took a seat next to them, and we chopped it up. One of the wide receivers named Chris looked over at me and said, "Aye, man, I don't know what's going on, but the worker just came to the window and pointed at you a few times." "For real?" I replied. I acted as if I didn't know. "Bro, did you pay for that?" he followed with a question. "Nahhh," I said while smirking. "You probably should get out of here then," he said while laughing. I left quickly. As I walked away, I heard him and a few other teammates laughing. I knew I was in trouble then. *I shouldn't have sat in front of the cafeteria.* It wasn't wise.

I was quite a distance away from the cafeteria. I was still visible, which was my second mistake. The employees weren't near the windows anymore, and my teammates looked like they were talking about something else. I leaned near a bench at the library while eating the burrito. I had a few bites left, and I had already trashed the wrapper. Suddenly a voice in my head said, *look up*. So, I did. It was the school Sheriff wandering around the top of the hill. It looked like he was looking for something, not someone. I couldn't really tell because he was wearing a pair of dark shades. My heart started racing, but since I was nervous and unsure, I didn't move. I had never felt my heart beat so fast before as it was at that moment.

My second mistake was just standing there. I don't know why but I thought it wasn't wise to leave or try to post up elsewhere. *Nahhh, he's not looking for me.* I was trying to convince myself. It genuinely looked as if he had lost something and was searching for it on the ground from the top of the hill slope. He was getting closer and closer to me. I started panicking, but I stood still. A few seconds later, he was on the same ground level I was on and headed in my direction.

Since he was wearing a dark pair of shades, I couldn't tell if he was looking at me or past me. I pulled out my phone and acted like I was scrolling through social media. When he got a few feet in distance, I put my phone up to my ear and started talking to myself to make it seem like I was on the phone. I thought he was just going to walk past me, but he didn't. The next thing I know, I heard, "Hello sir, were you just in the cafeteria about thirty minutes ago?"

This was my third and final mistake. I flat out said, "Yes, that was me." This was my first time having any real contact with the police, and I choked up because of it. "Turn around; you are under arrest." I complied. "You have the right to remain silent. Anything you say can and will be used against you in a court of law. You have the right to an attorney. If you cannot afford an attorney, one will be provided for you," he said. *F***, I could've gotten away. I'm going to jail...* I said to myself. I couldn't believe it. A nightmare, to say the least. I didn't think I would ever go to jail for stealing, but God clearly made a liar out of me.

F***! I kept thinking. I was scared, nervous, and embarrassed—a little bit of everything. The only thing I wasn't was hungry. The sheriff sat me on the curb, and that's where my thoughts started to hit me hard. I noticed people were staring at me, so I put my head down due to embarrassment. I didn't want to look anyone in the eyes. During that moment, I had another thought; *this dude played me.* I started blame-shifting because I was angry. He knew what he was doing. He wasn't lost or looking for anything besides me. He saw me before I saw him. Like a lion catching a gazelle, he plotted his catch. He was trained to do that.

I began to sweat through my hoodie while the Sheriff asked me random questions and reported everything over on his walkie-talkie radio. I was trying to figure out if he was trying to correlate the two; my answers and whoever was on the end of his radio. I couldn't call it. I sat on the curb for a good five minutes before he picked me up and walked me through what felt like across campus to his police car. He unlocked the door and put me in the backseat. *Man, I have no leg room!* He stood outside of his squad car while I sat in the back seat for another five to ten minutes. Within the first two minutes, my body temperature shot up again because of how nervous I was, my black hoodie, and how tight it was in the backseat. Mind you, my backpack was still on TIGHTLY, and it was about 90 degrees that day.

He finally got in the driver's seat and started up the car. "So, hey, man, I'm going to take you to my office towards the back of the campus, and we are going to talk. I just want to talk to you, that's all," he said. *Cool, I'm not going to jail.* I thought. I didn't even know the campus had a Sheriff or even a Sheriff's Office, but I found out that day. Once we made it to the parking lot of his office, he hopped out of the squad car but left me inside. My legs were in so much pain while he stood outside again, talking on his radio for about thirty minutes. *Man, what's going on.*

He opened up my door and walked me to his office. I swear we went through like five doors before we made it to where he was trying to take me. He pulled out my chair for me, and I sat down. He walked around the table and sat across from me. Someone started saying something on his radio, and he turned it down and all the way off. He pulled out some papers and a pen out of his shirt pocket. I was trying to read what he was writing, but I couldn't. It was a coded language that I had no idea how to decode. Suddenly he looked up at me after taking notes on his notepad, and no joke, this is what he said, "So you will be going to jail, but I want to talk about what happened out there today." *Thought he said I wasn't going to jail? MAN F***!* After hearing that, I felt defeated. I just remember sitting there thinking as he wrote down my answers… *man I'm really about to go to jail.*

"Do you know of anyone else who takes things from the cafeteria or bookstore?" he asked. "No, I don't know," I replied in a very low, monotone voice. I didn't want to snitch on anyone.

I don't know what this police officer thought of me, who he thought I was, or what the employees told him in the cafeteria because he asked me some strange questions. "Do you bring lunch every day? Do you eat at home? Are you struggling financially? Did someone prompt you or suggest you do this? Hey, so I'm only asking you these questions because whenever I catch most people who stole or are in the act of stealing, they are struggling and do it out of need," he said. *He's trying to get me to talk.* I wasn't buying what he was selling, but I knew it was best to comply. "Nah, I didn't need it," I replied back in the same monotone.

From that point on, it was hell for me mentally. I couldn't stop thinking about how much trouble I got myself into. The one thing I kept thinking about the most was how hard others would judge me. I wasn't certain, but it wasn't a bad assumption to make. He sat me in the backseat, and one of his buddies showed up and took up the spot in the passenger seat, and from there, they headed downtown with me.

In a weird way, the ride was kind of exciting because I got to experience what law enforcement talks about. Mainly, there was silence, but then there was a moment in particular when we were passing exits to get off of the freeway. The sheriff in the passenger seat said to the driver, "Hey man, was he getting undressed back there?" I didn't see anyone, but I guess they had seen someone homeless on the side of the freeway but kept going anyway. The ride was about twelve to fifteen minutes. We then pulled into a tunnel somewhere downtown, and then it got dark, pitch black.

I remember both sheriffs walking with me side-by-side until we made it to this door that looked very randomly placed. (Similar to a hole in a wall.) For a second, it looked like we were in a parking garage with no cars in it and no poles. Just concrete and walls, and then I saw a door on a wall, and that's the direction we were headed in. I never said a word to either of them, and neither did they say anything to me.

The sheriff, who was in the passenger seat of the vehicle, unlocked the door and opened it up. The sheriff who arrested me walked me in. Everything began after that. All of the awkwardness and uncomfortableness were just getting started. My thumbprint was taken, and so was my picture. I didn't smile or try to mean mug into the camera. I just stared dead into the tiny lens because I didn't really know what to do, plus it happened so fast. The lady behind the desk gave me instructions that I almost missed. It was approximately 3 p.m. (I was assuming). Here I was, right in the middle of the day, sitting in a holding cell.

The holding cells were very cold. The lady who took down my thumbprint and my mugshot opened up the holding cell using a system that opened and closed doors. As soon as the door opened, I saw five other guys in there who looked completely unbothered, so I took a seat in the corner. Different ethnicities and age groups, but other than that, I didn't know anything. I didn't know what the rules were or how the laws worked. All I could assume was that I had committed a petty theft crime, and I would be out soon. But the real question I continued to ask myself was… *when is soon?*

I was moved from holding cell to holding cell. I sat in three different holding cells with different groups of younger and older men for Lord knows how long. I had no idea what time it was, and I was still wearing the hoodie and jeans I had put on for school that morning. I looked over at a random guy sitting next to me, and I asked him what time it was, and he just looked at me and didn't say a word. I'm glad he didn't because it answered my own question. *How would he know?*

Holding cells A, B, and C, was the order of the holding cells each person had to go through when they first entered the jail. I found this out by the time I got into holding cell C. Guys were conversing in there. Friendly conversation and nothing too heavy. Words were flying back and forth about when they would get out and how much their bail was. I met this guy in cell C whose name, to this day, I don't recall. He was talking out loud about how much he didn't deserve to be in there, and it looked like he was fishing for a conversation with someone else. Since I saw guys going and coming from the phone, I asked him, "Aye, can we call someone?"

"Yeah, bro!" He was being very hostile, and he was sweating a little bit. He had on a white t-shirt and a pair of jeans, and scuffed-up tennis shoes. He was talking to me as if he knew me already. He started to explain to me how the bailing system works. He stopped explaining and suddenly asked me why I was there. I told him. "Mannnn! Bro! You can't get your time back! You can get your bread back up, but not your time! Call your lawyer! Here bro, take the phone! Take the phone, G!" he yelled out loud. I walked over to the phone and grabbed it. I had no idea what I was about to do because I didn't pay attention to the information he was giving me regarding the bailing system. All I could really process was his body language, energy, and emotion.

I picked up the phone and listened to the lady talk me through the instructions on the automatic system. If you have a lawyer or need one, press one. If you are calling to reach your lawyer, press two...blah blah. I hung the phone up. *I'll just do the time. It was a breakfast burrito. I'll be out soon. There's no way I will do any real time for that.* I sat in the holding cell for what felt like years before being asked to step out by a few guards along with the rest of the guys in *the C.* I complied.

It was time to change out of my clothes. That's when I freaked out because I knew then that I would be there overnight with no chance of making it home in time. The guards lined up me and another seven guys, and we stood on a number. I was number three. The guards went down the line and asked us to remove our clothing one piece at a time. I complied. After all of our clothing was removed, they had access to stand on our number. I complied. One out of the few officers in the glass-windowed room went down the line number by number with the same instructions. "Bend over... Spread them open... Cough. All right, back up. Step forward."

After I was all dressed up in my blues, I was given a pair of sandals that weren't even my size. If I had to make a guess, they were a size 10. That was the day that I learned that a size 10 is nowhere close to a size 13. My heel was hanging off of my sandals, so every step I took sounded like I was dragging my feet because if I picked my feet too high up, my sandals would go sliding. I was given a thick mat that looked like a yoga mat but felt like a piece of cardboard.

I was ordered to keep it rolled up with my blanket on the inside until the guy released me to my actual cell. I complied. All eight of us were sent back to the holding cell until someone came and got us. Once we arrived back at the holding cell, I thought it was nighttime because when I left, it was cold, but when I came back, it was extremely cold. The only thing I could rely on was my clothes to keep me warm because there wasn't enough space to lay my mat out. I stuck my arms into my sleeves and used my arms to grip my body. I curled up my toes inside my socks and laid on the bench in a fetal position. Maybe two or three hours went by before I heard the keys coming to the door. It was the guards coming to move us to our individual cells.

I noticed something. The section I was going to didn't look like it was for those charged with misdemeanors. I examined through the glass, trying not to get intimidated. I started seeing guys with tattoos all over. Tattoos on their faces, tattoos covering their upper bodies, and their demeanors said everything. These dudes looked like they had been in there for years. The closer I got, the more scared I got. The only difference was I refused to show it, so I didn't smile or look away. I just kept a straight face.

It all looked the same as it did on TV. That upstairs and

downstairs mall-looking complex where the inmates lived on TV shows such as "Lock Up" was right in front of my face. I was living it. The guard unlocked the door, and the first thing I saw were the tables on the first level. He walked me up the steps, and then we were on the second level. Once he unlocked the door, he slammed it as soon as I made it in. The door was close to hitting me, but of course, I didn't say anything. This was the second phase of the day.

The cell was the size of a standard-sized kitchen. It was just as small as everyone said they were—three bunks, a toilet, and a sink that barely stuck out of the wall. There were already two dudes on the inside who, from the looks of it, were using the bottom and the top bunk. After the guard let me in, it took them a few seconds to look at me. The bottom bunk was occupied by a homeless-looking guy using a paste to build some square-looking thing. He said it was a trash can (although I didn't ask). He and I didn't talk much, but he kind of just looked up at me and said something under his breath, and we didn't pay any attention to each other after that. *I guess that was his way of introducing yourself.*

The other guy was Mexican. He jumped off the top bunk and introduced himself to me by a nickname that I couldn't pronounce. "Sup Dog!?" We made eye contact while he was in midair. I almost dropped my mat and blanket because I was startled by his large leap. I was thinking the worst. *Fight?* That wasn't the case. He was being friendly. After that day, the three of us didn't speak at all—three different generations, three different age groups, and probably three different lifestyles. If I had to guess, the homeless guy had to be somewhere in his fifties or sixties, and the Mexican guy was in his thirties if not late twenties.

I was sleepy, but I still had hope. I was hoping that a guard would come by my door and say, "Ransom, it's time to go, or hey, you in the middle bunk, let's go. Come out." It was such a surreal moment. I never thought I would go to jail for stealing. I never thought that being in jail would look like this. *My mom is probably disappointed in me right now. My brothers too. Derrell and the rest of the team probably already know what happened by now. I'm probably kicked off the team. I'm probably suspended from school. Can you get suspended from junior college?* I ran out of thoughts, so I tried fighting my sleep because I didn't want to fall asleep.

Although my cellmates seemed to be cool with me just as I was with them, I didn't trust it. This was a jail, so I had to sleep with one eye open. Whenever I got close to falling asleep, I'd turn from laying on my right side (which was facing the door) to laying on my left side so I could look at the stained-glass window. The windows looked just like the ones you'd see at a Baptist church, but without all of those angelic designs on them, just clear, but you couldn't see through them. It was good while it lasted because a few minutes later, I was asleep. I also remember having a dream that night which I do not recall much of.

The next day was by far the longest day of my life. I was still not used to not knowing the time of the day and just sitting there doing nothing. So far, I haven't had any urine or bowel movements. I ate nothing. I was hungry, and I was running off four hours of sleep. The mat was extremely hard. It was rock-solid, but my blanket was alright. Without it, I probably would've never fallen asleep. My clothes were too tight, and my sandals were still too little. I just wanted to go home.

At around, what I believed to be noon, guards came to open up the cell. They were looking for me. When the door opened, I turned my head so fast because I thought I was going home, but really I was just going to court. I was just getting started. I, along with another twenty guys, were being hauled off into a bus right outside the door I had entered yesterday around 3 p.m. The twenty of us were chained together by our ankles and monitored and watched by guards walking by our sides as we stepped onto the bus. Once we were seated on the bus, the guards came by and chained us together foot to foot and wrist to wrist.

The ride took about thirty minutes. I don't know where I was, but I was nowhere near downtown San Diego anymore. I remember getting off the bus slowly. Whatever building I was in looked much nicer than the county jail downtown. The holding cells had clear glass windows and more room. The floors were cleaner, and oddly enough, the staff was kinder too. When I heard the words court, I thought I was actually going to court where I would see a judge (face-to-face), the jury, and hear a gavel, but that wasn't the case. It was more of a court hearing.

My court hearing started. I was moved to another room. It was another holding cell, but it was much tighter. Within the first five minutes, two guys started arguing. I quickly lifted my head out of my lap and paid attention. I never knew what I could have gotten myself involved with unintentionally. I wasn't a fighter at heart, but I was willing to defend myself at whatever cost if necessary. I caught on to the funk too late to tell what was really going on, but all I knew was it escalated quickly.

Punches were exchanged, and no one was stopping it. *Who's gonna stop this? The guards can't see this. Can they hear it?* These two guys fought for at least five minutes straight. Right around the fourth minute, fatigue started to kick in, and one of the guys asked the other guy if he was good. He threw in the towel. You know, signaling that he was done, waving the white flag. The two of them connected almost all of their punches and were red in the face by the time they agreed to stop. To this day, that was the most spontaneous act of violence I've ever seen in my life. Two hours went by after that, and before I knew it, I was back on the bus headed back to County Jail. I didn't see a judge, my mom, or anyone, so I wasn't sure what the point of that was. No one explained anything to me.

On the ride back, I sat towards the end of the aisle, unlike on the way there. Also, I was a few seats behind the driver. *Lucky me.* Using my peripheral vision to the right of me, I noticed an older Black man who was also sitting adjacent to me in the inner part of the aisle. He kept looking at me. He stopped for a few seconds after noticing my head turning to look in his direction, and then he would start again after my head turned the opposite way. I wasn't trying to make eye contact with him because I knew that would start a conversation. I just wanted to look outside of the windows. That happened four times before he decided to break the ice.

"Sup, young brotha? What's your name? How old are you?" he asked very calmly. Initially, I didn't want to say anything. I wanted to stick to the script of not speaking to anyone while I was there, but something told me that he had good intentions, exceptionally good intentions. So, I said back, "Chris and 18," in a short manner. I remained nonchalant. I couldn't allow him to think that I was soft or that I was afraid of him. I played it how I wanted to play it. "Oh… You a young buck. Listen, I don't even want to know what you did because it was probably minor but let me tell you something, don't you ever come back here again. I can tell that you're bright and have a very bright future, so you don't belong here," he advised.

As he was talking, I noticed that he was missing one ear, so it drew me into what he was saying. *He's been through some stuff.* "I went to Hoover High school over there in the inner city, and I have been through some stuff, so trust me, this is not the right place to be for you. Don't come back, you hear me?" he said. "Yeah, I won't come back," I replied. I was right, and so was he. I never forgot him or his words. I regret the body language I used towards him, but if he only knew how much I received from what he said at that moment.

I was escorted back to my cell after getting off the bus and unshackled from the crew. I lay back in my bed for four hours and did absolutely nothing, looking at the stained glass window. The funny thing about that window was that although I knew for a fact I would never be able to see what was going on outside and what time of day it was, it made me never lose hope. It was like my imagination wouldn't allow me to believe that I couldn't see anything. My mind was stronger on the second day.

I was let out along with the other cellmates on both levels for one hour of dinner, a bologna sandwich, one orange (that I couldn't stick my nails into to peel open), some type of sauce, a drink, and a piece of banana bread. I ate none of it. The risk wasn't worth it. I sat on the first floor at the end of one of the tables by myself. The table was full, and guys could tell that I was new because I sat there staring off into space while they were looking in my direction. I was waiting for one of them to ask me if I was going to eat my food, so I would gladly give it to them so that they would stop looking at me. One of the guys asked, and I pushed my whole tray towards him, and the rest of the guys scattered over like seagulls grabbing what I had given. I sat there, not saying or looking at anyone until that hour went by.

I daydreamed in my cell to pass the time. My stomach was growling so loud my cellmates could hear it. I hadn't eaten anything since the burrito at Grossmont. I was officially starving, and I needed to pee pretty badly. I told myself that if I were going to stay another night, I would handle business while everyone was asleep.

While the Mexican guy was doing push-ups and the homeless guy fiddled with his arts in crafts, I spent time thinking. *Man, I shouldn't have done that. I'm not doing that again. I'm never coming back here. EVER.*

While I was daydreaming, I heard the keys in the lock again. It was a guard. He pointed in our direction and said, "Shower?" The homeless dude completely ignored him; the Mexican guy accepted it and jumped out of his bed again. I calmly said, "No." It was hard to do that. I couldn't think of the last time I passed up on taking a shower, but it wasn't worth the risk. *I heard about what they do to men who drop the soap.* The door to my cell remained open, and I stared at it the entire time because the last thing I wanted was for anyone to come in there to start any trouble.

After my cellmate came back, the door closed by itself. *Woah.* It was being monitored. One hour went by, and a guard came back, but it was a different guard this time. He was Black and had a very enthusiastic energy about him. "Hey, Ransom!" he yelled. I just looked at him because I wasn't exactly sure how to respond. "Ransom! Let's go!" he yelled even louder with a smile on his face. Like a dad coming to pick his son up from his first day of kindergarten, I was overjoyed. *Oh, shoot.* I started smiling, but I wanted to cry. "Grab your mat, and cover. It's time to go." I was so happy. I leaped from my bunk as fast as I could and walked out. The fellas told me goodbye, but I ignored them and kept walking. I threw my hand up as a way of saying, "Bye."

I thought it was just as simple as being escorted out of that same door I entered, but it wasn't. First, they sent me back to a holding cell after changing into the clothes I was wearing on Monday. After that, I sat in another holding cell for a few hours. It was harder to be patient now than at the beginning of this ordeal because I knew I was going home, and I was ready for it. I was so happy on the inside, but I didn't show it. I had been looking forward to this moment and hoping for it to happen that entire day.

Many of the guys were friendly on the way out, and it made sense why. We had started getting comfortable with one another. I met another Black guy who was a lot shorter than me, and I could tell he was from out of town because he was wearing a pair of wheat-colored Timberland boots. (In San Diego, it can be anywhere from 75 to 90 degrees in September. Not many people are wearing boots.) He was also wearing two long-sleeved shirts under a thick hoodie. *He's gotta be from the east coast. I know he's hot.*

He was from North Carolina. He introduced himself to me and told me all about how he got locked up. "See, bruh, in North Carolina, since it's in the south, you can get away with things that you can't in San Diego," he said. All he did was tamper with a beehive, and the police saw him do it, so they arrested him for it. That's legal in North Carolina but not so much in California. *Really?* It blew my mind to hear something like that.

In the holding cell, it was super cold, but I was getting closer and closer to freedom. They were calling names one by one in the holding cell where papers were being processed, and I was next up. What I learned next broke me, discouraged me, and made me feel slightly emasculated. I was mad and didn't know what to do with my anger. The lady at the desk explained to me my written charge summary. My bail was set at $2,500, and the petty crime that I figured would be handled as a misdemeanor was being charged as a felony.

She then said, "You are responsible for 1,000 community service hours, and then you will have the opportunity to have the felony dropped to a misdemeanor if you complete an eight-hour day of shoplifting class online by the printed date in November." Her words were fast and difficult to process all at once, so I was a bit puzzled. *Wait, what? A FELONY?!*

The People of the state of California v.
Christopher Dominique Ransom

Bail: $2,500
Case#: C344128 DOB: 052696 BKG#: 14766328
Count Charge Issue 1: PC459 Count Charge Issue
2: PC484 Count Charge Issue 3: PC1054.3

As I sat back in the last holding cell waiting to be released, I said to myself, a*re they serious?* My blood was boiling, and I wanted to punch a hole in the wall. I knew what I did was wrong, and I deserved some type of punishment but sitting in jail for one day and the expectations of embarrassment were enough. The punishment didn't fit the crime. I was livid. *That officer played me!* I was released on Wednesday, September 24th, at 1:36 a.m.

I was as mad as I ever was, so the next decision I made was probably dumber than the one I made on Monday. One of the guys I met inside my last holding cell told me all about the 7-Eleven a few blocks down, which allowed all of the folks who got released to grab a few things "on the house." The story sounded beautiful to a guy whose stomach was eating itself, so I prepared to grab a few things to eat before figuring out my next move. He and I walked a few blocks while he talked my head off.

We made it to 7-Eleven, and to my surprise, no one was even at the counter. It was just him and I in the back grabbing a few things. "See, I told you, man," he assured me. I walked out with a honey bun, a bag of chips, and a few donuts. I finished it all and asked him if I could use his cell phone to make a call. I called my mom, and she didn't say much after I asked if she could pick me up, but I knew she was coming. Fifteen minutes later, I saw her truck pulling up, and my heart started to beat just as fast as it did when I saw that sheriff walking up to me.

I hopped in the truck, and for the first two minutes, I didn't say anything. She broke the ice by explaining how disappointed in me she was. Rightfully so. I didn't waste any time defending myself. I was tired, and so was she, and it felt like that was the longest car ride home I ever had with her. I wouldn't say I was sorry, but I was aware that I had made a mistake, and from that day forward, I promised myself that I wouldn't steal anymore or get in trouble with the law ever again. I kept my promise. That was the end of my five-finger era.

Once I made it home, I took a very long shower and ignored the hundreds of notifications. At a glance, nearly fifty notifications were coming from social media that read #FREECHRISRANSOM. *Oh, they thought it was funny; that s*** wasn't funny.* I just went straight to bed. I slept great and almost missed my bus to get to the trolley the next morning. I made it to school, and when I was walking up the steps, the air felt different. I was afraid to look anyone in the eye, although I hadn't bumped into any teammates just yet. I looked up for a few seconds, and I started to notice a few kids who weren't even athletes staring and taking double-takes. *Everyone knows.*

The first thing I did was walk to the men's football locker room so I could hide if it were empty. I thought detouring into the library was too open, but I probably shouldn't have chosen the football locker room either. I was fiddling through my locker, and a few seconds later, I heard, "Blood hahaha...my nigga...c'mon blood," it was Derrell. I laughed with him. That was just Derrell; his personality disabled me from getting offended. Although I didn't naturally find it funny, I went along with it. A lot of guys started to show up in the locker room, some players I knew and some I didn't know. I was embarrassed, and I'm sure that they could see that, but a football team will be a football team, so I had to take the heat that came along with walking inside the locker room.

One of my teammates came into the locker room and said, "Hey, Coach Jordan wants to see you in his office." Immediately the laughs turned into a cold silence. Everyone looked at me. I knew what this meant. I knew exactly what this meant. *He's going to kick me off of the team for sure.* Once I made it to his office, he wasted no time. He gave it to me raw and didn't try to make it sound sweet, "As of right now, you are suspended from the team until I figure out the next step. You will travel with the team until I say otherwise. Understood?" "Understood," I replied. I walked out.

I didn't mind being suspended. That was fair, but what really bothered me the most was that he and I never formed any type of relationship, so that was the first time the two of us actually spoke. *I'm sure I'm just a thief to him.* He didn't know me, and neither did I know him. It sucked that he never took the time to get to know me for himself or even through Coach Bullard, but he handled it as if he did. That was a painful moment.

15

DEPRESSION

Over the following weeks, I became depressed. Depression wasn't my only new problem; my self-esteem was too. I was at my lowest. My peers didn't seem to desire to hang around me anymore, especially the few I had gotten to know or already knew personally. I was hearing things about myself in person and on social media from people I knew and didn't know. From what I know, Derell stuck up for me behind my back. Since I had always relied on what other people thought about me, I was beginning to feel like I was a failure, and I didn't see any value in myself anymore.

I got "the eye" from many people around campus. People didn't trust me anymore. Whenever I was around folks, I could see people looking at their belongings, looking at me, and then looking back at their belongings as if I was going to take something of theirs. *Did I feel like I deserved it? No. Were they wrong? No.* I didn't know how to approach anyone about how I felt, so instead of venting or opening up to anyone, I stomached the feelings. I was pretty good at hiding my true feelings.

I traveled with the team for the remainder of the football season until it became the perfect time for me to finish up the Offender Solutions program for my online theft shoplifting class. The least I wanted to do for myself was make sure my felony dropped to a misdemeanor. That was the first step because if I didn't complete the program by the end of November, then I was guaranteed to have a felony on my record. I completed it in time. It was hard and tiring, but I did it. It took me almost twelve hours to finish an eight-hour online program, but I got it done. The next step was one thousand community service hours.

My mom drew up a list of places I needed to catch the bus around San Diego to ask for help. I asked everywhere we could possibly think of: recreational centers, detention centers, sweeping hair at barbershops, beauty salons, libraries, schools, and small businesses. No one was willing to allow me to complete my hours, and it was super frustrating. One day it dawned on me, *what about the church?* Then I had a second thought, *ain't no way I'm letting people at my church know about my personal business.* I couldn't fight the feeling for long because I didn't have many options or time.

Since the fall of 2007, I had been a member of a church named the City Of Hope International Church (COHI). From the day I was born until the time I went to jail, I grew up in church. My family and I were members of This Is The Way until 2003, and from then until 2007, I was a member of North Park Apostolic Church. Neither church had happy endings, so we tried a baptist church until the fall of 2007. I had tons of church experience, but I never let anyone in on my personal life.

I was a familiar face in my church. One of the church's associate pastors was pretty cool with my mom. His name was Pastor B. His first name was William, but everyone called him Bill, but since he and I were familiar with each other, he was cool with dropping the "ill" and going by Pastor B. From the time I had known him being a member, he was pretty cool and had a balanced personality.

When my mom told him, he reached out to me. I was wrong. He wasn't judging me at all about my circumstances. In fact, it seemed as if he was eager to help me get back on my feet. I aimed to treat my service as if it were just business. I felt like he was only there to help me clean my hours up so I could submit it to the courts. Instead, he gave me advice and taught me a few things here and there that I should know. He wasn't afraid to put me to work, though. Whenever he needed me, he was going to call me, and if I wasn't around, he was going to find me. The perfect example of that was when COHI decided to have service in a high school auditorium for a month or so.

It was at Lincoln High, which was actually right next to COHI. Lincoln's auditorium was huge. You could've mistaken it for a junior college or maybe even a division one university auditorium. It was that big. We had a lot of members who attended every Sunday, so he made me responsible for cleaning up the stadium and unplugging all the speakers on the stage to load up in the U-Haul. Every Sunday until my hours were up, I made it to church around 8 a.m. before start time (which was 10 a.m.) to help set up. I didn't leave church until around 2 p.m. or sometimes 3 p.m. By that time, I was tired and sweating after carrying so much equipment. He rewarded me with lunch afterward, which he didn't have to do, but he did it anyway.

I didn't think people like Pastor B were out there. I didn't think there were people in the world who were willing to give someone a second chance like he was giving me. Pastor B's actions toward me opened my eyes to the men and women in the church. The more Pastor B did for me, the more I wanted to get around him and other church folks. Over time he started calling me "nephew," and I returned it with an "Unc." He and I formed a relationship that I'm still proud of to this day. On the 12th of December, Pastor B printed out my official letter that I took to the courts that stated the completion of my community service work.

I remember going to court feeling relieved. My mom was with me that morning. When my name was called in the waiting hall, we jumped up and made our way to the door. We were both escorted to two different sections. She asked to sit towards the back while I was next to the stand. The judge then called for me to stand. I stood there saying nothing but staring him in his eyes, awaiting his first words. He looked like a modern version of George Washington because of his long gray pigtails hanging down his back, an older White man with a gray mullet that curled on the sides of his face. He spoke with the accent of a man born in the 1800s. He began to read my charge summary.

> "Mr. Ransom, you completed the assignments as instructed in the time assigned. We will start the process of dropping the felony charge to a misdemeanor and then to an infraction. Stay out of trouble, sir." *Slams the gavel*

2015

I was free within the system but not between my own two ears: I was still slightly depressed due to my new social norm. I felt unmotivated, and to escape my reality, sometimes I would leave class early to catch the bus just so I could stop by Derrell's house, who was already home, and smoke weed with him. This is when I picked up my habit of smoking weed and blowing at hookah lounges near his house. He was the only friend I had left.

On most nights, I wouldn't tell my mom where I was going. One minute she saw me, and the next, she didn't. Derrell was always outside waiting for me. He never honked his horn. He just sent me a text that said, "I'm outside, bro," and then boom, I was out in a flash. He always had some weed on him. (I never asked him where he got the weed from because it didn't matter. I just wanted to smoke). We had a routine; blunt first, and then hopefully, we'd stumble across girls at the hookah lounge. I remember sitting in the hookah lounge at one and sometimes two in the morning, dizzy, sweating, and thinking to myself...*How did I get here?*

I started to drink often too. Derell always knew a friend that knew someone that knew him. He was a very social person and had the gift of gab, so whenever I was around him, I met plenty of people as well. He knew this girl named Bailey, who hosted a birthday kickback at a hotel in Mission Valley. I got word that she thought I was cute, so I put on one of the flyest outfits I had in my closet that night before leaving (which was a very cheap outfit). Derrell came by and picked me up, and we planned on spending the night at her hotel for her birthday. It was alcohol, weed, girls, and a few other guys there when we arrived.

I masked my pain through the fun. By the end of the night, Bailey and I were in her master bedroom, and she ended up on top of me. I don't know how all of that escalated, but nothing happened. (At least that's how I remembered it). Derrell and I ended up leaving the hotel suite at about three in the morning, and since we were both high and drunk, we decided to sleep in his car in the parking lot. We dodged a bullet that night because cops drove in and out of the parking lot throughout the morning. Derrell and I had plenty of nights like that, and although we made risky decisions, his presence was comforting. It meant the world to me, knowing he was still my friend.

The more fun I had, the more I lost my focus, but the more fun I had, the less I focused on how depressed I was on the inside. It was like I was winning and losing at the same time. I barely showed up to school anymore, but no one noticed. On the inside, I was screaming for help, but I don't think anyone could tell. I didn't point the finger, and that's probably because I knew I couldn't. It was all on me. My grades were starting to resemble my lack of attendance. In all of my classes, I had failing grades. *I might as well drop out.* So, I did. I sat down with my mom after and told her the decision I had made. She didn't look so happy about it. I never went back to college after that.

When I became an adult, my mom wasn't the type to force anything upon me. She let me make my own decisions, but the one thing she made clear was that there would always be rules and regulations. "If you don't want to go to school anymore, Chris, you're going to have to start looking for a job. And I'm not going to let you borrow or give you any money anymore. All of your bills are your responsibility now. Find a job," she demanded. *Cool.* Instead of actually saying that I said, "Alright, I understand."

I had $1,000 left in my bank account, which was the remaining financial aid I was granted from the government. Once my mom made it clear that she wasn't going to give me a dime, I knew I had to hold onto my $1,000 tightly. So, I pulled back on the amount of partying I was doing with Derrell and hanging out. Derrell and I went out still but just not often. Whenever I needed my haircut or when my phone bill was due, I was responsible for that. (I didn't realize how fast $1,000 could be spent, but I learned then.) Money started to become a little tight, so I started job searching.

I learned this: How much money a person has is less important in comparison to how the person spends. I was learning gradually through my own lack. I also learned this: not having a job is one thing, but not having transportation is another problem in itself. Job hunting was extremely hard. My mom was giving me hell about it. "Ten applications a day, Chris! Nothing more, nothing less," she yelled at me while walking through the hall and crossing my bedroom door.

She was as serious as cancer, but it didn't help much because I wasn't having the best of luck. So, she reached out to one of the pastors at COHI at the time to help me find a job. This time it wasn't Pastor B. It was Pastor Ericka. She went by PEP, an acronym for her first and last name, "Pastor Ericka Parker." If it weren't for her, I would've probably taken the chances of selling drugs or going into the military.

Pastor Ericka Parker met with me at one of the thousands of Starbucks locations in the inner city of San Diego on a Saturday morning. I had always listened to her sermons whenever she preached on Sundays, but when I met with her one-on-one, her voice sounded different than it did through the microphone. Her voice had so much hope in it, or at least that's what it felt like. "Looking for a job, Chris, is a job," she said in a soft voice. If there was anything about me, I could always tell when someone cared or did not care. Pastor Ericka cared, and from that day on, we kept in contact while I remained persistent in my job search.

I hate catching this dang bus. I was all too familiar with it. Woodman St. was the start of every interview. One day, when I least expected it, I got a call from Walmart. The manager was interested and interviewed me for an overnight stocking position. I definitely didn't want that job because I had no interest in working overnight, so I was hoping I didn't get it. (I put my best foot forward during the interview, though).

The bus took me to the Orange Line, and instead of going past the Lemon Grove Dpt stop, I got off and walked to a nearby bus stop. The bus took me straight to Walmart. The interview went by quickly, and I took the same route back. It took all day, and I was mad because it felt like it was a waste of time. I didn't end up getting the position.

The very next week, I had another interview in the same area, Lemon Grove. Once I hopped off of the Lemon Grove Dpt stop, I walked to my destination since it wasn't too far. Chuck E. Cheese. They were looking for a floor assistant and a mascot. I chose the floor assistant position because there wasn't any way I was going to dress up in their hot suit. The interview went well, but I didn't get the job because I couldn't convince the manager that I was willing to pick up human feces from the floor. I took my route back home. I was getting tired of it, and there were many days when I didn't want to talk to anyone, and I just hung out in my room all day until I fell asleep.

Towards the end of March, I had my first fast-food restaurant interview. It was a KFC and Taco Bell location combined that served both venues. Growing up, my mom took my brothers to this location, and we got full off of tacos, burritos, and chicken strips. I never thought I would one day potentially work for the company. The interview didn't go well at all. The manager who was interviewing me didn't seem too interested in me from the jump. I'm not sure what it was. I could've made one thousand guesses, but it didn't really matter. I left within thirty minutes of arriving.

16

THE FIRST

On April 4th, I caught a huge break. It was my mom's birthday, and she and her friend were seated in the driver and passenger seats while my brothers and I were in the back of her truck when my phone started to ring. We were on our way to go bowling to celebrate her birthday when a Target location asked if I was available for an interview on the 6th. Without thinking or letting the human resources employee finish their question, I said, "Yes, I can." I'm glad I answered that call because I was broke and was borrowing money from others to go places. Target was officially my first job.

It was clear to me that I was turning a curve and that I was about to start breaking ground finically. Target hired me after the first interview to work in the "backroom" located in the basement, counting inventory. They didn't want to interview me a second time. All I had to do was count and store the product that wasn't on the shelves for the customers to see. The "backroom" position wasn't usually given to those who'd never had any working experience, so there must've been something about me they liked or something I said that won them over. Either way, I was pretty excited, so I began to prepare by opening up my first bank account.

I had big shoes to fill, and I wanted to live up to that expectation. I was asked to start on the following Monday, so I bought a few pairs of khakis and red shirts to work in. I forgot about one thing: my way to work. I always left two hours before my shift because my shift started in the morning. I hopped on the bus on Woodman St., plugged my ears up, laid my head back, and closed my eyes. I had a long route to and from.

When I made it to the Orange line located on 62nd St., I made sure to check when the next trolley would be showing up. Usually, it was only fifteen minutes. I waited and then hopped on it. Just as if I were going towards Grossmont College, I passed the same exits: Massachusetts Ave., Lemon Grove Dpt, Spring St., and La Mesa Blvd. I hopped off at the Grossmont Transit Center stop. Instead of taking any bus, I waited for the Green line trolley that took me in the opposite direction towards Mission Valley.

On the Green line, I had to pass 70th Street, Alvarado Medical Center, SDSU, Grandville, Mission in San Diego, Qualcomm Stadium, Fenton Parkway, and Rio Vista. I got off at Mission Valley Center, and J walked across a few streets until I was in Target's parking lot. The day had just begun, and I was already sweating. Most of the time, when I arrived, I had another fifteen to thirty minutes to relax, and I used that time to stay off of my feet until it was time to punch the clock.

I met my first coworker, who was responsible for training me on the first day. His name was Brandon, and he was at least ten years older than I was at the time, and he walked ten times faster than anyone I had met at the time. (I think the number of monster energy drinks he drank played a part in that). He asked me all of those additional probing questions to get to know me better. "Oh, you went to Mission Bay. I did, too, man! But this was back in the 2000's man!" he yelled aloud. He was a friendly person, and he even introduced me to the rest of my coworkers and showed me around the basement, where I spent the rest of the spring and the beginning of the summer. "Aye, man, by the way, we don't call customers 'customers'; we call them guests, cool?" he informed me. "Yeah, no problem," I replied.

My job in the basement was to count inventory by the hour so that my coworkers who worked on the floor could have enough for the guests. If a guest asked a coworker on the floor for something that wasn't on the floor, it was my job to bring it up to my coworker so that they could hand it to the guest. If a guest needed help with an item being carried to the car, sometimes they would call me for that too. (On a good day, I'd receive $30 in tips and not tell anyone). When you're new, you handle everything until they decide to lay off you. No one told me that, but it was what it was.

I was adjusting to a new wind of adulting in the summer of 2016. My feet were on fire at the end of every shift, and I could feel a sharp pain in both of my knees and shin bones from all of the walking and jogging I did. I had a huge sweat stain on both my back and between my thighs. I was beat up and out of shape. *Dang, man, this is a lot.* I thought twice about coming back the next day but wasn't dumb enough not to show. The sweat and pain went on for weeks until I decided to see my local physician, who I hadn't seen since my physical appointment prior to making the Grossmont football team.

I went to see my primary physician; her name was Tess. "Currently, you are in the early stages of diabetes," she told me during my appointment. I looked at her with a blank stare hoping that she was wrong. She wasn't wrong; I was. I didn't realize until my appointment that from the time I was released from jail, I picked up stress eating habits. All of the processed meat, fast food, and Sprite was sitting on me. Luckily after that appointment, I had my own transportation, so I didn't have to worry about being on my feet before my shift. My 2003 silver Ford Expedition truck was my very first purchased set of wheels at the time. I had a lot of memories in that truck.

Trying to remain optimistic was easy until Target cut my hours without warning. So I made a request to my manager, Josh, at the time to see if they needed more cart pushers. No one liked being the guy who stood outside all day and grabbed the carts, but for some reason, I found it fascinating, and I wanted in. I figured it would be a good investment because I could get all three in: exercise, freedom, and more hours. About a week went by, and Josh reached back out to me and said he was willing to have me try it out. He couldn't make me any promises, but one day would be a good start.

It was. I loved it. I was still out of shape, but the time moved by much faster than stalling in the basement when I didn't have anything to do. The only difference was in being a cart pusher, you're responsible for more than just the collecting carts outside of the store. It was another one of those things no one told me about. I was responsible for not only grabbing every single cart outside that I could possibly find and bringing it inside but other tasks as well.

The handheld baskets guests used to hold their items were my responsibility too. There were about four different stations downstairs that needed to be filled with handheld baskets at all times; I had to make sure they were filled up. The same applied for upstairs. In addition to that, whenever a customer needed help carrying their new TV they just purchased or their new piece of furniture to the car, I was the one who needed to help. Last but not least, I had to clean both the men's and women's restrooms at least twice a day. After one week, I asked myself, *Man, why did I switch?*

Luckily, I met my help. Ramon showed me the ropes for the first two weeks. Ramon was the first coworker who turned into my friend outside of work. He was about 5'8 and tattooed from nearly head to toe. He was a lot older than I was, and he didn't come from the same background as I did, but I got along with him because he was authentic and didn't care about what others thought of him. He didn't just show me how to do the job, but how to do it in a smart, fast, and easy way. Ramon had been employed at Target for years, so he knew exactly what to do.

"Look, man; we don't have to get all of these carts right now. There aren't many guests inside right now, so let's just stay outside. When it picks up, we can move," he'd say. "Alright," I'd say back. He showed me who the snitches were, who to trust and not to trust. He also showed me how to catch a manager snitching on us to another manager through the walkie-talkie radios. Channel four was where all of the dry snitching went down, which didn't bother me in the beginning, but over time it did. That's when I first learned never to trust a manager.

Ramon was the coworker who made sure I was being wise. He always kept me laughing and curious with all his knowledge about women. He had more dating experience than I had life experience, literally. Like a baby learning how to walk, Ramon was one of the first men to expose me to the pros and cons of dealing with women.

It was nothing for us to peel off and out of sight and just sit somewhere near the parking structure and either crack jokes, talk about music, or discuss women. If there was a time that I got in trouble or was caught sitting down when I was supposed to be working, it was usually when I was with Ramon, and it was worth it because we always had fun.

I met Sergio next. Sergio had been an employee longer than I had been alive. (I was 19 at the time.) Half man, half robot. He was the oldest out of all of us, and he didn't do too much talking. While Ramon and I were outside, he was on the inside, making sure everything was steady and ready. I could always count on him to pick up when I was slacking—going through the motions, minute by minute. Since he was the veteran out of us, he took the a.m. shifts along with Ramon. Whenever I'd come in around the afternoon, he'd greet me the same way, with a wave. Sergio was a cool guy.

Michael was another partner I met who I didn't get to know much. Michael was Black, but I could tell we grew up a tad bit differently. I got to know more about the Packers and Eminem through him because that's all he ever talked about. Whenever we crossed paths, that was the basis of our conversation and his desire to be a police officer. Usually, he would work on the inside like Sergio, and he didn't mind being passive. It's safe to say that he and I spoke the least but were just as cool as I was with Ramon. He went on to be a police officer after he left Target.

Having those three guys as co-laborers made it seem like less of a job, and I couldn't ask for any more than that, especially once I met Carlos and Brandon H. I clicked with Carlos and Brandon H. instantly. The three of us were around the same age, which made everything easier. Carlos was Mexican, and Brandon H. was Honduran, but the three of us got along as if we came from the same home.

The three of us formed platonic friendships. We knew about each other's backgrounds, goals, and desires. Carlos was from Sacramento, and he grew up in a rough environment. He didn't respect his father, and I could relate to that in a sense. He moved to San Diego shortly after high school with his older sister and her fiancé. I would always clown on him a little bit because he stayed not too far from the job, yet he was always late or calling in sick. Sometimes I would text him, "Really? lol." He'd hit me back very nonchalantly. That's just who he was, relaxed and easy-going, which I admired about him.

Brandon H. wasn't as quiet as Carlos, but there were a few similarities. Brandon H. had a bigger sense of humor and was just as easy-going as Carlos. I could tell he was a trustworthy person from the jump, and he meant well. But the best thing about him was his loyalty. He was very loyal. Along with Carlos, he opened up about his casual flaws. He was very conversational, and even on my bad days when I just woke up out of bed and didn't feel like talking to anyone, he was someone I wouldn't mind talking to.

It seemed like every other week during the summer, I met someone new who I connected with. By the middle of July, I met another Black guy from New York who had a huge personality. His name was Norman, but he told me he was from Harlem shortly after we met, so I started calling him "Harlem" or "Harlem World." His New York accent was heavy, and it was my first time hearing it. It wasn't hard to tell why he became a manager there; it had to be the gift of gab he possessed.

"Yo... my goodness." "Ayo listen, word to my muva." "Oh yeah? For real? Word." It was my first time actually meeting someone from the projects of New York City, so it was fascinating. There were many times when I would start a conversation or just ask him a random question just so I could hear him talk, and he never knew it. He introduced me to other coworkers who I usually walked past. He stretched me into being more social throughout the store. Knowing who I was, made me spot out those who were outgoing and had big personalities. Norman was that guy.

One day while I was inside chasing hand baskets, I spotted Norman. "Norman...Aye Harlem... Harlem! Who's that girl that comes downstairs every so often? The Black girl? Does she have a boyfriend?" I whispered. "Who? Trinity???" he replied, with a squint on his face. "She doesn't have a boyfriend. I mean c'mon, he's in Colorado because he's in the military, and she's here. She doesn't have a boyfriend. Want me to get her math for you?" he said. *Math? Oh, her number?* I fumbled out a few yes's and no's, but I couldn't front. I wanted her number, so I gave him the right away. Norman called me later that night.

"Yo bro, wyd right now?" he asked. Right then and there, I knew what time it was. *Dang, he really exchanged our numbers.* I laughed. He gave me the rundown on what it was going to be, "So, listen, because she and her man broke things apart, I told her you're single. So y'all two should talk it up and see where it goes." There was no way I could back out now. There were just a few things I blew right past, and they were: we were all coworkers, she worked in the Human Resources department, and Norman and Trinity had a cozy friendship.

Trinity was the first girl I ever pursued (if this counts). She was Black, five feet even, and had a smile that I couldn't stop staring at. From afar, I could tell that she was confident, and I liked that. She seemed very outgoing, funny, and smart. As we began to communicate, I learned things about her I wouldn't have assumed. She was driven by her desire to be a psychologist while studying in junior college. We started off talking on the phone every night, which was my first time. (A lot of the time, I didn't know exactly what to say, so there was a lot of dead air.) We kept each other up late at night until one or two in the morning. We'd ask each other tons of questions and flirted with each other until one of us fell asleep. Usually, it was me who fell asleep first.

Her: "You look like a baby, but you come off as mature. I'm not going to guess. How old are you?"
Me: "Sounds like it, but I'm not a baby, but I'm 19. U?"
Her: "Boy, you're a man-child! I'm 23."
Me: "Man, enough for you…."
Her: "Oh really???"

Being the serious person I was, her sense of humor was probably the most attractive thing about her. Plus, she got a kick out of making me laugh, and I didn't mind it. However, I knew I had to make a move or else she and I wouldn't become. I mean, since we were always in the work environment, and she worked upstairs in an office while I was outside, we said as much as we could through text to keep in touch. Since it was my first time, I didn't really know when to ask her on a date or when to create chemistry outside of work, so I waited until I felt comfortable enough. *I gotta make a move.*

"Are you free to go on a date this weekend?" In return, I didn't get a direct answer, but since it was all too new to me, I didn't feel compelled to try again. I didn't want to assume, but I was thinking the worst. *She's probably going back and forth with her ex-boyfriend in Colorado.* I was confused, so I thought about dropping her plenty of times until she did just enough to keep me around.

One day she sent me a text that raised not only my eyebrows but elsewhere. The text read, "Meet me in the downstairs bathroom. I have a sweet surprise for you." I was outside when I read that text. I was too green behind the ears to realize that she was just teasing me, so I stood by the bathroom until she texted me back, "I'm just joking, hahaha; why would I do that at the job?" "I don't know… why wouldn't you?" I replied. Afterwhile I started to question if she was ever serious about getting to know me as I was about her.

2016

Early New Years, I spotted her walking out of the store to what I believed was her headed home after her shift. She worked in the mornings, so she usually got off around 3 p.m. I just so happened to see her from a distance holding a shiny dress, so I immediately became curious. Shortly after, I was told that she was headed to a military ball. I knew exactly what that meant, so I officially let it go. Moving forward was all I could really do. I was bitter, very bitter. She and I never spoke again.

The upside to my first experience with Trinity was realizing a rule Pops taught me long ago in the bathroom during "man talk." Growing up, he'd always tell me, "Girls are just like buses. If one leaves or you miss one, wait for the next one. It'll come to you." I didn't understand that ideology growing up, but I fully understood it after Trinity and I parted ways. *Pops was right.* I might have beaten myself up over Trinity for a few weeks until I met a different girl.

17

SAVANNAH

Savannah was biracial - her father (who was never in her life) was Korean, and her mother was Black. She and I had been friends on social media for years; that's where she and I started communicating. We knew each other because we grew up going to the City Of Hope International Church. She and her family were regular attendees, just as my family and I were, so there was some familiarity. She had always been pretty to me, so if ever given the opportunity, I was going to capitalize on it.

She and her boyfriend broke up on Valentine's Day, which is right around the time Trinity and I stopped communicating. We began texting each other from March through April. I was planning on asking her out, but I never said anything. The small effort was evident, and I knew she liked it. One day, before heading to Bible Study, I said to myself... *just do it. Ask her.*

At the end of Bible Study, Savannah stood in the lobby by herself, waiting for her mom, and I saw that as an opportunity to make my move. I started a conversation, and then we began conversing for a few minutes. Suddenly I went for it, "So if you're always bored on Saturdays, then that means I can take you out on a date." I didn't ask her; I told her. She was shocked. Her reaction was just what I expected, "Yeah, I mean, I didn't know you liked me like that. Yeah, I don't mind, but you have to ask my mom, though. She's coming now." Both of our parents showed up and exchanged numbers.

"Hi... I'm LaTracey, but you can call me Ms. Tracey," I shook hands with her mom. Her sister, Sophia, extended her hand to shake mine. I never thought I'd be meeting someone's family on my first attempt, but it was what it was. "Where are you gonna take her?" her mom asked me. "The movies." I wasn't expecting her to ask me that, but it let me know at that moment what type of mom she was. I was nineteen, turning twenty, and Savannah was seventeen. I wasn't sure if her mom knew or cared about our age difference, but I didn't ask. What I didn't realize at that moment was that she cared about her daughter as a whole, not just her safety. Soon, I would find out more about that.

I remember being anxious to go on my first date that weekend. I didn't know what to wear, what to ask her, or what to expect. I didn't have a plan at all, but I went anyway. (I should've given it more thought than I did, but I didn't have much time, so I hopped in my truck and drove north to meet Savannah.) It was the longest drive I had made at the time.

Savannah lived pretty far from me in a neighborhood named Mira Mesa. Mira Mesa was nowhere near where I grew up, but it had everything, especially on Mira Mesa Blvd. There were tons of restaurants to choose from, and the theater we were going to that evening was close to where she lived. She lived on the end of Mira Mesa Boulevard in a set of condominium homes. I was reading her text messages while I was on the freeway, "When you get here, park in the visitor's parking spaces on the second floor." I thought that would be easy to find, but the Casa Mira View lot was huge, and it had about four different levels of parking structure, so I accidentally parked in her mom's spot.

It wasn't a big deal because she just wanted me to come in really quick before we left. Her grandmother wanted to meet me. I wasn't ready for it, but it would've looked bad if I didn't go in, so I went inside their home. I rang the doorbell, and it took a few minutes before I heard the door latch unlock. It was her, and she looked ten times prettier than she did on Wednesday night. *Woah.*

I was offered a seat at the dining table, which was right next to the door and the kitchen. "Heyyyy!" Ms. Tracey said. She held the same smile on her face, and her greeting was warm. *She's gonna like me.* Her grandmother and I got to know each other better within those thirty minutes I spent in the home.

As we walked down the hall, there was silence. A good silence. I was shy, and I knew she could tell, but I don't think she was. She was waiting for me to kick off the conversation, so I started with the movie we were going to see. We went back and forth with questions and answers as we got closer to my truck. "Wait, where did you park? Here? Haha... this is my mom's spot." My innocence made her laugh. *She didn't tell me to park here.*

I'd be lying if I said I remember what movie we watched and what it was about. The feeling of being on my first date was a feeling I had never felt before, so it was hard to focus on the movie. *So this is what it feels like? This is what other men feel like.* It wasn't long before Savannah went from laughing to locking her arm into mine. She was touchy, but it wasn't a big deal because I loved it. Whatever I was doing, I assumed I was doing it right.

After the movie was over, we walked back to my truck to make the five-minute drive back to her home. I asked her, "How did you like it?" I didn't care if she liked it or not because I wasn't paying attention. I just hoped she had a good time, and she did. We didn't talk much, and the mutual silence during the car ride didn't help much either, but I had to remind myself that it was still the beginning and to cut myself some slack. Overall I was optimistic that the date went well and that there would be many more to come.

Once we made it to the parking structure, instead of parking in her mom's spot again, she showed me where to park. I thought level two was on the same floor that she was on, but I was supposed to go down a few floors. Parking structures were my weakness out of all things as a fairly new driver. Thankfully, the lower levels had a lot of empty guest parking spaces available. She guided me down the lower levels and said, "You can park down there at the end." "Alright," I replied. I parked, turned my car off, and reached for my door handle.

Right before Savannah extended her door handle to hop out, she said, "Wait," in a soft voice. She slammed the door and leaned in for a kiss. It was my first time kissing a girl. My door was still cracked open, but I was so into it that I closed the door completely while we were in the middle of kissing. We kissed for at least five minutes before one thing turned into the next. It was my first time being physically intimate with the opposite sex so fast. Chills ran down my spine, my body temperature rose, and my hands started shaking. By the time we were unclothed and in my back seat, I didn't feel like I had control over myself. I could feel my hormones raging. It almost felt like I was having an out-of-body experience.

Once she got on top of me, it was over. I ended up losing my virginity on my first date in the back of my truck. I wanted to stop, but my desire for more was much stronger than it was for me to stop. *This is what it feels like?* So many thoughts. So many feelings.

So many wonders. It was ongoing. In the moment, I wasn't thinking about whether I was in the right or in the wrong. I didn't even wonder what she was thinking. I was conscious of only two things: my truck and getting caught. I didn't want to break anything, and I didn't want to hurt her, and Lord knows I didn't want to go back to jail. It was a costly moment, but a moment that left me thirsty for more.

I drove home in shock at what I had just done. My heart was racing, and I kept playing what just had happened over and over in my head. My back was covered in sweat. I never thought that day would come and how I would react to it when it did. I didn't tell anyone what had happened, and I didn't ever plan on it. That night, I lay in my bed thinking to myself, *how did I get here?* Everything happened so fast, and it was a lot to process. I looked over at my phone, and it was a text from her that read, "Hey, I'm sorry. I couldn't control myself." I wasn't mad at her, but instead, I was curious. Since I was still processing the moment, I didn't feel comfortable expressing anything. I texted her back, "It's all good. That was my first time." "Really?!" she replied quickly. "Yeah," I said. I thought about that evening for days.

After that day, I craved that same level of intimacy with her. It was like a drug. Sex was the driving force behind my decision in wanting to make things between Savannah and me official. On May 7th, she said yes to it. Since we were together, I expected to have sex with her whenever I saw her, and we met up often. The seats in my truck became the designated area, and we parked in the same old parking spot every time. I even moved the last three seats out of the back and kept the truck empty so that I could have easier access. Our daily routine didn't change. On my off days, it was hanging out in the pool (which is what led to sex), and after having sex a bunch of times, we grabbed a bite to eat from whatever we were craving on Mira Mesa Blvd. It was a very intimate spring, to say the least.

Savannah didn't have many interests, but she was passionate about a few things. From animals to nature and feminism. She took all three seriously. It was a part of who she was, and the fact that she stood for something made me like her all the more. My plan was to fall in love, so when she uttered the words "I love you" to me, I didn't waste time saying it back, whether I did or didn't. I even went out and bought the most expensive promise ring I could afford and had it custom engraved *CR & SW 05.07.16* on the inside and gifted it to her. She loved it.

I quickly became head over heels for Savannah because I assumed she loved me. Later on in life, I found out my love languages are physical touch and time spent, which makes sense because I spent three to four days out of the week hanging with Savannah. Her presence was all I wanted at the time, so we spent a lot of time around each other. I was learning her as she was learning me. One day I learned of one of her friends that struck me with curiosity. She informed me of a male best friend who liked her, but she didn't have the same affection for him. *Who is that?* I wasn't aware of him and their relations from the beginning, but I let it be since there wasn't a reason to make a big deal.

I rarely hung out with my family while I was dating Savannah because I struggled with making time for both sides. I never learned how to balance life outside of being in a relationship while spending hours with Savannah. There was a Japanese Friendship Garden in a well-known area in San Diego named Balboa Park. That's where we went. She loved it. We walked a few laps around the garden while talking about everything under the sun. That was one of our most memorable dates.

"Hey, my mom wants to know if you want to go to the street fair with us?" she asked. "Yeah, I'll go. What time do I have to get ready?" I answered. She and her family were like four peas in a pod. I was always willing to hang with her, her sister, mom, and grandmother because I learned a lot around them. It was my first time hanging around so many women at the same time. I didn't realize how much I didn't know about women until moments like the day at the street fair. I realized growing up without sister or female friends was a con for me. Every time the family invited me, I learned something new.

Right before the summer was coming to an end, Ms. Tracey thought it would be a great idea to go on a hike with her and her family in Big Bear, California. I was invited. It was August, and anyone who knows about the dog days of summer in San Diego knows how hot August is. We decided to make a road trip of it since it was a one-hour drive there and one hour back. I threw on the closest thing I had to hiking clothing, grabbed my backpack, and loaded it with essentials before heading to Savannah's house.

The drive exposed my lack of traveling experience. Everything turned my head. We were headed to the woods, so the difference in nature was apparent in every nine miles we gained. The trees were ten times thicker and taller than the ones in San Diego. The roads started looking a lot thinner, and so was the air. Grandma and Ms. Tracey were telling me I needed to step my game up. I didn't want to agree, but they were right.

The hike was cool — for me. We started on top of the trail and made our way down to a huge lake. We rested for about thirty minutes before heading back. We talked about so many hot topics and shared quite a few laughs. It was then that I realized how much of a unique family they were; Savannah was just the one who stood out.

About one month into dating Savannah, her mom and I formed a bond of our own. I was no longer Chris; instead, she started calling me "Son-n-law," and she was "Ms. Tracey." That's when Savannah's house became my house. I ate, drank, and watched whatever at her residence. That's just how Ms. Tracey was, as a person, freelance. She served in the Navy for a long time, so she shared many stories with me. I enjoyed hearing them too. We laughed, laughed, and laughed some more. I felt like I had a personal space of freedom around Ms. Tracey that I had never experienced before. No one else knew about my freedom, but her and I liked it that way.

One day she asked me if I was free on the 5th of November because she had two tickets to see Katt Williams live in the Viejas Area (where the San Diego State Aztecs basketball team played). Without any hesitation, I said, "Yeah, I'm free; let's do it." I didn't even check to see if I was scheduled to work before answering her because I didn't want to pass up the opportunity. I had never seen any comedian live before, let alone Katt Williams. I was more of a Kevin Hart type of guy, but if there was anyone I was down to laugh with, it was Ms. Tracey. Luckily, I wasn't scheduled to work that day, so I drove to Savannah's house that evening, and Ms. Tracey and I departed.

We sat down, and I looked up and saw the words in huge font above the stage "Conspiracy Theory." We had a pair of fairly good seats. I was impressed. From the moment the undercard comedians came out, Ms. Tracey started laughing. That was her thing, laughter. A lot of those guys weren't funny to me, but her laugh made me laugh. Once Katt Williams came out, I was proven wrong. For years, I thought he was just a vulgar person who portrayed himself as funny, but I was wrong. He was hilarious. I'm not sure if the fact that it was a live show changed my mind or that I just flat out judged him, but I enjoyed myself, to say the least.

During the holidays, I was excited to see Savannah's and my family sharing Christmas together. We spent Thanksgiving apart but made Christmas shared as one. She and her household family opened up their gifts early that morning before coming to my mom and I's home to watch us open up ours. The room was packed. It was Savannah, Sophia, Ms. Tracey, Grandma, and Savannah's cousin John John on one side of the room. On the other side, it was my mom, Pops, granny, Donte, Tanya (Donte's wife), SaNay, Alofamoni (my nieces), Jhamir, Kenetta (Jhamir's girlfriend), Jhaylen, Sabina (Jaylen's wife), Jhavari, and I. The living room never looked as packed as it did on that day, and I loved it.

We ate breakfast first. My mom cooked for everyone. A lot of smiles and laughter went around the room that day as gifts were being opened. Savannah gifted me my first Kobe Bryant jersey. After all of the gifts were opened, Savannah and her family wanted to join my family's Christmas family tradition: movies and dinner. We all went to see Fences starring Denzel Washington and then went to a restaurant named Sizzler for dinner. That was one of the best Christmas days I have had since I was a kid.

2017

I never really cared for setting a New Year's resolution. I just wasn't a big fan of it or the fresh start cliche until Savannah and I discussed goal-setting. She was thinking about going into the military. Maybe the Navy like her mom or the Army like her grandma, but she wasn't sure yet (or at least that's what she said).

Meanwhile, I went car shopping to save myself some gas money. I sold my 2003 Ford Expedition truck and purchased a 2007

Mitsubishi Galant. I fell in love with the way the Galant looked. It was silver, and it sat low to the street. The Galant was my first small four-door vehicle. The same day I bought it, I took it to a detailer and got my windows tinted 100% dark. By the end of the week, I moved into my own apartment as well. Savannah and I saw each other more since I had a place of my own. We had the freedom to do whatever and make our own decisions. It felt like we were taking things to the next level.

18

WEARING A MASK

Savannah and I were coming to an end, but I didn't see it coming. On May 11th, we woke up, and I dropped her off at home. After I dropped her off, I headed to work. We had been arguing ever since I moved into my own apartment. I wasn't feeling like myself because it was difficult not to talk to someone I had such strong feelings for. I hadn't heard from her all day, but just a few hours before my work shift was ending, she texted me:

Her: "I'm done with this relationship, and please don't come by."
Me: "What? Why?"
no reply
Me: "Savannah?"
Her: "I don't want to be in this relationship anymore. It's over. I'm sorry, Chris."

I can't believe this. I didn't see it coming, but it was over just like that. I never saw Savannah or her family again. Immediately

I entered a stage of grief. I hadn't had experience with grief before, but the very first stage was denial. I wasn't willing to accept it, so I tried calling her hundreds of times, and it wasn't long before I was blocked. I was in complete disbelief, so I sat in my car and cried hard.

Day after day after day, I cried. If I wasn't crying, I was trying to contact Savannah from different phone numbers. One day I asked a random coworker, "Aye, can I borrow your phone really quickly? Mine is dead. I just have to make a call to a family member at the airport soon." I made up a story out of desperation. Most of the time, she'd answer, "Hello?" Then I'd try to get every word off before she hung up. It never worked. If she could just explain, then I'd be okay. I wanted closure. I just wasn't willing to accept what Savannah had done.

Denial made me do things out of character. *Was she seeing someone else? Check her social media accounts.* I became anxious, so I quickly grabbed my phone with hopes that she wasn't wise enough to change her passwords. *She probably didn't remember that we swapped usernames and passwords months ago.* Although I was blocked from all of her social media accounts, I knew her username and password to her accounts. *Log in and see what's up.* I was right; she wasn't that wise.

I pressed the 'my story' icon, and there it was. On her latest story of the day was a photo and video of her and her male best friend with a caption that read, "no face, no case." Instantly, I became sick. *She told me he was just a friend.* I felt the insides of my stomach turning and my heart bouncing within my rib cage. I started sweating. It wasn't what I was expecting — hell, I didn't have any expectations. *Is this real? I thought they were friends.* I replayed the story over and over and over and over again. At least fifty times. I was hoping it wasn't real, but it was.

The promise ring for her birthday? The amount of sex we had. The stuff I bought. The time we spent. Was I not enough? I began to have many more thoughts just like that. I felt like I just wasn't enough, and because of that, my self-esteem lowered, and I became sad and very angry, and self-destructive. I was pissed off. I wasn't Chris. I was someone else.

I usually grabbed groceries on Thursday nights, so I kept my routine going, but it took me an extra hour to finish everything. Folks were looking at me crazy, and they had every right to because I was spilling and slamming stuff in my shopping cart. I couldn't keep it together, and it was evident. While packing my trunk with the groceries I purchased, the milk carton busted wide open. I just left it there and flew down the street doing 55 mph on a 25-mph two-way street. I was furious in public spaces and sad in private ones. I had trouble getting my emotions under control, which led me to thoughts of driving my car off the highway. I contemplated suicide for about a week.

"Son, you seem so closed off. Why?" my mom would ask.

It was difficult because I didn't know how to process what I felt, so I didn't talk to anyone. Once I made it home, I headed to bed, hoping the feelings would go away. Many nights I cried myself to sleep. I'd start to sweat at random times, and my bedsheets would be moist by the morning because of the sweat coming from my body. To cope, I slept on my side with a pillow in between my legs. When trying to cry my feelings away didn't work, I ate obsessively. I was nearly obese, and my face was practically covered with acne.

For the first time in my life, I felt a taste of abandonment. I didn't just feel abandoned by Savannah; I felt abandoned by her family as well. I didn't realize how attached I became to Ms. Tracey and the rest of Savannah's family. This was the first group of Black women I thought loved me (outside my family). I constantly questioned myself and wondered if something was wrong with me and if I was good enough for Black women. Those thoughts and feelings caused me to put into perspective what abandonment was. I didn't understand the idea of abandonment, but I understood it fully after Savannah left. I felt abandoned by someone I thought loved me and would never leave. My heart was bleeding, and I didn't know how to stop the blood.

As the summer began to roll in, I began to slowly accept that Savannah wasn't coming back. It hurt, but what hurt even more was the new perception I had of women. I never saw women the way I once did. To this very day, my mom believes the ending between Savannah and I changed parts of me for good. She's right. (It's something I still struggle with to this very day.) My utopian mindset of the opposite sex was destroyed. Subconsciously, I felt as if society taught me that if I treated a girl correctly, she'd never leave, but obviously, that wasn't true. *Someone was in debt for what she did to me.* I had to accept a new reality that I didn't want to accept. I swallowed a hard truth that I didn't want to believe. I wanted a way out of my head, but I didn't know what direction to turn.

The last stage of the grieving process was reaching out to someone who I thought at the time would help me cope, so I did. One of the most enlightening moments of this emotional struggle was meeting Joseph. His name was Joseph, but he went by Joe. Joe was Black, about five-feet-eleven inches, funny, and very laid back. He reminded me of someone born and raised in New York because of how he carried himself. He was a smooth character, and I was about to find out how smooth he was. One day he sent me a message, "Yo bro, let's slide out to the bar this weekend. Get this stuff off of your chest." He was a complete stranger to me, but from the time we met until this current day, we have been friends.

It was never a dull moment with Joe. Joe worked downtown doing security but was passionate about music production, and he was dang good at it too. Joe was four years older than I and was much more socially experienced. There I was, one day after turning twenty-one standing in line to get into a bar with someone who was turning twenty-four in July. *How did I get here?* This was the beginning of many fun nights with Joe.

Joe lived in Eastlake. Eastlake was a city of its own but adjacent to Chula Vista, so he met me at the trolley parking lot and headed downtown. He knew all of the little shortcuts and places to park where it was free and not crowded. I knew it wasn't his first time doing this. We stood in line to get into a bar called Shore Club. We made small talk for thirty minutes just to pass the time. Once we were checked for identification, I walked into a nightclub for the first time.

Woooooah. I said under my breath. I couldn't hear myself talk, so I had to learn how to use my eyes. Everyone, whether they like it or not, becomes great with eye contact in the club or bar. It's one of those unspoken things. It didn't help being 6'4, because it brought a lot of attention to me. "You wanna drink, bro?" Joe asked. I proceeded with a slow, "Yeah." "Tell her what you want. It's on my tab," he said. "Alright," I replied. I asked the bartender what she was serving, and she gave me a list of stuff, but I was overtaken, and I couldn't hear all of what she said. All I could recall was her yelling in my ear two words: cranberry juice and vodka. "Cape Cod!?" she yelled. "Yeah, yeah, that's cool," I replied. I had no idea what that was going to taste like, but I agreed to it. I didn't care what it was either because I just wanted to have a good time.

The setting was going to take some getting used to, but I was more than willing because I couldn't go another day with the pain I was enduring. Joe and I tore up the city every weekend. He was an extrovert; I was an introvert. It wasn't long before I started to become acquainted with everyone he knew. I'm glad he introduced me whenever we came across a group of women or some fellas he knew because I didn't have it in me to speak up. I met one of his closest friends, named Trevon, but we called him Trey, and his cousin, named Richard, but we called him Rich.

The four of us ventured out every Saturday night. It was almost like a tradition and a part of our Saturday routine. Joe got off at 3 p.m., but I was at work until 7 p.m. So when I got home, I had just enough time to cook a few hotdogs to eat, take a shower, change clothes, and walk to the trolley stop. The guys met me there, and then we left. Backyard was the name of one of the clubs we went to frequently. There were so many women and so many drinks that I was starting to like the routine.

Backyard was pretty soothing, just like Shore Club. Shore Club was a few feet away from the beach, but Backyard was near Mission Bay High School, so it brought back a lot of memories being in that area. By the time I had finished my second vodka cranberry drink, I was drunk and had already danced with two different girls.

Backyard was the perfect setting for a lightweight like myself because the women were easier to talk to. I only approached or started a conversation with a woman next to me rather than going out of my way. I'd probably dance with five to six girls before the night was over. I never asked for her phone number or tried to bring them back to my apartment for sex. I only enjoyed them for the spare moment because that's all I really wanted, a quick satisfaction.

Sometimes we got tired of seeing the same old women and

hearing the same old songs at Backyard, so we switched it up. F6ix was one of the best alternatives. It was downtown on F St., one of the busiest streets on a Saturday night, so we had to park pretty far and walk to it. "How many girls are you getting tonight, Chris?" Joe asked sarcastically. "All of 'em," I would reply sarcastically. Joe laughed, "You're the goat man, you're the goat man." He got a kick out of pumping me up. Trey brought me back to reality, "They don't be on you, bro!" We all laughed. For the first time in a long time, I felt like I was having fun. Sometimes the walk to the club was just as fun as the club itself.

F6ix's setting was relatable; it was more of what I was used to. Once we made it past the ropes and walked down the stairs into the basement, it was like we were in another world. Backyard played pop music, but F6ix played all of the latest and greatest rap and R&B tracks, artists like Rihanna, Tee Grizzley, Kendrick Lamar, Migos, and a bunch of other artists that were hot that year. Not to mention, the women were down to do anything — or at least dressed and behaved like it. Unfortunately, there were more men than women who showed up on Saturday nights, so I was only able to get a few women to dance with me. Women who didn't even know my first name were dancing on me as if I were married to them. I left a lot of memories at F6ix; a lot of unspoken things happened in that basement that I won't share in this book.

There was one problem with F6ix... it always got hot quickly! After my first time going, I knew not to wear a long-sleeved shirt again. So, we left and walked into a bar named Analog. It was a very mellow setting, and it kept my body temperature down. The doors were always wide open, and we weren't at the bottom of the basement anymore, so I cooled off quickly. Whether I was drunk or not, I ordered another glass of vodka and cranberry just so my hands weren't empty. I couldn't afford to stand there with my hands in my pocket while a woman was eyeing me.

After Analog became boring, we drove back to Mission Bay to check out a club named Avenue the next weekend. Out of the few years Joe had been clubbing, he had never been, so I suggested it. Something about it caught my eye, so I couldn't help but persuade the guys into it. It worked. When we walked in, the energy that was already in the room latched on to us. We were the only Black guys on the dance floor, but you couldn't really tell. The music was blaring, and the ratio of women to men in the room was perfect.

We spent most of July at a sports bar named PB Cantina until Joe's 25th birthday. Joe's birthday was on July 31st. He had planned to go to one of the biggest nightclubs downtown named Parq. It just so happened that one music producer named DJ Mustard was going to be on the turntables on the night of Joe's birthday. Parq was the plan. Some of Joe's friends (whom I hadn't met yet) called the club and reserved a table for that night.

I was one of the last guys to show up at Joe's table, but all of his friends knew who I was, so they let me in without hesitation. The tables were roped off, and in our section, there was a good ratio between men and women. It didn't take much for me to get action because women flock toward men who have reserved tables. I'm guessing that meant we had money and could afford a section to ourselves, unlike the dudes who just stood in the middle of the dance floor like we once did in the earlier parts of the summer.

We were deep in a far-left corner of the club. There was a sectional couch at our table that sat high off of the ground. Joe, Trey, Rich, a few other guys, and I sat on the couch while women mingled at the bottom, and every now and then, the ladies would come up to dance and drink. I watched women come up and down, back and forth, before I asked one of them if they could pour me a shot of Hennessy. That was very courageous of me. I had never drank Hennessy before, nor had I asked a woman to pour me a shot.

"Yeah, I got you," she replied. She seemed really enthusiastic about doing it, so I took that as a sign that she may have been interested. *Got 'em.* I watched to see how much she was going to pour up. *Dang, that's a lot.* I bit off more than I could chew, and now I had to own it. I didn't ask her to pour it back or for a chaser because I didn't want her to think I was some punk, so I grabbed the shot out of her hand as if it wasn't my first time. She stood there looking me in the eye until I finished it, and suddenly she asked, "Wanna dance?" Without thinking, I immediately said, "Yep."

We danced to quite a few different tracks that DJ Mustard spun that night. There I was again grinding on someone who I had never met. After each song, she turned her head and gave me a very seductive look. I was turned on, so things could've escalated. By this time, I was drunk (or at least felt like I was drunk) and could barely hold my glass of Hennessy. Without any warning, some spilled out of my glass and landed in her weave. It was a large portion of Hennesy. Luckily, she didn't feel it because she was also drunk, and no one saw it. I dodged a bullet that night, thanks to DJ Mustard.

19

NOISY HEART

THE CLUBBING WAS COOL AND ALL, BUT AFTER A WHILE, I realized that I wasn't healing, and the wound Savannah left me was still very fresh. It was frustrating because I thought healing emotionally was a linear process, but it wasn't. Hell — I hadn't experienced this type of pain, so I branched out. So instead of just drinking, I started smoking marijuana again.

Clubbing, drinking, smoking, and something else…meeting up with women. *If I just find another girl, I'll be alright…I hope.* As crazy as this may sound, clubbing helped me get rid of being shy around women. It gave me confidence, a little too much. I was still craving the energy and presence of a woman, so I tried to make as many companions as I could to see where things would go. Any woman that caught my eye, I went for.

The first girl I met was named Carrington. She was nineteen, biracial (Black and White), short and skinny. She and I communicated back and forth for about two weeks before she told me that she lived in Northridge, California. At first, I had no idea where that was. When I searched for the location through maps on the phone, I learned exactly where Northridge was. *Man, she's trippin'. I'm not driving three hours just to take her on a date.* That's what I said to myself, but in reality, I did the total opposite. Thirsty, to say the least, I left work three hours early on a Saturday evening and drove to Northridge Fashion Center to meet her. (I still can't believe I actually did this.)

I was expecting to be at the Fashion Center at 7 p.m. Northridge Fashion Center was a mall where the movie theater was. I arrived there and sat for a few minutes to wait for her to come out of the bathroom. I remember sitting on one of the couches in the lounging area, thinking to myself, *man, I'm thirsty for this.* I was in disbelief that I had driven hours just to meet a stranger.

I was taken away by her beauty when she came out of the bathroom. We took a seat and started talking about some of everything. We had a few awkward minutes of silence, but overall, she knew how to keep up a conversation. I was impressed. We shared the same religious beliefs and future plans, but neither one of us was willing to relocate. I'm sure she figured I lived too far, just as I figured the same about her. We went on and on and on while the theaters were being cleaned.

Our conversation went on for about forty-five minutes until the lines opened back up, and we were able to purchase our seats. Looking back, this is arguably where I ruined my chances with her if I ever had any. I stood behind her while I was texting. My head was down, and the bib of my hat was covering my vision. Not to mention I couldn't hear. Unbeknownst to me, the cashier yelled, "Next customer!" and she stepped forward to buy her ticket. She expected me to buy both, which I did as well. When I looked up, she was already at the counter and made her purchase. *Shoot.* It was too late.

She didn't say a word to me after that. Her body language changed — she didn't seem as open as she was minutes ago. After the movie ended, I asked her how she liked it. She replied, "It was okay," in a very monotone voice. *Yep, I messed up.* I knew it. Since I didn't know her well enough, I chalked it up as a loss. We walked out. I hugged her slightly and said, "I'll talk to you later." She didn't say anything back. She took an Uber home, and I hopped in my car and left.

I guessed correctly. I tried to reach out to her a few days later, and she didn't reply. A few more days went by, and I realized that I was blocked from all of her social media accounts. If I could only explain why I didn't buy her ticket. All I needed was a few minutes. Unfortunately, I didn't get that, and I had to live with it. I didn't let it bother me; instead, I moved on to the next girl.

Eden was another girl I met through social media. Eden was biracial as well (Creole and Black), a little over five feet, and had a smile that was to die for. Out of all of the girls I met, Eden knew how to hold a nice conversation. We started by having an innocent and casual conversation. I could tell she was mature for our age, and I liked it. I arranged a day for us to meet, and we did just that. She lived in Oceanside, California, which was right next to a pier, so we met at the pier.

It was a forty-minute drive, but I didn't mind (after all, I previously drove three hours, so forty didn't make much of a difference.) Her personality was something I hadn't seen in a girl before. She was very calm, confident, and upbeat. It was very attractive. I knew nothing about her background, but within the first few minutes, I said to myself, *someone raised this girl correctly.* I was more impressed with her than I was with Carrington or any other girl I knew at the time.

We sat on a bench staring out at the water while talking about everything. We touched on family and dating more than anything else. The two of us were the same age and were going through a rough breakup from a one-year relationship at the same time. I assumed she was special, but I just didn't know how specifically she would be to me and for how long. That was the first and last time I saw Eden. We never actually dated, but we remained cool through social media.

I hit a hard stop after Eden. I questioned my motives. I felt like I needed to take a step back. I also wasn't clubbing as much as I was with Joe and the rest of the guys. Whenever Joe and I saw each other, it was more so to play basketball or hang out. I did everything possible to numb my feelings, but overall, I was still searching for that same level of intimacy I had with Savannah.

I had a lot of time to sit around and think while I wasn't at work. *I can't believe I allowed my emotions to get me out of character.* I started to feel a little guilty while still in pain. In one moment, I was fine, and in the next, I was a mess. *When will this end?* What I didn't realize was Savannah needing me (or sex from me, I should say) made me feel secure about myself. Her need became my identity, and once she didn't need me, I didn't know who I was. That was the problem. I needed to find out who I was. In my mind, the world was ending, but in reality, I was just deeply hurt.

I was feeling so much that I didn't know whether the next person had the answer for me or whether I should just sit back and heal as time went on. Maybe I needed both; I wasn't sure. I thought of the possibility of seeking a mentor that would help me, but that required being vulnerable again. The last thing I wanted was to be vulnerable with anyone else. I developed a huge fear of opening up to anyone, so I knew it was going to be a hard task regardless of who I spoke with.

20

JORDAN

Jordan (Yarden) - *"descend" or "flow down"*

IN THE SUMMER OF 2017, I REACHED OUT TO JORDAN. JORDAN was like my God cousin. We weren't related by blood, but we were kin because our moms had been best friends before we were born, and our families knew each other pretty well. He was about eight years older than me. He was outspoken about his faith, and he attended a church that was actually near my apartment, unbeknownst to me. I needed someone to help me figure it all out, and for some reason, after seeing a post of his on social media, I sent him a message, a very vulnerable message. It was a risk.

He was someone I watched from afar. I had never heard of or seen a Black fitness trainer before, so he stood out. His family stood out even more so. There were times when my family would travel up north to a city named Temecula for occasions or just to fellowship with his family. He came from a smaller family than me. It was him, his mother named Carolyn (who I called Auntie

Carolyn), Mr. Torrance (his stepfather), and his younger sister Tabitha (who was my God cousin as well). Jordan had a sense of wholeness about him, and I wanted to be just like that but in my own way.

I opened up to Jordan about my past and my current state. If there was anything I knew and understood about vulnerability, you can't fake it because you won't be able to receive the help needed. I had to let him know about my truest thoughts and feelings. There came a point in our conversation where I just didn't care because I needed help, not an image to uphold. "So, I go to church on Sundays at a friend's house. There are a lot of brothas there I feel like you could learn from. You should come," he said. *Church? I didn't ask about going to church. I already go to church.* I started to rethink the whole Jordan thing after that.

That wasn't the best assumption to make because I'm glad I went. He was right too. This wasn't like anyone's traditional church service. This was being held at the chief of the San Diego firefighter's home. His name was Jason, but out of respect, I called him Mr. Jason since he was a lot older than Jordan and I. Mr. Jason was nearly the same age as my mom. In fact, the two actually went to high school together. Mr. Jason and Jordan were members of a church before going independent; that's how they met.

I stayed after service just to chop it up with Jordan. Jordan was a man of few words, but if you watched him long enough, you could learn a lot rather than listening to him talk. One of the few things I paid close attention to was his lifestyle. As a trainer, he was very organized and had a very high self-esteem. The way he carried himself was pretty eye-opening. I wanted that, but I was barely fitting into my clothes. I had gained nearly a total of sixty pounds while dating Savannah and drinking alcohol during those Saturday nights with

Joe. I was huge and the heaviest I'd ever been. One day before it was time to part ways, I asked the question I needed to ask:

> Me: "Yo, Jordan, I need to lose weight. I'm a few pounds away from two-forty."
> He turned around slowly, cocked a smirk, and asked, "How much do you weigh?"

I'm not sure if he asked intentionally or if I said two-forty too fast, but the two of us ended up answering his question at the same time.

> Him: "240?"
> Me: "240."

His smirk turned into a smile. He began nodding his head slowly while saying, "Okay, okay."

> Me: "How much are your sessions?"
> Him: "Uh, I can work out a deal with you for like $35 or $40 per session. Something like that. Cool?"
> Me: "Yeah, what's your schedule like? I'm free today and tomorrow mostly. Early mornings on other days."
> Him: "Does tomorrow around 12 work for you?"
> Me: "Yeah, that'll work."
> Him: "Alright yeah… cool. Get a lot of sleep tonight. Bring a towel and some water. I'll see you then."
> Me: "Alright."

I didn't realize what I was about to get myself into until I started thinking. As time went by, I began to overthink. It became hard to finish the day. All I could think about was how hard the next day was going to be. Asking that question was a risk, but I didn't expect to be afraid of actually exercising. *I should've thought it through.*

I was nervous, extremely nervous. That night I had everything laid out next to my bed. Trying to find what to wear helped me realize that I didn't have anything close to exercising. Most of my sneakers were either casual or too clean to get dirty, but luckily I had a pair of Nikes I used to go hiking in with Savannah's family that one time in Big Bear.

I remember sitting on the side of my bed the next morning, thinking to myself...*Just cancel and make up an excuse.*

I'll text him that I'm not going to make it. My digital clock in the corner of my room read 10:06 a.m. I had a decision to make, and I needed to make one fast. Without thinking any further, I reached across my bed, grabbed my phone, and went into my text messages. When I found Jordan's name, I opened up the thread and began typing up an explanation as to why I couldn't make it. *Jordan, just a heads up....* then I stopped. My guilty conscience kicked in, so I started hitting the backspace key to delete one letter at a time. *Forget it, just go.* By 11:20 a.m. I was on the highway.

The drive from my apartment to Jordan's workplace was about forty minutes. I didn't realize it until I typed his address into my GPS. I started to find every reason to turn around and go home, but something inside me held me together. I continued to place one foot in front of the other until I made it to my car. Once I got in my car, there was no turning back. I started my engine and hit the freeway, driving at about 80 mph. Thank God I didn't get pulled over.

The further I drove, the more I tried to fight the feeling of being nervous. I kept two hands on the wheel because my left shoulder became numb. (I never drove with two hands on the wheel.) My shoulders stiffened up, and I couldn't take my foot off the gas. Every other minute I watched my GPS, thinking to myself...*I'm getting closer.* I could feel the anticipation, but I was also curious. I made it ten minutes before the session began.

Jordan worked in a gym space at a Boys and Girls Club in Solana Beach. Solana Beach was fairly close to Mira Mesa Blvd., but I had never been in the area because I had no reason to. When I arrived, I expected to see a bunch of Black folks who were fit as well but instead, it was just Jordan and me. He and I were probably the only Black people in that part of town at the moment. It's safe to say that Solana Beach wasn't a Black community.

"Sup, Jordan!" I yelled out, trying to fake confidence. I walked in with a fake enthusiastic attitude because I didn't want him to see any signs or traits of weakness or intimidation. "Yo, wassup Chris," he replied with a serious look on his face. This time, there was no smirk or smile, so I knew I was in for a long workout. As he was finishing up with a client, I observed his body language. I knew he wasn't much of a talker, but this was different. I hadn't seen him so focused like how I was witnessing. This wasn't the Jordan I was hanging with yesterday. Whoever he was on Sunday was cool, but this Monday guy was a serious act. It had only been ten minutes, and I could already tell what type of fitness trainer he was.

Just like a rookie on the job, my weaknesses were exposed. The funny thing is he didn't even have me touch a single dumbbell or barbell at the beginning—every exercise he had me do required body weight for the most part. "Yo, so...hop on the treadmill," Jordan said. I stepped on it, and he turned the speed up pretty high. I ran for about five minutes until he walked back in and turned the speed up even higher for the last three minutes. I thought I was going to die.

I jumped off, and when I landed, a few drops of sweat slid off my shiny skin. *Ah, man.* I hadn't experienced that in a very long time. I was a little dizzy, and my arms were shaking a little bit. I went from nervous to scared, but I refused to say anything because I was in it knee-deep. After the treadmill, I was instructed on the basics such as push-ups, wall sits, ball slams, and deadlifts. In that order, I began.

Luckily, I had been doing a few push-ups in my apartment from time to time, so the ones he had me do weren't that hard. Although I could only do ten in my room because of how much body fat surrounded my chest, I couldn't allow him to see that. I started pushing up with every ounce of strength I had. I completed forty-five push-ups with a block that sat between my chest and the floor, saving me some space from going all the way down. "Dang, I didn't know you could do that much!" I looked up and saw a huge smile on his face. He was already getting a kick out of killing me—two out of two.

The ball slam was what almost did it. I could've passed out. The objective was to pick up a ten-pound medicine ball and slam it on the floor as hard and fast as I could and then repeat it over and over and over. My heart was beating so fast that I thought it was going to burst through my rib cage and out of my chest. (I might be adding a few details to this story for some dramatic flair, but you get the drift. It was difficult.) I could hardly breathe while picking the ball back up from slamming it down. At this point, I wanted it to be over. I was tasting defeat while covered in sweat, and I felt a little wheezy in my stomach.

"I'll be right back. You can grab some water," he said hastily. Whoever called his name or whatever he had to do, I thank God for it because I wasn't going to make it any further if I wasn't offered a break. I chugged all of the water in my water bottle until it was gone and tossed the bottle by my soaked towel. *That wasn't even enough water.* My mouth dried back up quickly, so I caught my break just in time before his return. "So now we have wall sits...right over here," he said as he walked through the door. *Mannn.*

This huge pillar was placed in the middle of the gym that he used for wall sits. The objective was to sit with my back up against the wall and my legs at a ninety-degree angled position for as long as possible. Within the first twenty seconds, I started to break. I wasn't satisfied, and I slightly started to feel soft, so I kept telling myself to *hold on.* At about fifty seconds, I gave out and rose up. Before I could stand up, Jordan grabbed both my shoulders and pushed them back down into my sitting position, and said, "No, back down. Back down. Sit back down." That made me angry.

This was supposed to be a thirty-minute session. I was trying to find an excuse to quit because I didn't feel like I could go any further. *I guess you can do a lot in thirty minutes.* He didn't tell me what was on the menu. The exercises were being revealed as time went on. "We're almost done. We have deadlifts." Deadlifts were the hardest by far. I thought it would be so easy to bend my knees, arch my back, and pull a barbell off of the floor, but it looked a lot harder than it actually was.

I felt a throbbing pain exhilarate through my stomach every time I pulled the bar up. "Ahhhhhh!!!" I yelled. Each set was heavier than the previous set. By this time, I was drenched in sweat from head to toe. My socks were even wet. With each repetition, the pain became more intense, so I stalled after dropping the bar. I contemplated. "Don't think about it! Just do it, Chris! Don't think about it!" he yelled. The last thing I wanted to do was upset the man who had my well-being in the palm of his hand, so I lifted the bar off of the ground as fast as I possibly could while grunting loudly, *Agggghhhhhhh!!!!!!*

There were roughly five minutes left until 12:30 p.m., and his next client showed up, so I thought he was going to let me off of the hook, but he didn't. He made me run three laps around the parking lot. "Start at the door and stay close to the corner and edges. No cheating." I squinted with sweat covering over fifty percent of my vision to see how much the run was. *Ahhh shoot.* I hung my head low because I knew this was my last straw. I had no wind left in me or energy. Somehow I mustered up enough energy to run as hard as I could. *Just put one foot in front of the other.* I kept telling myself that until it became hard to think.

My vision was blurry, and I was about to fall over. As I walked on my second lap, my mouth became a little watery, and I could hardly breathe. There was no way I was going to stop the vomit from coming out, so I just let it go. *There goes that bowl of Cookie Crisp.* All on the pavement of the parking lot. I had one more lap to go, so I stalled, put my head down, and then took off. I thought I was running pretty fast, but apparently, I was running in slow motion. "That's not running, Chris! You call that running?" Jordan yelled from the doorway. Thankfully, when I looked back, he was gone, so I jogged it in until I made my way back inside. I was done.

I was done for that day, but Jordan wasn't going to let me loose. He asked if I was going to train some more, predominantly in the morning just before work. I said, "Yeah" (out of fear), but really I was thinking...*never again*. He said, "So, we can train together for the same price on Mondays, Wednesdays, and Fridays at 7 a.m. at the LA Fitness down the street from here. I have a membership there. Grab a membership. It should be like twenty-something." "Alright," I said back.

Truthfully, I walked out of the Boys and Girls Club feeling like the weight I had been carrying on my shoulders for months had finally been removed. It was such a strange feeling because, while

I was working out, I didn't feel good, and I was uncertain, but the reward came after. Plus, in the back of my mind, I knew I needed Jordan. I had a strange feeling that the only way I was going to get to the next stage of my life was if he got me there. *Maybe God is going to use him to help me.* I drove home feeling and slightly thinking like a brand-new person. For the first time in a long time, I felt strong.

Jordan held me accountable to a routine from September throughout the winter. I knew he wasn't going to let me slack, so I woke up with the same thing on my mind every day...*show up and get it done.* Work for me started at 10 a.m., but Jordan's day started earlier than mine, so we met at the LA Fitness on Mira Mesa Blvd. at 7 a.m. Since my commute was thirty minutes plus, I woke up at 5:30 a.m. I hated it at first because I wasn't used to it, and sometimes I would fight my sleep while driving, but this was my only hope of shaking off the person I was.

He'd shoot me a text, "Hop on the treadmill for eight minutes if you get there before me. The last two minutes are full speed." I always made it to the gym before him. I'd be upstairs already sweating by the time I saw him walking through the door. He never saw me, but I saw him. He walked straight to the lockers to store his backpack, and then I'd meet him downstairs.

It was my first time being in the gym around folks who were committed to a fit lifestyle, so I was easily intimidated. Truthfully, if it had not been for Jordan, I wouldn't have signed up. I followed his lead. "Just follow me, and I will show you what to do," he said. Every day was like the first day on the job. He instructed me on how to use the equipment and the purpose of the equipment served. I learned quickly that I had to pay attention because he moved fast and didn't like to explain it twice.

After every workout, I was covered in sweat. I couldn't keep up with the game plan, so I just did whatever was assigned. He mixed it up. On Mondays, we trained lower body; on Wednesdays, we trained upper body, and Fridays were a little bit of everything. Tuesday, Thursday, and Saturday, I showed up and did a little bit of everything. Cardio was the starter and finisher of every session. The routine was simple and kept me going. After every workout, I felt the same way I did after that day at the Boys and Girls Club. Although it was hard, and I barely completed the pushups, sit-ups, and squats assigned, I felt good physically and mentally. *I think I like this.*

Within just one month, I lost nine pounds. When the weight started to fall, I became more comfortable and confident. I started to like LA Fitness and the folks I met there. LA Fitness had nearly everything: a pool and jacuzzi, dumbbells, barbells, squat racks, benches, a basketball court, a turf area, a sauna, a cafe, etc. A lot came for twenty-plus dollars a month. I was getting a lot for what I was paying, so it was worth it.

Jordan wasn't one of those guys who liked to talk at the gym, so I followed suit. The two of us were naturally introverted, so with us, it was easier said than done, but every so often, Jordan would unplug his ears and introduce me to someone important to him. One day he bumped into another him. At a glance, he looked Indian or was of Indian descent because of his tattoos, man bun, and complexion. "Yo, Chris, this is the last Mohican," he said, laughing while dapping him up. "Is this your family?" he asked. "Yeah, this is Chris," Jordan replied. We shook hands, and I laughed with them.

It was evident that I was growing in my new habitat because I kept hitting the gym hard every morning, and the results were coming in weekly. Time flew by, and I looked up one day and realized that I could complete twenty-plus pushups without the block that created space between my chest and the floor. I could run faster and much longer too. When visiting Tess, my physician, I learned that I was no longer in a pre-diabetic stage, and my blood pressure was at its best, which was 110 systolic over 80 diastolic. My heart rate was at 60. (Athletes and people who are very fit can have a resting heart of 40 bpm. The range is between 60-100.) By Thanksgiving Day, I was down twenty-five pounds and had only 18% of body fat. I was proud to be in better shape, but I wasn't content.

I wonder if things would've turned out different for me back in high school had I been in this shape.

San Diego in December can get really cold in the morning, so on some mornings, I woke up scraping ice off of my windshield because it was 37 degrees. Running on the treadmill usually warmed my body up quickly, but it got boring quickly too, so I became creative. Before hitting the treadmill, I'd jump rope or grab the battle ropes and go at it. Sometimes after jumping rope or battle ropes, I'd skip the treadmill and hop in the pool and do a few laps or run a few runs on the court with a bunch of strangers. Basketball usually was my go-to. Usually, I was the only Black guy on the court and the tallest too, so I used that to my advantage. A lot of guys would pick me because, at a glance, I looked like I could ball (although I was average). The games got physical, and they went down to the wire, so I burned a bunch of calories.

The plus of playing ball with guys at the gym was the opportunity to grow socially. All of my life, I had been a soft-spoken please-and-thank-you kind of guy, and I was far from an extrovert, but for whatever reason, I left a mark on strangers. I learned that Jordan fell in that category to some degree. We were thinkers and doers, not talkers. He became my source of accountability both in and outside the gym. He even invited me to many places and continued to introduce me to people he knew. He was busy, so his investment and concern meant something.

One day he texted me, "Yo, are you free after our workout?" This was after a workout we had scheduled on a Monday afternoon. I wouldn't love anything more than to go back home and get some rest, watch a movie, or read a book, but instead, I texted him back, "Yeah, what's up." He wanted me to go with him to support his friend, who planned to stand with Colin Kaepernick's protest against police brutality by kneeling during the national anthem. I agreed to go.

I left my car at the Boys and Girls Club and carpooled with him to the game. It was further north in a city named Vista. His friend's name was Josh, who coached high school football. For the next thirty minutes, we picked each other's brains. We challenged each other as much as we could. As two dudes who thought so much, the conversation started in one place and ended in another. I'd share a story about a time with Savannah and my days at Target that he knew nothing about, and then he'd double back with a few dating stories of his. We'd finish the convo by laughing it off like two eighty-nine-year-old men. To this day, our conversations are a lot like this.

"Mann! Out of nowhere, my jeans didn't fit. That was the worst part of it all. She left me like that," I said while laughing. Jordan took his time before saying anything back; he always did. It was intriguing to me to see someone who took their time before responding to a statement. Since I grew up in a household full of noise, I wasn't used to the silence. As he was focusing on the road, he did the grin-to-smile ratio thing as he always did, started laughing, and then he said, "A relationship can make you fat, Chris," sarcastically while shaking his head. We both started laughing uncontrollably.

That was the dopest yet uneasy part of being God cousins. When the conversation took a turn, it took a huge turn for the better. As kids born and raised as Christians, it was hard to avoid topics centered around our faith. Whenever I mentioned the benefits of the new job I started earlier in the year, he'd mention the importance of giving. "Make sure you're saving money and giving ten percent of what you make because if it weren't for God, you wouldn't have it," Jordan kept me on track.

The more we talked, the shorter the trip felt. The further we drove, the whiter it got. Not the weather, but the people. We had to have been the only Black men in that city that night—us and Josh, who was biracial. Don't get me wrong, I never had a problem with White people or being in their presence. However, it was evident that it intimidated White people. Why? I don't know. No one had ever said anything racist to me before in my life, but the body language of White people spoke louder than anything they could've said.

"Yo, man, can I ask you a question?" I asked. "Yeah, what's up?" he replied. "How did you get so comfortable being around White people all of the time? I get a lot of weird looks," I asked. "It makes me uncomfortable," I said again. He gave me a simple answer. "You have to learn how to develop a presence around them. Be confident in who you are. It happens over time," he said. "Ahh, okay," I replied. I didn't get it then, but I knew I would eventually. After parking, we stopped to use the restroom and made it to the game to watch Josh protest. I had been concerned with my interactions with White people practically my whole life until that conversation with Jordan. Since he believed in himself, I believed him when he said to develop a presence. That was a very impactful day for me.

I kept the focus and a weighing scale in my room — a cheap one I picked up at a local department store that was a few miles away from my apartment. I weighed myself twice a week. By the middle of January, I weighed in at 200 lbs. I had lost 40 lbs. Since I had a bad habit of being cheap, it showed up in my clothes before it did on the scale. Everything had a baggy fit to it, but for whatever reason, I didn't care as much as I did about losing the weight.

Every day I stepped out of the shower and gazed at my sculpted chest and broadened shoulders. I'd look down at my quad and calf muscles and notice how strong my bones felt. It was new to me, so I could hardly believe it. That was the difficult part, believing it. Since I had never had a muscular build before, I checked myself out often, as much as I could wherever I could. I purchased a huge body mirror and placed it in my room near my bed. I stared at myself through my bathroom mirror both morning and night.

I kept going. I didn't stop at 200 lbs. Although Jordan and I parted ways from mornings at LA Fitness on Mira Mesa Blvd., we stayed in touch, and he continued to hold me accountable. I migrated from that LA Fitness to another LA Fitness gym located in National City, which wasn't too far from Chula Vista.

It was perfect; I left at 6 a.m., worked out for about two hours, showered, and then left for work. I arrived about thirty minutes before my shift, which was just enough time for me to collect my thoughts before starting work. Since I didn't have much of a social life or any friends, I walked three slow laps around the building while eating a bowl of my homemade tuna and crackers on my lunch break. I was still heavily dedicated.

By Valentine's Day, I was down another fifteen pounds. *185.* A total of fifty-five pounds of body fat was gone. I looked even better than I did at 200, and I was lean and stronger than I had ever been.

To save money, I ended my membership with LA Fitness as a whole and joined a YMCA branch named after Jackie Robinson that was a little further out in my community but worth it. The Y was cheaper because I was on a family plan. My family chipped in, so I was only responsible for my piece of the pie, which was $12. This gym felt more like a home than anything else.

It had everything LA Fitness had but had a different structure, and it wasn't as crowded. I loved it. The YMCA became my sanctuary. Every day, I couldn't wait to wake up and go lift and shoot some hoops, more so the hoops than anything else. It was just me, my ball, an empty court, my gym playlist, and my imagination. It brought me so much joy and peace that there were days that I thought to myself... *Just call in sick from work and stay here.* I was reminded of my days as a boy and teenager who couldn't and wouldn't play on the court. It got so bad that I had to set a timer so I could know when it was time to shower and leave. I was late to work a few times, but I didn't care.

A few months later, I was headed back towards the 200s, full of muscle. To this day, I can bench press 245 pounds, squat 275 pounds, and deadlift 405 pounds. My weight fluctuates between 215 pounds and 220 pounds. I didn't know getting in shape was going to affect other areas of my life. My way of thinking changed drastically. It was an overwhelming feeling (in a good way), but I embraced it because I began to realize who I was becoming and was required to get rid of the old way of thinking, especially since Jordan pitched me an offer.

Jordan and I had been discussing the possibility of me training others full time after being shepherded by him. It would be wiser and less time-consuming to start from the ground up rather than going back to school for a degree in Kinesiology. I earned the tools of the assistant he was looking for, so the offer was on the table, and I wasn't going to pass it up. I knew it was a real investment the day he invited me out to a client's birthday party.

"Yo, you wanna go to a rich person's party?" Knowing Jordan, I knew he wasn't playing. I had a fair understanding of the type of guy Jordan was so far. He was a lot like me, and knowing me, I wouldn't text anyone that type of question in a joking matter. He didn't have to ask me twice. "Yeah. When is it?" I replied. I had never been around rich people and definitely not at a rich person's party. "Saturday at 7:30 p.m. when you get off. In Del Mar. It's business casual attire," he replied. "Alright," I said in return. I tried to play it cool, but deep down on the inside, I was moved. *Me? At a rich person's party?*

Friday evening, I prepared to clock out of work a little sooner than usual. At 6:30, I clocked out and headed straight to the showers downstairs next door to the gym. I cleaned up and headed to the exit. By 6:55 p.m. I was on the road. Jordan and I met at the Boys and Girls Club. I followed him to the party from there. Jordan knew his way around the area, so it didn't take us long to get to the party. When we arrived, I realized that we were at someone's home and not a building. That's how rich this person was; the party was in their home. On top of that, we weren't allowed to park our cars because there was valet parking. *Is this real?* I was in awe.

We walked in slowly while catching up with each other through conversation. He was a new father, so we had a lot to chat about. The two of us were proud of each other. *These folks must be RICH rich. Like super-rich.* The entrance was as long as the distance between the sand at the beach and the actual tide. I couldn't help but look around while he was talking. Some of what he was telling me didn't make it in one ear because I was so thrilled to be in a rich person's house. Inwardly, I was doing backflips.

It turned out to be two of Jordan's longtime coupled clients: Harvey and Shirley White. "Harvey is the president of Qualcomm Stadium," Jordan said. I was speechless. When we walked in, we were greeted by Shirley White; it was her birthday. She was wearing a very elegant white dress, white heels to match, and a pair of white pearls. Her outfit probably cost more than my Mitsubishi Galant. She greeted Jordan with such a warm smile and hug.

Jordan introduced me to Shirley, "Shirley, this is another trainer of the Body Architect company, Chris." That was the moment when I knew Jordan believed and trusted in me without a shadow of a doubt. He gave me the stamp of approval for his assistance right in front of not only a very wealthy client but one of his first clients. I couldn't believe it, but I followed suit. After that, he introduced me to everyone else without me having to say a word.

Although Jordan and I were the only Black people at the party, we made our presence felt. The hospitality was warm, and Shirley showed us around. She made sure that we knew how to get around. "There's a live band in the corner, and all of the bars are free to the two of you, so enjoy whatever you like!" she said. I was glad to hear that because I was starving. Jordan and I walked around while catching up some more. The home looked brand new, polished, and spacious. There were three floors, and we were on the third.

"Yeah, man, so there's an underground gym right below us. I've trained Harvey down there earlier in the morning sometimes," Jordan abruptly said. "Really? ... How much are these paintings?" I asked. "Mhmm, maybe like a couple million dollars. High thousands maybe," he replied. I didn't even know what to say but stared at the art. "Did he go to college?" I asked. "Harvey? Nope, uh, no, he didn't," he answered. *Wow.*

We grabbed a seat and chopped it up some more. "Yo, did you see the dunk I posted on my Instagram story? Hahaha," I asked. He nodded his head while smirking. "Soaring. I see you," he responded. I continued on to another subject. "How was it watching your daughter come out?" I asked. He started laughing. "Man, the funny thing is, she was crying the entire time until I cut the umbilical cord. She stopped as soon as she saw me," he replied. "Dang, man, that means something. I'm glad you had that experience," I said. "Yep, yep. Are you hungry? he asked. "Yeah, let's get something," I replied.

There were tons of choices. The seafood bar caught my attention, and Jordan could tell. "Have you ever tried sushi?" he asked. "Nah, never," I replied. There he went again, smirking. "Let's try it!" he exclaimed. I wasn't too sure about it because most people had horrible things to say about sushi, so I almost backed out. "What flavor should I try? What's in them?" I asked. "Well, there are different rolls that are filled with different ingredients. The California roll is the most common and probably the best to start with. Let's ask the chef," Jordan replied. There were Dragon rolls, California rolls, and a few other rolls I didn't give too much of my attention to. "Yeah, I'll go with the California roll," I said. After my first bite, the rest was history. *Man, this is good.* Sushi became one of my favorite foods that day.

We left the party around 10 p.m. because we had long commutes. We hugged Shirley and thanked her for hospitality. On the way out, Jordan said, "See Chris, look. I just want you to see this." He lifted his arm and pointed at the luxury cars lined up facing the White's driveway. There were about five back-to-back in two different rows. I didn't notice them on the way in for whatever reason. "See, man, and this is just the first row. Chris, it's possible," he said. I didn't have a dream car and never had been a fan of cars, but the Aston Martin caught my eye because of the vanilla chrome paint job. We continued to walk slower so we could get an eyeful. I was truly inspired.

The attendants brought my vehicle back, and I dropped Jordan off at his car. Before I took off, I saw him flagging me down in my rear-view mirror, so I stopped. "Yo, try this on really quick. It should fit you because it's too small for me," he said. It was a baby blue Tommy Hilfiger suit jacket. "This is fly. When do you want me to give it back?" I asked. "It's yours. Keep it. Welcome to the team," he replied. My eyes got big. No one ever randomly gave me a fairly new suit jacket, and I didn't think anyone ever would. Watching him freely give it to me was what I took away from it. In fact, the entire night, he gave to me. He gave me my first experience around rich people, my first taste of sushi, and my first suit jacket. That was a night I will never to forget.

After that night, Jordan and I discussed the ins and outs, my role, and future plans for the company he created from the ground up, Body Architect. It worked for him, and it worked for me. A few weeks later, my photo and background were added to the "about me section" on the Body Architect website. I was officially a member of the Body Architect company: Jordan, a very fast woman from Ghana named Nafisa, a strong younger guy named Malikia, and myself. Shortly after that night, I had a handful of clients to train.

It's funny to me that I tried everything I never thought I'd try after Savannah's exit from my life. Clubbing, women, smoking, and then exercising. I was trying to escape from the pain, and I found freedom in my effort to escape.

I'm not sure if I would be the man I am today without the help of Jordan. Before we built a relationship, I was broken and lost, but after receiving redirection from Jordan, I changed drastically. I was able to spot my own weaknesses and turn some of them into strengths. I no longer lacked confidence, my self-esteem was high, I became more accepting of myself and others around me, and I also became more patient. In addition, I learned how to play chess, box, and a little jujitsu moves.

In a sense, exercise and lifting weights made me feel like a man, and because of that, I formed a healthy addiction. To this very day, there isn't a place I'd rather be but in the gym. Most importantly, I began to take my relationship with God seriously, so I began to read and study scripture on my own for the first time in my life. As crazy as it may sound, if it wasn't for Jordan, I'm not sure if I would've pursued God or developed masculine traits like assertiveness and courage. In the first twenty-one years of my life, it's safe to say he's had the biggest impact, and I think most of that has to do with the way he descended to the level I was on and brought me up. A father figure indeed.

JEFF

Jeff short for Jefferey (Variant: Geoffrey) - *"peace"*

After connecting with Jordan, I started to build other meaningful relationships with people I had never met before. A specific deacon at COHI had his eye on me. His name was Deacon Cartwright, and he had been looking for me. He was a positive, well-rounded, and upbeat type of guy in his seventies. One day while visiting my mom's house, I received information from him. "Chris, Deacon Cartwright at the church, said he wants you to start going to the community organizing meetings at the church," my mom yelled from the kitchen.

My mom continued, "He said he noticed your growth and sees an emerging leader in you, so he thinks you'd be a good fit," she said again. I had no idea what to think or say because Deacon Cartwright and I had never really had a conversation over ten seconds, so I wasn't too familiar with him personally. To hear a compliment like that followed by an invite was surprising and intriguing, so I showed up to the first meeting.

Deacon Cartwright sent me a text. The meetings were held every last Monday of each month in the Fellowship Hall located in the church basement, along with other faith leaders who showed up from different districts in San Diego. COHI was the location for the meetings, but it was open for anyone to show up. As soon as I showed up, Deacon Cartwright introduced me to Jeff. Jeff was a community organizer who had years of organizing experience with a company named SDOP (San Diego Organizing Project). I didn't even know community organizers or faith leaders existed in communities at the time.

Jeffery Alonzo Karahamuheto was his full name. "You can just call me Jeff," he said. We shook hands and talked before the meeting began. Jeff was in his early thirties and well-spoken, but I could tell he had a young spirit because of his yellow-dyed flat top. Jeff and I clicked instantly. After conversing with Jeff, I learned that we shared similar experiences as Black men in America who desired a heart for change. I walked away from our first meeting, thinking about how intentional, passionate, and energetic he was. His aura inspired me.

Every meeting was different based on the needs of district four (where I grew up). However, the energy was always the same level — powerful. I began to take lots of notes and share my opinion on what needed attention, but I listened to learn for the most part because I knew I was inexperienced. Sometimes the room was filled with high-level local positions like bishops, pastors, clergy members, and board members. It was easy for me to get intimidated at times, but I knew I brought my heart to the table, which was enough for me to have a seat.

I didn't realize that I was needed. Deacon Cartwright was

looking for not just emerging leaders to represent COHI but *young* emerging leaders. That wasn't mentioned to me by my mom. She must've forgotten, but once I figured that out, I walked around with more confidence as if I belonged. There were lots of older men and women in the room who had years of experience that I learned from. In fact, a grandmother named Ms. Gloria was someone who brought both of her granddaughters to the meetings. One named Temple, who attended Lincoln High School, and the other named Zion graduated from Lincoln High, was a teacher and a year older than I.

Homelessness, affordable housing, and police reform were some of the biggest issues in San Diego. Primarily because nearly every district had issues concerning those three topics, especially in the southeastern section of San Diego, where most Black and brown people lived. It didn't take me too long to gravitate toward police reform. After opening up about my experience at Grossmont College, Jeff was furious.

"Fam, that shouldn't have happened to you. You shouldn't have gone to jail that day, and you definitely shouldn't have been charged with a felony. You were profiled," he demanded. *He's right.* I didn't know what to say back because I had never thought about it that way. I knew it was an act of injustice by the system, but I only had focused on learning the lesson in the past. The way he said it had a revolutionary touch to it. It was electrifying, and it opened my eyes to the change that was needed. "We are going to use this moving forward. We will tell this story," he said in a calmer tone. "Alright," I replied. I had a simple reply because I was speechless.

After that day, I found my lane, and it was advocating for police reform, so I was excited to learn and push the envelope for a new Assembly Bill that was brought to my attention. Assembly Bill 392 was the name of it. The bill was introduced by a local

Assembly Member at the time by the name of Dr. Shirley Weber as well as Kevin McCarty. To what some would say, Shirley Weber was an ally with SDOP and the Black soul of many communities. The bill was liberating, so liberating, that at first, I didn't think it was real.

> AB 392, Weber. Peace officers: deadly force.
>
> "Existing law authorizes a peace officer to make an arrest pursuant to a warrant or based upon probable cause, as specified. Under existing law, an arrest is made by the actual restraint of the person or by submission to the custody of the arresting officer.
>
> Existing law authorizes a peace officer to use reasonable force to effect the arrest, to prevent escape, or to overcome resistance. Existing law does not require an officer to retreat or desist from an attempt to make an arrest because of resistance or threatened resistance of the person being arrested.
>
> Under existing law, a homicide committed by a peace officer is justifiable when necessarily committed in arresting a person who has committed a felony, and the person is fleeing or resisting such arrest.
>
> Existing case law deems such a homicide to be a seizure under the Fourth Amendment of the Constitution of the United States, and as such, requires the actions to be reasonable."

Quickly, I texted Jeff back, "I want in." Plain and simple. I knew this bill was going to potentially change the trajectory of a lot of police stops and altercations, as well as better relationships between officers and citizens. This was an opportunity I couldn't afford to fumble.

I was then invited to sit down with Dr. Shirley Weber in her office. When she introduced the bill back in February of 2019, she wasn't sure how it would play out, but it excelled. It was passed by the Assembly Public Safety Committee in April, which was right around the time I sat down with Board of Supervisor member Nathan Fletcher and drilled him on his agenda and plans for the bill if passed. Towards the end of the meeting, he walked over to me while I was still sitting in my seat, crouched down, and said, "I'm allies with Dr. Weber. I've gotten word that it will most likely pass."

Within the same month, I chaired my first Leadership of Conference (LOC) evening meeting through SDOP on a Monday night. I was also mentioned in a Fox News article regarding my conversation with Board of Supervisor member Nathan Fletcher. It was a very empowering feeling, but it made me hungry for more. I knew it was just the beginning of what God was preparing me for. After being mentioned in the online article, I knew then, without a doubt, that I was in my lane. In May, the bill was completed by the assembly, and on July 9th, it was officially passed by the Senate.

On Tuesday, July 30th, I woke up at 6:30 a.m., but this time it wasn't for myself or an appointment or a client but to Dr. Weber's office downtown. I parked at a local ACE parking lot near Front Street in downtown San Diego. I gave Jeff a call to see where he was, and it turned out that he was a few minutes behind. I was okay with that because I was a bit early anyway. After catching up on sleep in my car, I hopped out, paid for my parking spot, and walked toward the building. This was going to be my first time sharing my arrest story with a politician, and I was ready to finally share my story.

The building was huge, and it appeared to be about six stories high. The entire building was covered in bronze marble-coated paint besides the doors. The doors were tinted black, but just enough for you to wonder who was on the inside. On the top left border of the door read the number *1350*, and on the top border of the right door read *Front St*. I was familiar with the ways and views of downtown, but this was the most official building I had ever seen downtown.

I stood there for no longer than thirty seconds before noticing other faith leaders walking toward me. It was about ten of us: Jeff, Ms. Gloria, Reverend Mark, Temple, Zion, Tanya, myself, and a few others. Tanya Patterson and I were the ones who were assigned to share our experiences with improper policing with Dr. Weber. The two of us were assigned about five minutes to speak. Reverend Mark gathered us all together to pray before walking into the building. I looked at Tanya and asked her, "Are you ready?" She gave me a noticeably confident nod.

We walked in as a group and met the first elevator, which wasn't too far from the entrance. Jeff had a relationship with Dr. Weber, so he knew his way around the building. We arrived on the third floor and met Dr. Weber's assistant named Edmond. Dr. Weber had just arrived, and she needed a minute or two to settle in, so we patiently waited to be escorted to her office. We all had to take a second elevator to her office, including her. Edmond assured us, "There's room for a few more to hop on." Everyone looked around. I didn't hesitate. I hopped on. I stood in the elevator with Dr. Weber and Edmond. That was my way of trying to leave a good first impression, and it worked.

Shirley N. Weber
Assembly Member, 79th District
Chair of Budget Subcommittee #5 on Public Safety
Member of the Committees on Banking and Finance; Budget; Budget Subcommittee #6 on Budget Process; Education: Elections and Redistricting; and Higher Education
Chair of the Select Committee on Campus Climate
Represents: Chula Vista, La Mesa, Lemon Grove, National City, Bonita, and San Diego

Wow. The huge sign next to her door caught my attention. I thought it was pretty dope, but the energy shifted once everyone made it to her office. The air in the room thinned, and it made me tense up. I was nervous. On top of that, I was sitting close to her. She sat at the end of the table while I was sitting on the corner closest to her. She had an extraordinarily strong presence that seized my desire to talk. When she began to talk, I sank my back into my chair and listened to her. I was processing every word, every sentence, and every phrase, but it was difficult. She talked for at least the first thirty minutes.

It was my first time hearing a Black woman in her age group speak so eloquently and confidently. Every other ten seconds, my eyes would glance out of the window. The morning downtown skyline was lovely. By the time I began searching her bookshelf without moving my head, she had given the floor over to Jeff. I snapped out of my daydream. Jeff began to delegate, and before I knew it and could mentally prepare for it, I was sharing my testimony.

I removed my back from my seat and leaned forward towards her. I unhooked my fingers, placed my elbows in my lap, and cleared my throat. "Good morning, Dr. Weber. My name is Chris, as I said earlier. I had an encounter with a sheriff at Grossmont College back in 2014 that I perceived as unjust," I said. I forgot my script, but I didn't care because my intro was great, and I knew God would fill me with the right words if I spoke from the heart. As I was speaking, I watched her body language shift. After the first few sentences, she did something she hadn't done during the meeting by leaning back instead of forwards. *Is she copying me?* She did as I did. Instead of sitting up as I was, she leaned backward in her chair and propped her fist on her right cheek. The eye contact was pretty intense, but I continued.

My words moved her, and that morning was completed. I left her office in disbelief as to what I had done. I thanked Jeff as I had always done. Many people would have loved to sit down with Dr. Weber, share their story, and pick her brains, too; being a part of a team to do so was nothing short of a blessing. Once the group of us made it to the lobby level, we debriefed, prayed, and left the building.

A few weeks later, Jeff contacted me to see if I wanted to fly out to Sacramento, California, to be present for the signing of the bill. *Sacramento? Are we driving?* Those were my first thoughts. I sent him a text to get more information. He replied immediately, "Hahahaha, nah, man. We are flying. It's on Monday. U in?" To be completely honest, once I knew that I was going to catch my first flight ever, I was in. This was another one of those unbelievable moments, but I was ready for it. It took a few days for me to process the idea that I was going to experience my first plane ride and another city.

Monday, August 19th, was the big day. It was the day I was going to witness history be made, catch my first flight, and experience another city at the same time. It was one of those days I was looking forward to during the prior week. Excited is an understatement;

I was thrilled. Jeff shot me a text the evening before asking if he could ride with me to the airport. I was glad he asked because I didn't know my way or the airport protocol. I went to bed that night around 8 p.m. and woke up at 3 a.m.

Jeff wanted me to meet him at his address at around 4 a.m., so I only had about forty-five minutes to get ready. I wasn't sure what to wear, so I kept it simple, maybe a little too simple. I pulled out a pair of grey sweatpants, a white Body Architect shirt, and a pair of Nike Air Max. My hair hadn't been cut, so I grabbed my navy-blue SD 59fifty hat and hit the door. *Dang, it's dark out.* I hadn't been up that early in a while. *Good thing it isn't cold.*

I left around 3:40 a.m. and made it to Jeff's house around 4:06 a.m. He was still inside, so I shot him a text. "I'm outside," I said. A few minutes later, he walked out wearing a suit jacket, slacks, and casual tennis shoes. *Dang, man, I'm wearing the wrong clothes.* I should've known better. "Good morning, bro! Let's get it!" he said. That energized, purpose-filled spirit he always had was working even at 4 a.m. We fled to the airport, which was only ten minutes away.

Once we made it to the airport, we had already been in deep conversation about how the day was going to go, its importance, and what it meant to the two of us. Neither of us had heard from Ms. Gloria, Temple, Zion, Reverend Mark, Bishop Bowser, or the rest of the crew. The airport was practically empty. We could hear our own footsteps on the freshly polished floor. Since our boarding time was at 5:50 a.m., we had nothing but time to converse. "Have you had breakfast?" Jeff asked me.

All of us boarded the flight at 5:55 a.m. I was one of the first to enter the Southwest airline plane, and since I was unaware of the best seating options, I walked straight to the back. For whatever reason, I chose the right window seat. *I enjoyed the flight.* We landed at the

Sacramento International Airport at about 7:40 a.m., and that's when I learned that there was a waiting period before actually getting off the plane. My knees were in pain, but when I finally stood up and took a few steps, it felt good. I was impressed by Sacramento's Airport because of the glass-windowed tunnel used as a shuttle walk-through to get to the Lyft and Uber drivers. The fellas took a Lyft to downtown: Jeff, Bishop Bowser, Tony, Reverend Mark, and I. We were about twenty-plus minutes away from Sacramento City Hall. That's where the celebration was.

Once we arrived at the Sacramento City Hall, all five of us became jammed by the crowds of people waiting to enter the Hall. Luckily, Jeff's name was on the list of organizers who had priority, so we met up with ladies and headed to the front of the line. While many of us stood around, I felt many people brushing past me, some even bumping me. One of the many people who bumped my shoulder by mistake was Bobby Seale of the Black Panthers. Bobby walked right past me, and some didn't even know who he was. In fact, he blew right past everyone and was one of the first to be let through the gates.

It wasn't long before the crew and I were inside and seated at our seat of choice. The Bill signing ceremony began on time, and Dr. Weber was the intro speaker, followed by the mother of Oscar Grant. I could still see the pain in her eyes as she was speaking. It was disheartening to witness. She walked past me on her way back to her seat, and when she swiftly passed me, I could feel the energy of a deeply saddened woman. The entire ceremony lasted about two hours, and when it was over, many people rushed to the stage to take photos.

"I am proud of all of us. Why? Because that was the first time I ever saw an Assembly Bill we actually finished from start to end, all of the years I began working as an organizer. Today was powerful. All of you are powerful. I want you to know that," Jeff said. I always took Jeff's heart-to-heart moments very seriously because he was just as genuine as I was. I could see myself in him.

See, when I first met Jeff, he didn't know a thing about me, and neither did I of him. Deacon Cartwright connected a bridge when the two of us met. He had no idea how much of a force the two of us would be after meeting and working together. For the first time in my life, I felt like I was recognized not for my disability but for my abilities, for my strengths. I continued my research and became a foot soldier of the movement SDOP symbolized and would walk through doors of opportunity made possible by that movement. If it had not been for Jeff anwakening the mind of justice and the heart peace in me, I wouldn't have discovered this hidden passion of mine. A brother indeed.

22

LONGING FOR A HAPPY ENDING

I WAS A TWENTY-THREE-YEAR-OLD YOUNG MAN WITH A LOT going for myself. My confidence was at an all-time high. I was optimistic, driven, and filled with faith. My relationship with God was in great harmony. I was in the very best shape of my life. Man, I was so athletic and my fast twitch muscles were so sharp that I almost threw down back to back windmill dunks in an empty basketball gym. I had read so many books I could literally feel how sharp my mind was. I had a handful of clients, a new car, and new goals. I was grinding and living well, but all of that went crashing and burning when I met another girl.

Her name was Ashlyn. My experience with Ashlyn brewed an anger within me for a long time. She was a stallion, standing at almost six feet tall, with a smooth caramel complexion and a smile that aroused me into wanting to do a lot of stuff I wouldn't naturally want to do. This girl was fine, and plus, she was super sweet.

She paid for nearly everything. Her hip to waist ratio was perfect, like the ones you'd see on those girls in the WWE or professional cheerleaders back in the day. Not to mention, everything she wore was tight to her skin and revealing, so I couldn't keep my hands off of her. I was so overtaken by her appearance that by the time I began learning about her ways, it was too late. I was truly captivated by her appearance. Within one month, we went from communicating through social media, dating, and sleeping with each other.

I had a tough time deciding if I wanted to keep her or not because I knew I shouldn't have slept with her. I was ashamed of myself. I truly didn't want to, but again I felt like I had to for her to respect me, stay, and or not leave me for another guy. The only problem was she left me after a few months for her ex that she wasn't entirely over and pissed me off. Once things ended, I was convinced that she never had any intentions of actually being with me. You know, like a rebound, that's what I was to her. I didn't like that. I felt entitled. *Nah, f*** that. How you just gon come into my life, and then leave for that clown?* I was hurt and pissed off at the same time. This experience with her created a two-year situation that ultimately turned me into a very angry person. My anger turned into depression, and after battling depression for so long, I started to lose the desire to be genuine with people.

I was losing hope as the days went by during the winter of 2019. Without any closure, AGAIN, I was left to overthink so I started to feel like my true genuine self wasn't desired by the world, particularly women. These feelings made me very sad because I didn't know how to be anyone else but myself; hell, I didn't want to be anyone else. All I knew was that I hated this girl with a passion, and if I could've gotten revenge, I would've.

Things between Ashlyn and I ended a few days before December

31, 2019, so I entered the new year feeling like a failure. The timing was what made it all worse. And then, twenty-six days later, my childhood favorite, Kobe Bryant, loses his life in a helicopter accident. I still remember crying on that day. I could've used a beach towel instead of Kleenex to wipe the snot from my nose and tears from my eyes. That's how much I cried. Kobe Bryant was someone I never thought I'd see die in my lifetime (as odd as that may sound, it's true), so the pain was doubled. A lot was going on in my heart and in my head that raised many questions. *Why is all of this happening?*

I couldn't find a place to rest in my mind, and I felt myself slipping into depression again, especially when the spread of Covid-19 reached San Diego. California Governor Gavin Newsom called for a mandatory stay-at-home order and mask mandate. It was shocking to see everything close down. COHI closed, and because of that, I felt disconnected from God even more than I already did. I was torn because I felt like it was the safest thing to do to close the church doors, but for me personally, it wasn't.

I didn't realize it at the moment but bearing much pain in the pandemic was teaching and redirecting me in a different direction. In fact, I met a girl who, this time, wasn't going to be my girlfriend but my sister and serve as a bridge to the next season of my life. Her name was Amanda, and I got an invite from her on my 24th birthday. I felt like she was such an angel for that. She came from a very strong Mexican cultured background and was passionate about living for God. She shined her light wherever and whenever, and there was great proof in that when she asked to celebrate my birthday with me. My 24th birthday was the beginning of a platonic friendship between Amanda and me.

I didn't have many birthday plans due to the pandemic until she sent me a text asking what I'd like to eat for dinner and suggested we watch the movie that we didn't get to finish. I was more than grateful to join, so I texted her back and told her to surprise me. She cooked salmon and asparagus and poured us a glass of wine. I hadn't eaten salmon in so long, so its taste made my mouth water like a flowing river. The asparagus was cooked to a perfect crisp, and together we finished the bottle of red wine. We topped it off with Ben & Jerry's Cherry Garcia flavored ice cream bowl.

While we were enjoying the ice cream, she abruptly changed the plans. "Hey! So instead of the movie tonight, I have a better idea. A friend of mine named Eric is hosting a Bible Study today, and I want us to go. He sent out a text today. Wanna go?" she asked. That was exactly what I needed and was the perfect way to end the night. "Yeah, let's do that," I said. She looked up at me and said, "You know it's funny because today is his birthday too, so he didn't plan on having Bible Study tonight." *That's interesting.*

I hopped in my driver's seat, and Amanda sat in the passenger's seat. Amanda's younger sister, Yessi, was with us as well. She sat in the back. Since we were ahead of time, Amanda directed me to a local spot to watch the sunset. I parked my car on top of a hill I never knew existed, and the three of us enjoyed each other for a few minutes. The sun was setting, and it felt like I was watching it for the first time since I wasn't leaving home much. Once Amanda received a text from Eric letting her know he was at his house, we headed towards his address.

When we arrived, Amanda introduced me to Eric. "This is my friend Chris. Today's his birthday," she said in an extremely excited voice. Eric and I shook hands, and then he looked me dead in the eye and said, "Man, the Lord is going to release some things to me today for you." His voice was just as deep as mine, if not deeper. He maintained a serious look on his face, and he walked away with his shoulders back, chest up, and head up. There was no doubt in my mind that whatever he was going to say was indeed prophetic based on his confidence.

His home was huge, and his backyard was just as big. Bible Study was held on the patio just before the backyard. It was only a handful of us: me, Amanda, Yessi, Eric, and a middle-aged couple. Eric's style of teaching gave me flashbacks of the days at This Is The Way. He resembled Pastor Taylor, who was also very straightforward, loud, and bold. There was no doubt in my mind that Eric's neighbors who were far off could hear him; that's how loud he was. I sat in my seat like a kid at the theater watching a scary movie that wondered what was going to happen next. I was overtaken by Eric's confidence and energy.

Eric played a few worship songs towards the end of the study, and during the time of worship, he walked over to me, tapped my shoulder, and said, "Follow me. I want to pray for you." I didn't say anything. Instead, I got up and followed him. For the first time in my life, I felt like I was going to hear from God in a way I hadn't heard from Him before, I don't know why but I believed it. I didn't know how or why, but I could feel it. It just felt different. Everything about the night felt different. As I was walking, I felt an uneasy feeling in my stomach. The anticipation was heavy, and it grew heavier as I continued to follow Eric.

He led me to an empty room in his large home. The room had a bunch of junk on the floor and a spare piano that looked broken. No one was in the room besides the two of us, and a standard school-looking four-legged chair was placed jam smack in the middle of the room. "Okay, sit right there for me," he said. I sat. I hadn't said a word because I didn't know what to say at that point. "Now you're gonna feel a heavy wind blowing by as I pray, okay?" he asked. "Yeah," I replied.

He asked a question that completely threw me off. "Do you have anything on your body that needs healing?" he asked. I was a few split seconds away from saying no until I remembered the pain of a toothache I was having on the upper left side of my mouth. Still, I wanted just to say no because I had a dentist appointment set for a month from that exact day. Without thinking any further, I replied, "Yeah." He asked me where the pain was and when I told him, he asked me to close my eyes and put my hands on my heart and repeat after him. I did as he asked.

"Heavenly Father, we come humble before you right now."

Eric began to pray, and that's when I felt the heavy wind blowing that he warned me about. I wasn't sure if he was causing it or what was causing it, but all I knew was I felt it. *Yoooooo*. The not-so-smart thing to do was to open my eyes, so I kept them closed, but I was concerned about what was going on, why it was happening, and what was going to happen next. No one had ever prayed for me the way Eric was praying.

> "At six years old, you were compassionate! You
> have always been for the hurting, the crying,
> and the voiceless. He placed that in you.
> At eleven years old, you had visions! God is
> gonna bring those visions back around.
> I see a new wave of finances coming into your life."

I just knew Eric didn't come with that information on his own. The two of us never met, so I knew this was God speaking through him. As those words came flying out of his mouth, tears rolled down my face, and I became deeply humbled by what I was hearing. God was reminding me that He never forgot about me. I continued to feel pain in my tooth for a few days, and then it vanished on its own. That shocked me. I was in awe of what God showed me, and it made me more curious than I ever was. I began to be honest with myself. I began to ask God real questions with the intent and readiness to receive real answers.

> *God, what is Your plan for my life? Did I make a wrong turn somewhere? Why am I here?*

I prayed about many things I was afraid to express to others in the summer of 2020. I continued to ask God, *where do I go from here? Why am I here?* I never felt like He was answering me, but I kept praying, hoping that He would somehow. One of the many things I prayed about was my life's purpose. Maybe I was overthinking, but there was just so much that happened in my past that I didn't understand. I wanted to know why it happened or why am I so impulsive. I wanted to know why I was the way I was. I prayed about it for weeks until one day, I received a text message I never thought I'd receive.

Back in 2018, my mom found my biological father through social media, but it never went any further than that, and I didn't tell many people about it either, just my family. His name was Eddie, and on that day, he texted me out of the blue. "Hey son, wyd? I have news for you. When can we talk?" it read. *Why does he keep calling me son?* I was a little thrown off, so it took me hours to reply. "Sup? I'm free," I finally replied. I didn't hear anything back, so I called a few hours later. He picked up after the third ring, which was unusual, so that appeared to me as a sign that he had something important he wanted to tell me. I was right. He answered the phone and went straight to the point. "I have a plan. Are you free in September?" he asked.

He thought it would be a great idea for us to meet at a neutral spot and on a neutral occasion, so he booked a flight to Los Angeles to tailgate a Chargers game. On Sunday, September 20th, the Los Angeles Chargers hosted the Kansas Chiefs. The plan was for us to have a two-day vacation on both Saturday the 19th and Sunday the 20th so we could talk. Although I wasn't a fan of the NFL, I knew this was an opportunity I needed to capitalize on, so I planned to go. I also wasn't sure if he was serious or not, but instead of asking a bunch of questions, I just replied to him, "Yeah, I'm cool with that."

Maybe this is the answer to my prayer?

The following week he sent me a screenshot of his plane tickets, and that's when I knew he was serious. *Are you really going to do this?* I began to overthink. I tried to play it cool, but I was nervous and afraid of what could go wrong and what others would think about me. *What if he avoids your questions?* I was taking a huge risk that could have either gone bad or well, but I wasn't prepared to expect the possibilities of what it would become.

Day after day, I drowned in my thoughts of overthinking, but I caught a huge break one day when I got a text from Brandon H. We spoke briefly throughout the years, but we hadn't seen each other since our days of kicking up trouble at Target. He wanted to sit down and catch up. He sent a message to me through social media that read, "Yo bro, I need some advice from you." I was more than happy to meet up and give whatever advice I had to give, so we met up.

It was Father's Day, and we met up at a local sandwich shop just near the golf course Dré introduced me to. I sat and waited since he was just a few minutes behind. When he arrived immediately, it felt like old times again. "Bro, your son looks just like you," I said. "Nah, bro, he looks like his mom. Look…" he replied while flashing me a picture on his phone. That was how the beginning of our conversation kicked off, fatherhood. Brandon H. wanted a little guidance as a new father.

"Actually, this is perfect timing because I'm actually going to meet and talk to my biological father soon. Any advice?" I asked. "Go, bro. Tomorrow isn't promised. I wanted to meet mine in person but never did," he replied. Although Brandon H. was a new father, he longed to have a relationship with his own, so he sought after him earlier that year. The two met virtually, and just before he made plans to meet him, he tragically caught the coronavirus and passed away. I saw the pain in his eyes when he said to me, "Go, bro."

I didn't plan on sharing that with Brandon H. that day, but I'm glad I did because it gave me the energy I needed to go. September felt like it was miles away because the days were going by so slowly. I counted down each day and remained in deep contemplation. I had so much on my mind that on some nights, I had awkward dreams about the day I'd sit down and talk to Eddie in person. The rest of June ended, and July was present. July finally finished out, and August felt like the longest month ever.

When September finally came, Eddie and I hadn't spoken in weeks because we anticipated the day we'd actually see each other (or at least that's what I assumed). One day he sent a text of the address to the Airbnb he was staying at. It was located in Anaheim, which sat on the outskirts of Los Angeles. *Bet.* I made sure I had the weekend cleared on my schedule because I planned on staying for the weekend.

I remember waking up on the morning of September 19th. My entire bed was damp, and it scared the mess out of me. *Cold sweat.* My body was fed up with my level of nervousness. Initially, I thought it only happened when hormones changed, but apparently, I was nervous, so my body began to sweat in my sleep. Either way, I couldn't tell the difference. Before leaving, I hugged and kissed my mom. She knew where I was going and who I was meeting, so I didn't say anything to her about it. I was just glad to feel her support and see her smile.

Leaving no stone unturned, I hit the road at about 11:30 a.m. to meet my biological father for the first time in my life. My GPS gave me an estimated time of two hours and forty-five minutes. *Alright... I guess.* I wasn't expecting it to be that long, but I got comfortable since I knew I had no control over it. Time was all I had, so I began to think of ways to help the time pass. Nothing came to mind, so I settled with my thoughts because, for the first thirty minutes of the ride, I couldn't believe that I was actually about to meet my father. After years of curiosity and questions, the wait was almost over.

I thought back. I thought back to when I wished I knew where I came from, those days in middle school but especially high school when I learned from Derrell and Dre', who had their dads in their lives. It made me think of the times when I was dating and felt like I didn't know how to exemplify masculinity to my companion. I couldn't stop thinking about those times and how they made me feel because I was about to step into another side of those times, or at least I thought. *After this, I'll be whole...I'll be a lot better.*

I made sure to clock my speed because the last thing I wanted was to get pulled over. My speed read a little over 75 mph, which was still speeding in most parts of Southern California. Reframing from checking my cell phone wasn't so easy after Eddie texted me. I spotted the text from the corner of my eye, and it read, "Hey son, the guys and I found a better-looking Airbnb, so here's the address. Wya? How close are you to LA?". "43 minutes", I replied. Things were getting real, really quick.

After I typed the new address into my GPS, it shortened my time by roughly fifteen minutes. *New arrival time: 1:13 p.m. It's getting real.* My body started to sweat again, but slowly. The steering wheel felt moist, and I didn't know why until it dawned on me that I was sweating. There was no way I couldn't numb my feelings anymore because my body was making me aware of them.

Nearly another hour flew by because when I looked down at my cell phone, it read twenty minutes to the destination. Subconsciously I released my foot from pressing so hard on my gas pedal, and then my speed decreased. The closer I got, the more I couldn't believe it. *This is unreal.* It felt like watching the ball drop on New Year's Eve. I had ten minutes left when I was officially coasting through the busy streets of Los Angeles, so I let my window down and enjoyed the breeze.

When I was a few blocks away from the location, I began to drive even slower than I was before. That didn't help because I was driving down one of the longest streets in Los Angeles named Slauson Ave. It was my first time actually driving down Slauson Ave, so I took in the sites and attractions. Soon enough, I made a right turn at a stoplight and was officially in the right neighborhood. *Woah.*

From afar, you would have mistaken me as someone planning a drive-by; that's how slow I was driving. I gazed at the houses one by one. The neighborhood was beautiful. All of the houses were huge and had nice clean cut grass front yards. It was so quiet that the only noise was coming from my quiet engine (which naturally wasn't loud) and birds chirping in the trees. After figuring out which house was my destination, I stopped in the middle of the street to figure out my next move. My hand was on the steering wheel, and my eyes were glued to the huge two-story house.

Just park right here. I didn't want to park near the home because

I felt more comfortable walking up to the home rather than driving up. So, I parked a few houses down and hopped out of the car. As soon as the bottom of the sole of my shoes touched the floor, I felt my phone vibrating. It was Eddie. He was calling me. I picked it up. "Hey son, wya?" he said. "I'm walking towards the house right now," I said back. "Okay, I'm coming through the garage right now. Imma let it up," he said back to me. "Aight," I said back to him. I hung up and continued walking toward the house.

As soon as I was within a few steps from the second house closest to the address, I saw the car garage rolling up slowly. My heart skipped a few beats. For the first few seconds, there was nothing, and then suddenly, a head full of dreads covered by a head wrap ducked under the garage door. It was him. Still a few feet away, he walked toward me as I walked towards him. For the first five seconds of walking toward each other, we stared and didn't say a word. "Wassup, son!" he yelled out loud. I didn't know what to say because I was extremely nervous and didn't want to refer to him as "Dad", so I didn't say much except "Wassup?" It was a surreal moment that I knew I wouldn't ever forget.

The first thing I noticed was his bowed legs and how he walked. They looked just like mine, but his legs were even more bowed than mine. Our walking pattern was remarkably similar. The second thing I noticed was the rest of his body structure. His forearms were shaped and angled in the same direction as mine. His hands were just as large as mine and both of our fingers spread apart pretty far. Although our face masks were covering the majority of our faces, it looked like I was looking at the old version of myself because his eyes looked exactly like mine. *What...the...heck.*

Once we got closer to each other, everything was put into perspective. We were just seconds away from each other, and I had already felt sweat running down my face and marinating on my neck. Since I was nervous and didn't know where he stood as far as physical contact in the middle of the pandemic, I didn't know what to do. Thankfully, he made the first move by putting his hand out to shake mine. "What's up, man!" he said aggressively while gripping my hand and squeezing it tight. The handshake quickly turned into a reach for a hug. I didn't hug him back. Instead, I just stood there with my hands by my side. "D***, you're handsome! You're just as handsome as you are on Instagram!" he yelled aloud while laughing. I stood still, emotionless, while he hugged me tightly how military parents hug their children once they return from deployment.

I wasn't emotional because I didn't know how to feel exactly. I didn't cry or feel the sensation of crying. I was bemused and probably wouldn't process what just had happened until months down the line, but I was okay with that. Once he released me from the hug, I felt a huge weight removed from my shoulders. My biological brother was behind him and stood there and waited for us to have our moment. Eddie kept his hand on top of my shoulder but turned to the side and said, "This is your older brother, Eddie Jr. or Lil Eddie."

He let my shoulder go, and I walked towards Lil Eddie, and the two of us graced each other with a handshake followed by a hug. "Sup, bruh?" he said in a deep Midwest accent. The look in his eyes let me know that he was also awaiting this moment. "Wassup, bro?" I said back. After all the hugging was over, Eddie invited me to come inside. "Come on. My crew is inside; they want to meet you too," he said. As I walked across the thick bright green grassy lawn and into the car garage, I couldn't believe what had just happened. I didn't know what to say, and I didn't know how to feel.

23

FREE

I never went into full depth with Eddie about what happened between him and my mom on September 9, 1995, because it only had so much to do with me. Besides, meeting him didn't solve my problem. Instead, it allowed God to relieve answers. After the weekend I spent in the presence of my biological father, I drove back to San Diego from Los Angeles in deep silence. It was 4:00 a.m., foggy, and I could feel the cold, dry weather seeping through my skin and into my bones.

I remember driving home in such deep thought that I gave myself a headache. God revealed something to me in a matter of seconds while I pulled over to pump gas. I heard the Holy Spirit whisper to me, "I have always been your Father, and I always will be." I knew that it came from the same Holy Spirit my mom talked about growing up and I learned about at COHI, because it was the answer to my question that I was too afraid to ask. Hearing from God in such an affirming way made me emotional, so it took me some time to pull off from the gas station. Eventually, I acknowledged it once I hit the road. *God is my Father...always has been...always will be.* I said those very words back to myself while behind the wheel.

I get it; sometimes, people pull the "God is my Father" card. It can be such an annoying cliche because it may feel as if one is neglecting or avoiding the importance of their earthly father and the experience of having one. But what was I supposed to believe? Who was I supposed to call "Dad"? Who was my father? Do you see what I'm saying? It all began to make sense. *Not only did I never have a complete father and son relationship with a man...It was never designed for me to have.* If He wanted me to have one, He would've given me one in the beginning.

See, though I am a carrier of my brother's father's last name, "Ransom " I am not of his gene pool. Not only are we not biologically connected, but I also didn't feel connected relationally during the time he was in my life. I didn't feel as if he invested in me or made the time to discover who I was. I felt indifferent about the relationship. It didn't matter to me. Don't get me wrong, he and I never had an issue, and he was an amazing father to my brothers, but I was not bothered by his absence. His departure from the home didn't sadden me. It just pained me to know I was stuck with another man's last name to whom I never felt connected.

Mike wasn't the father who knew much about my bone diseases, surgery dates, personal likes, dislikes, or anything regarding my physical health, etc. He didn't keep up with it (from what I remember), so I didn't feel like he knew much about me. In fact, I have one vivid memory of a moment I had with Mike, my brothers, and me. It could have been anywhere in the early 2000s; I'm not sure. However, I do remember that it was after I had surgery, and Mike decided to schedule a motocross event for us to go to. It wasn't our first rodeo, and I loved going to see the motocross events at Qualcomm Stadium as a kid until the night Mike left me hanging.

He didn't leave me hanging completely, but he did leave me behind. It probably wasn't intentional, but I expected more from him, considering the fact that I was a week out of the hospital, on crutches, and had blood rushing to the tip of my toes from sitting all night. Mike was one of those guys who always had to use the restroom, and I remember there was a moment when he got up to use it, and my brothers and I followed him. Second by second, Mike was drifting further away. There were tons of people who I couldn't maneuver through to catch up. I began to sob from afar while trying my best to catch up. I didn't feel safe. I was angry, vulnerable, and felt misunderstood.

Growing up, Mike was a great family man who didn't disappoint in the aspect of providing for my mom and brothers, and me. He wasn't perfect, but he did what he needed to do. He showed my brothers and me an equal amount of affection. He always supported us in whatever we did, and he never put work over his family. I've always respected him for that, but I quickly lost a sense of connection with him as I grew up once I realized he and I never formed an intimate relationship. To me, it always felt like Mike plus my brothers and me, not Mike and I. I didn't feel very known or understood by Mike, which is something I longed for and found in my relationship with God over time.

As for Mr. Chris, he and I were like big and little homies back in the day because he was more of a friend than a parent to me. He let me do whatever I wanted. I referred to him as "dad" a few times out of confusion, but I never truly meant it. I never genuinely saw him as my father, just an older buddy who let me get away with a lot of crazy stuff I enjoyed. He was a great guy with bad habits, so when we parted ways, I never had any harsh feelings toward him, nor did I feel like I was his son.

Mr. Chris never had the capacity to fulfill the disciplinary role in my life as God does to those He loves. As much as I was taking belongings from stores and other children at school, I knew I needed someone other than mom to discipline me. Something more concrete, aggressive, masculine, if you will. I couldn't take my mom seriously during the few moments I got in trouble, so I needed Mr. Chris.

I needed someone (outside my mom) to knuckle me up (as the older generation would say) or punch me in the throat for creating a habit of theft. I needed a man to do it because I knew I probably would have stopped much sooner if he did. Looking back, it's a crazy feeling to know that he was encouraging my brothers and me to steal as kids. I sit around thinking sometimes, *maybe I wouldn't have gone to jail.* The criminal justice system did me an injustice for slapping a felony on my record, but I'm thankful for it because I wouldn't have stopped. I know God allowed the sheriff to arrest me because He loved me enough to stop me from further destroying myself. I needed Mr. Chris to put some fire up under me, but he didn't, and because of that, he and I were buddies rather than father and son.

Pops was someone who taught me many lessons over the years, although we were two different types of men. He spent the largest amount of time in my life and played the role of a step-father for twelve years. If anyone has gotten to know me the most, it would be Pops. I respected him for who he was and what he taught me as a boy and as a young man, but unfortunately, he too did not provide the father-and-son connection I was missing. The connection wasn't there, not because he didn't want to be, but more so because the shoes were too big for him to fill.

The interesting thing about the relationship Pops and I built is he knows the most about me without actually knowing my inner being. He was connected with the stages and seasons of my life, and he always supported me. He corrected me and showed me just enough affection. He taught me how to drive. He taught me how to tie a tie. He taught me how to shave. He taught me how to fix broken objects around the house. He taught me about car parts I never knew. He gave me the best and worst dating advice a young man could receive. He watched me grow, but he couldn't empathize and guide me through wars that were waging inside me. Pops knew the levels, stages, and seasons but not my thoughts and emotions.

I am the offspring of Eddie, but God just used him to have me. Eddie and I are 100% genetically connected. I even have three brothers and two sisters who I am also related to through Eddie. An autopsy on his body would prove that I am his son biologically, but unfortunately, he wasn't the answer. The two of us remained in contact but not nearly as much as before we met. We are like two strangers who know each other without actually knowing each other. It's not easily explained and understood.

I've seen Eddie on a few other occasions since we met, and sometimes, it still feels like I'm shaking hands with a stranger. We have a lot in common: upright posture, speech fluency, creativity, and an odd obsession with hats. That's just how it feels because we've gotten to know each other a bit, but the hole that had been in my soul for so many years could never be aided by his presence. He just can't fix it, and I became okay with it because, after all, my birth wasn't planned through neither him nor my mom. I'm content with where we stand because I know it was all God's doing. Like I said, God just used him to have me.

Mike, Mr. Chris, Pops, and Eddie were the only options I had.

So, I turned to God for it all. Although I believed God when He said He was my Father and He had been fathering me through the obstacles of my life, it's still hard to believe at times because I felt like I was dealt a bad hand. If you ask me, others had a head start. I've always believed I started in the back, which sometimes made it difficult to believe that a perfect-loving God gave me this troubled life.

It's hard to make sense of it all because I was uncertain about my assignment on earth for the first twenty-four years of my life. I was made aware that I was born to be a pastor, and I recognize ministry is what I am most passionate about. However, there is a dilemma because my obstacles, errors, and shortcomings did not align with what I thought a pastor should be or was. On some days, I woke up and wondered if God was who He said He was because there were many times when I felt like I was just a living-breathing accident who would eventually, like everyone else, die.

I believed negatively about myself for many reasons. The biggest of the few was the knowing and feeling of growing up in special education. If there's anything I was most ashamed of, it would be that. I often asked myself: *Why would God allow a system to misinterpret my likes, dislikes, strengths, and weaknesses?* From being kicked out of school(s), failing classes, and the troubles of fitting in, it all wounded me emotionally.

In the 1800s various journals and newspapers shared this quote, most believed Albert Einstein is the originator of it but no one is for certain, anyway, it reads, "Everybody is a genius. But if you judge a fish by its ability to climb a tree, it will live its whole life believing that it is stupid." I second that. I lived the majority of my life believing I was stupid because of my errors. My failures still torment me to this day because I thought my grades were a reflection of how smart

I am, but that isn't true. I've always wrestled with my learning disability (or what the school system considered a learning dysfunction), and because of that, I've always had thoughts and plans of suicide. Being identified for disabilities and not abilities is a very painful feeling. It makes you feel less than human.

The second is just as hard as the first. Sports are huge in Black culture, and nearly every Black adolescent wants to be the best in the sport they choose. It can define your worth, which, in my case, made me feel worthless. However, I had to settle for never reaching any higher than I was able to do because I was born with a disease that prevented and delayed physical strength in my lower body. I knew I had rough from the start, and it didn't feel fair. At times it made me question if there was something I did that made me deserve my disease. In fact, at times, my disease made me question if God gave me any gifts.

Lastly, being adopted. Being adopted felt like the world said, "You didn't matter, but now you do." It's an awkward, uncomfortable, and quite embarrassing feeling. It's another way of saying, "You know what, never mind." I just wanted to come from one mother and father. I just wanted to be normal like everyone else. I just wanted it to all happen the "traditional" way. Adoption is something I was quite ashamed of because I thought I deserved less than the average child. The feelings of inadequacy then made me question the so-called plans God has for everyone. *Everyone* must've qualified for everyone else, not me.

So believing God fathered me through it all was the first step. The next was believing He planned my life, and the hand I was dealt was perfect to Him. However, the truth is this: the path to freedom is believing God planned my life and called it "good," whether it felt like it to me or not. It wasn't easy, but ultimately, I got tired of trying to decide between two truths. I had to make a decision. I had to make a decision that was not only going to set me free but help me walk in my designed destiny. Just as I believed God when He said He fathered me, I also made up my mind that He planned my life from start to finish.

I would be lying if I said I never struggled mentally after changing my beliefs about God's plan and thoughts towards me because, after all, I'm human. However, I gained a sense of peace that I didn't have before. *All I had to do was make a decision.* I know that one day I will be a pastor. I don't know why, when, or where, but I know who and what, and that's enough for me. It may or may not be in a pulpit, but whatever it looks like, I trust that I am fit for it. I no longer live under the expectations or standards of others because I wasn't born to be them. I don't have the capacity to be them. I'd go as far as saying it was never designed for me to be normal or like *normal people*. (Whatever the world considers being normal.)

I believe someone out there needed to hear my story so that their eyes would be open to a God who knows everything. Some people were never designed to be like everyone else, made mistakes, but don't realize it until God allows them to put themselves into a position that will provide the answer they were looking for, as I did. That was me. I unlearned who I thought I was. Someone out there needs to know that you may be misunderstood and or mislabelled by people, but God fully gets you. I came to a resolution that I'm good with what God gave me. Not only am I good with what God gave me, but I also started to grow into what He called me to be. After all, the only way I could step into my assignment boldly was by accepting the man I was created to be.

The truth is no matter how different we may be from each

other, we all trace back to one Creator. You may or may not come from a different walk of life than I. You may or may not come from Section 8 housing and food stamps. You may or may not come from a two-parent household. You may or may not have to endure a physical, social, and/or emotional struggle as I once did. Your errors may or may not look a lot different than mine. Your entire life filled with highs and lows may look closer or farther from mine. Either way, we slice it, we must know and remember who we belong to. Your father may have left at an early age, older age, or before your birth, but you've always had the father in heaven who sees, loves, and knows you. Resolve in that.

On November 14, 2021, I received a Minister's license from The City of Hope International Church.

ACKNOWLEDGMENTS

Without my Lord and Savior, Jesus Christ, I wouldn't be alive, and so this book wouldn't have come to be. It is very difficult to come up with the words to express how thankful to God I am for choosing and entrusting me with this story. All I can really say is it all started and ended with Him.

Before I list any names, I must immediately acknowledge Bishop Terrell Fletcher of The City Of Hope International Church. If it weren't for his obedience, the Holy Spirit wouldn't have constantly spoken the very words, "Some of you have books inside of you. Write the book." Without his obedience and willingness to inspire those in my generation, this memoir wouldn't have come to be.

My mom, Rotunda Cody, is responsible for the young man I have become. She's done so much for me over the years that it would be impossible to remember it all. Her unending support, love, and patience have shaped me greatly. I am forever in debt because of her sacrifice, grace, and mercy. I am thankful for her advice during the promise of telling my story. I haven't and highly doubt I will meet another woman like her. I love you, mom; thank you for being you.

To Donte, Jhamir, Jhavari, and Jhaylen, thank you for your brotherhood. The atmosphere is always at ease whenever we gather. I often believe that my childhood would have been a lot worse without you guys. I couldn't picture being the only child growing up. We did a lot of crazy stuff as kids. We saw a lot of things we didn't need to see. We got into many fistfights and had just as many laughs. We experienced things that made us want to stray away or draw closer to things in this world. We weren't and still aren't perfect, but we are brothers, and that'll never change. I love all of you. Oh, my aunts, uncles, cousins, family, and friends, thank you all too, love y'all as well.

Jesus had many followers, twelve disciples, but alone a few close friends. His inner circle was Peter, James, and John. That's who Dre' and Derrell represent to me, my inner circle. Ever since we were sixteen/seventeen, we've been best of friends. It wouldn't be right not to mention these two who've always remained true to our friendship, right or wrong, flaws and all. Thank you both for your endless laughs and moments of sacrifice. 92114 forever.

John being the third confidant, was actually Jesus's cousin. So, of course, Jordan Jackson (who is like my cousin) is someone I must acknowledge. Jordan exemplified healthy masculinity in my life during a time of confusion. Jordan single-handedly changed the trajectory of my life. How many people can say that about someone? He added ambition, mental fortitude, balance, and wisdom to my life. Tools I didn't have or understand. I'm not sure how my life would currently be had I not submitted to his leadership. Iron sharpened plastic in the fall of 2017, and because of that, the world was given this story. J-Jack, thank you, couso. Body Architect 4L.

Jeffery Alonzo Karahamuheto. If anyone has assisted me in growing into a well-rounded faith leader in my community, it would be Jeff. He's more than just a community organizing activist; he is selfless. I've learned a lot about myself, my community, politics, and leadership within a few minutes of conversing with Jeff. He has inspired and challenged me greatly to do and be more, and that's a gift I am not able to return.

My sister in Christ, Amanda Madera. Amanda has always held me responsible directly and indirectly for spreading the gospel of Jesus Christ. Because of her accountability, shared moments, and pure conversations, I've remained true to who I am and carried out assignments. She is a blessing to me and everyone who knows her intimately—big sis, in this life and in the next.

Pastor B and PEP (Pastor Ericka Parker) I don't know where to start with these two. If it weren't for Pastor B, I wouldn't have gotten my act together after my time spent in jail. If it wasn't for PEP, I don't know how else I wouldn't have gotten into ministry. Thank you for your endless sacrifice, concern, love, and patience with me. I will never forget the impact you've had on my life. Oh, and thank you for telling me about Prize Publishing House.

To Pastor Jeremy, James Wiley, and Coach Brandon, thank you for setting an example. As a kid, I didn't understand the sacrifice, patience, and persistence it took to keep my brothers and me out of trouble. Your stance and effort bled in my life, and my hope is that, by the grace of God, I do the same in other children's lives.

Nailah V. Leghon, an amazing Black woman I hand-selected to edit my story. She has been a stellar elementary educator of eight years, minored in English, has a Masters in Elementary Education, has a Bachelors in Child and Adolescent Development, and has served publicly for quite some time. Oh, and she loves Christ as well. Her friendship is uplifting, and her eagerness to assist with this story's coming meant a lot to me. Thank you, Nailah.

I couldn't close this without thanking all of the beautiful Black women at Prize Publishing House for their hospitality and willingness to take on the task of publishing my story. More specifically, I want to openly thank Tiffany Thomas, and Sana L. Cotten for her patience, enthusiasm, and trustworthiness. The sky's the limit for Prize Publishing House.

To anyone I missed, forgive me, thank you too.

> *"Look at the birds. They don't plant or harvest or store food in barns, for your heavenly Father feeds them. And aren't you far more valuable to him than they are?"*
> Matthew 6:26 (NLT)

www.ingramcontent.com/pod-product-compliance
Lightning Source LLC
Chambersburg PA
CBHW020338010526
44119CB00035B/448/J